The Power of Play in Higher Education

"Academics are a justifiably sceptical lot and love to privilege logical and analytical thinking. To get us out of our routinized ways of creating meaning, assigning merit and judging worth we need to draw senses and powers other than purely rational cognition. Play galvanizes creativity, inspires action and triggers different ways of building knowledge. It's also an insurrectionary force that challenges bureaucratized and siloed thinking and practice. In this visionary book packed with wonderful vignettes, exercises, techniques and suggestions you will find ways to rethink and broaden your teaching and academic practice. Product warning: this book changes lives."
—Professor Stephen Brookfield, *University of St Thomas, USA*

"The importance of play as an ecology for learning and discovery is often overlooked in tertiary education, so these author/editors are to be congratulated for bringing together such a diverse and valuable set of pedagogical narratives about how play is being used to encourage learning and creativity in higher education. This is a 'must read' book for tertiary educators who are interested in and who care about the creative development of learners and themselves."
—Professor Norman Jackson, *University of Surrey, UK*

"This book is a unique and timely contribution to the field of play and learning in Higher Education. It presents voices from practitioners across the sector demonstrating the extensive scope and scale of engagement with playful forms of learning. Through a series of in-depth case studies and vignettes of playful practice, this book inspires and convinces. It is packed full of examples and ideas, bringing together theory with experiences from the field. A must for creative educators everywhere!"
—Professor Nicola Whitton, *Durham University, UK*

"Learning through play is a powerful methodology: this invaluable guide illuminates through an excellent range of UK and North-American contributions how ludic approaches are used to good effect in higher education. This highly practical and evidence-informed volume illustrates how creativity can be boosted, fostering student engagement, and generating enthusiasm for learning."
—Professor Phil Race, *Edge Hill University, UK*; Professor Sally Brown, *Leeds Beckett University, UK*

Alison James · Chrissi Nerantzi
Editors

The Power of Play in Higher Education

Creativity in Tertiary Learning

Editors
Alison James
University of Winchester
Winchester, UK

Chrissi Nerantzi
Centre for Excellence in Learning
and Teaching
Manchester Metropolitan University
Manchester, UK

ISBN 978-3-319-95779-1   ISBN 978-3-319-95780-7 (eBook)
https://doi.org/10.1007/978-3-319-95780-7

Library of Congress Control Number: 2018958593

© The Editor(s) (if applicable) and The Author(s) 2019
This work is subject to copyright. All rights are solely and exclusively licensed by the Publisher, whether the whole or part of the material is concerned, specifically the rights of translation, reprinting, reuse of illustrations, recitation, broadcasting, reproduction on microfilms or in any other physical way, and transmission or information storage and retrieval, electronic adaptation, computer software, or by similar or dissimilar methodology now known or hereafter developed.
The use of general descriptive names, registered names, trademarks, service marks, etc. in this publication does not imply, even in the absence of a specific statement, that such names are exempt from the relevant protective laws and regulations and therefore free for general use.
The publisher, the authors and the editors are safe to assume that the advice and information in this book are believed to be true and accurate at the date of publication. Neither the publisher nor the authors or the editors give a warranty, express or implied, with respect to the material contained herein or for any errors or omissions that may have been made. The publisher remains neutral with regard to jurisdictional claims in published maps and institutional affiliations.

Cover image: © pchyburrs/Getty

This Palgrave Macmillan imprint is published by the registered company Springer Nature Switzerland AG
The registered company address is: Gewerbestrasse 11, 6330 Cham, Switzerland

This book is dedicated to Glyn and Adam and to all those who have stepped out along the play path

Foreword

A System Error

For some while now there's been an odd assumption about formal education. A curious belief has taken root in the heads of policy-makers and those working in schools and universities that higher levels of study should be a deadpan business with little time for fun. Apparently as you grow up, it's important to smile only occasionally and laugh a lot less than when you were younger. A stock rejoinder in any school classroom in response to behaviour which is seen as undesirable is to 'get on with your work'. Not 'get on with your learning'. Definitely not 'get on with your play'. For many children, education can all too easily be a journey of increasing seriousness from the exuberance of the playground to the silence of the examination hall. At university, it is all too easy for a learner's spirit of enquiry, playful experimentation and curiosity to be stifled by a misplaced perception that 'student engagement' and 'student satisfaction' will only be achieved if courses are delivered in certain unplayful ways.

In *Descartes Error* (2005), Antonio Damasio famously placed René Descartes in the dock for separating mind from body back in the sixteenth century. With the benefit of modern neuroscience, we now know that emotion, reason and the human brain are all intimately linked and that the philosophical assertions made by Descartes and others simply do not wash. Yet education still bears the mark of viewpoints like this in its separation between academic and practical learning, the former being of higher status.

Something similar has happened with the way play has been separated out from education, although this is not down to any one individual's influence. Rather, it has been a gradual cultural evolution towards a more serious version of learning. In early years, education play is virtually synonymous with learning. But, as pupils become older, play is increasingly removed from the experience of school. And, once at university, play can all too often be seen as unserious suggesting a lack of quality. Yet for some while now the learning sciences (Harrington 1990; Csikszentmihalyi 1999; Fullan and Langworthy 2013; Lucas and Spencer 2017) are increasingly showing us the importance of creative exploration, playful imagining and the kinds of perspective taking which play promotes throughout education.

Learning in the Not-So-Wild

Outside of school and university, life is also becoming less playful. Once upon a time, we used to run wild, returning to our homes only to be fed by our parents before heading back out again for second helpings of wildness and fun. Or at least this is the dream of the past that many of us still hold dear.

Sadly our memories on this occasion hold true. Today's young people do indeed have less freedom to play, more tests to complete, a lot of homework (that word 'work' again) and, if they enter higher education, a growing seriousness of intent as the amount of their financial investment becomes apparent. Such a serious view is reinforced by many institutions in their perception that quality is to be judged by the earnestness with which every waking student moment is filled with useful assignments.

Life outside school and university, like formal education itself, is tamer and much less free. It has never been more important for those students who make it to university to experience open-ended exploration and deep learning which is not immediately attached to some kind of measurement in order to keep a more balanced view of education and ultimately lifelong learning alive.

The Power of Play in Education

This fascinating collection shows us why higher education can be playful today. Each of the sketches and contributions holds out the hope that teaching and learning in higher education can be both excellent and playful, purposeful and creative, rigorous and surprising. Contributors explore playful spaces, playful methods, playful new roles and seriously playful games. Author after author challenges us all to relish the child in us and to use childish thinking to good effect at university. The thinking is by turns exploratory, curious, synthesising, compelling, disturbing, reassuring and always motivational. As I read it, I am reminded that our chronological age is much less important than our mental one. For, as George Bernard Shaw put it, 'We don't stop playing because we grow old; we grow old because we stop playing'.

So dive into this wonderful reservoir of ideas. Drink deeply. Remind yourself how important it is to keep a more expansive view of education alive and how many creative ways there are in which you can do this.

Winchester, England   Bill Lucas

References

Csikszentmihalyi, M. (1999). Implications of a Systems Perspective for the Study of Creativity. In R. Sternberg (Ed.), *The Handbook of Human Creativity* (pp. 313–338). New York: Cambridge University Press.

Damasio, A. (2005). *Descartes' Error: Emotion, Reason, and the Human Brain*. New York: Penguin Books.

Fullan, M., & Langworthy, M. (2013). *New Pedagogies for Deeper Learning*. Washington: Collaborative Impact.

Harrington, D. (1990). The Ecology of Human Creativity: A Psychological Perspective. In M. A. Runco & R. Albert (Eds.), *Theories of Creativity* (pp. 143–169). Newbury Park: Sage.

Lucas, B., & Spencer, E. (2017). *Teaching Creative Thinking: Developing Learners Who Generate Ideas and Can Think Critically.* Carmarthen: Crown House Publishing.

Professor Bill Lucas is Director of the Centre for Real-World Learning at the University of Winchester. His model of creative thinking, developed with colleagues at Winchester, was published by the OECD in 2013 to critical acclaim. It has led to a fourteen-country study by the OECD's Centre for Educational Research and Innovation into the development of creativity in schools and his appointment as the co-chair of the PISA 2021 test of creative thinking. Bill holds many external appointments including membership of LEGO® Foundation's advisory group and international adviser to Australia's Mitchell Institute. The author of more than forty books, Bill recently collaborated with Guy Claxton in *Educating Ruby: What Our Children Really Need to Learn*, to ask educators to put creativity and play at the heart of the school system.

Acknowledgements

We are grateful to all our authors for their time, patience and enlightening stories of play, without whom this collection would be the poorer. On their behalf too, we owe a special thank you to Professor Sally Brown for believing in this project and helping us find a way for *The Power of Play* to emerge in public. We wish also to acknowledge a group of people who have lent their voices and support to The Power of Play, in particular Professor Stephen Brookfield, Professor Phil Race, Professor Bill Lucas, Professor Nicola Whitton and Professor Norman Jackson. Our universities too—the University of Winchester and Manchester Metropolitan University—have provided rich arenas in which to try out play practices. We have been incredibly fortunate to find colleagues within them who have taught us so much about their ways of playing. Finally, over the years our play practices have been shaped by more people than we can name and by theorists on whose work we depend, but who, alas, we will never meet. We thank them all for their inspiration.

Contents

1 Making a Case for the Playful University 1
  Alison James

Part I Trainers and Developers

2 Exploration: Becoming Playful—The Power
  of a Ludic Module 23
  Sandra Sinfield, Tom Burns and Sandra Abegglen

3 Exploration: ESCAPE! Puzzling Out Learning
  Theories Through Play 33
  Jennie Mills and Emma King

4 Exploration: 'I Learned to Play Again' The Integration
  of Active Play as a Learning Experience for Sports
  Coaching Undergraduates 43
  Richard Cheetham

5   Sketch: The Training Game   55
    Scott Roberts

6   Exploration: Play in Practice—Innovation Through
    Play in the Postgraduate Curriculum   57
    Sophy Smith

7   Exploration: Experiences of Running a 'Play and
    Creativity' Module in a School of Art & Design   67
    Gareth Loudon

Part II   Wanderers and Wonderers

8   The Dark Would: Higher Education, Play
    and Playfulness [i]   77
    Rebecca Fisher and Philip Gaydon

9   Exploration: Playing with Place—Responding
    to Invitations   93
    Helen Clarke and Sharon Witt

10 Exploration: Cabinets of Curiosities—Playing with
    Artefacts in Professional Teacher Education   103
    Sarah Williamson

11 Sketch: Playful Pedagogies—Collaborations Between
    Undergraduates and School Pupils in the Outdoor
    Learning Centre and the Pop-Up "Playscape"   113
    Chantelle Haughton and Siân Sarwar

12 Sketch: Teaching and Learning Inside the Culture
    Shoe Box   117
    Hoda Wassif and Maged Zakher

Part III Experimenters and Engagers

13 Exploration: Dopamine and the Hard Work
of Learning Science　123
Lindsay Wheeler and Michael Palmer

14 Exploration: Play in Engineering Education　131
Bruce Kothmann

15 Experiencing the Necessity of Project Management
Through the Egg-Dropping-Challenge　141
Tobias Seidl

16 Exploration: Public Engagement Activities
for Chemistry Students　145
Dudley Shallcross and Tim Harrison

17 Sketch: Playful Maths　159
Chris Budd

18 Sketch: Connecting People and Places Using
Worms and Waste　163
Sharon Boyd and Andrea Roe

19 Sketch: Maths, Meccano® and Motivation　167
Judith McCullouch

20 Exploration: Playful Urban Learning Space—An
Indisciplinary Collaboration　171
Clive Holtham and Tine Bech

21 Sketch: Novelty Shakes Things Up in the History
Classroom　181
Carey Fleiner

Part IV Wordsmiths and Communicators

22 Exploration: Don't Write on Walls! Playing with Cityscapes in a Foreign Language Course   185
Mélanie Péron

23 Sketch: Poetry as Play—Using Riskless Poetry Writing to Support Instruction   195
Ann Marie Klein

24 Sketch: On Word Play in Support of Academic Development   199
Daphne Loads

25 Sketch: The Communications Factory   203
Suzanne Rankin-Dia and Rob Lakin

26 Sketch: Playful Writing with Writing PAD   207
Julia Reeve and Kaye Towlson

Part V Builders and Simulators

27 Exploration: Wigs, Brown Sauce and Theatrical Dames—Clinical Simulation as Play   213
Caroline Pelletier and Roger Kneebone

28 Sketch: Using Play to Bridge the Communication Divide   223
Jools Symons, Nancy Davies, Marc Walton and John Hudson

29 Exploration: Building the Abstract—Metaphorical Play-Doh® Modelling in Health Sciences   227
Rachel Stead

30 Sketch: Our Learning Journey with LEGO®   239
Alison James and Chrissi Nerantzi

31	Sketch: Using LEGO® to Explore 'Professional Love' as an Element of Youth Work Practice—Opportunities and Obstacles *Martin E. Purcell*	243
32	Sketch: Creating LEGO® Representations of Theory *Nicola Simmons*	247

Part VI Gamers and Puzzlers

33	Exploration: A Dancer and a Writer Walk into a Classroom *Seth Hudson and Boris Willis*	253
34	Exploration: From the Players Point of View *Maxwell Hartt and Hadi Hosseini*	263
35	Exploration: Wardopoly—Game-Based Experiential Learning in Nurse Leadership Education *Bernadette Henderson, Andrew Clements, Melanie Webb and Alexander Kofinas*	273
36	Exploration: Using Play to Design Play—Gamification and Student Involvement in the Production of Games-Based Learning Resources for Research Methods Teaching *Natalia Gerodetti and Darren Nixon*	283
37	Tabletop Gaming in Wildlife Conservation—'Park Life' *Louise Robinson and Ian Turner*	291
38	Sketch: 'Frogger It, I'd Rather Be Playing Computer Games Than Referencing My Assignment'—A Harvard Referencing Game *Tracy Dix*	295

39	Sketch: Using Play to Facilitate Faculty–Student Partnership—How Can You Co-design a Module? *Sarah Dyer and Tanya Lubicz-Nawrocka*	299
40	Sketch: Imagination Needs Moodling *Debra Josephson Abrams*	303
41	Exploration: It's a Serious Business Learning How to Reference—Playfully *Juliette Smeed*	307

The Playground Model Revisited: A Proposition for Playfulness to Boost Creativity in Academic Development 317
Chrissi Nerantzi

Coda 333

Index 337

Notes on Contributors

Sandra Abegglen is Senior Lecturer and Course Leader for B.A. Hons Education Studies at London Metropolitan University and is currently teaching on modules promoting peer-to-peer support and experiential learning. Her research interests are in peer mentoring, creative learning and teaching, visual narratives, identity and qualitative research methods. She has written about her teaching practice in a variety of journals and actively participated in creative learning events. Find her blog documenting her mentoring work at: http://peermentoringinpractice.com.

Dr. Tine Bech is a professional artist and researcher working at the intersection of art, technology and play. Bech's practice presents an aesthetic in which sculpture merges with the digital language of technology to create stunning large-scale public artworks, interactive spaces, participatory events and games. Play is the call to action within our emergent interactive environment. Ultimately, her practice aims to provoke curiosity and connect people with their immediate environment and with each other.

Sharon Boyd (@sboydie) is a Lecturer in Distance Student Learning at the Royal (Dick) School of Veterinary Studies. She is Director of the

Postgraduate Certificate in Advanced Veterinary Practice and Deputy Director for the online MVetSci in Advanced Clinical Practice. She was seconded from October 2014 to February 2016 on a project looking at methods for embedding Education for Sustainable Development in the veterinary medical curriculum. She is a part-time Ph.D. candidate at Moray House School of Education looking at digital narrative methods to capture a sense of 'place' in research with a particular focus on the distance learning student campus.

Professor Christopher (Chris) Budd, O.B.E. is a British mathematician known especially for his contribution to nonlinear differential equations and their applications in industry. He is currently Professor of Applied Mathematics at the University of Bath, and Professor of Geometry at Gresham College.

Tom Burns is co-author of *Teaching, Learning and Study Skills: A Guide for Tutors* and *Essential Study Skills: The Complete Guide to Success at University* (4th edn.). Always interested in theatre and the arts, Tom has set up adventure playgrounds, community events and festivals; produced the first and only International Dario Fo Festival while still a student at Essex University; and taken Godber's 'Bouncers' to Crete dance venues.

Tom is a Senior Lecturer and University Teaching Fellow in the Centre for Professional and Educational Development at LondonMet, with a special focus on praxes that ignite student curiosity, harness creativity and develop power and voice.

Richard Cheetham, M.B.E. has a reputation at national and international level in coach education and development with his work ranging from rugby union to triathlon and professional cycling with the UCI. His research, publications and conference presentations have focussed on developing a more holistic approach to coaching as well as encouraging creativity and innovation in practice session design. The important role of play in sport at all levels of performance and across all ages has been a specific area of research with his work contributing to a regional primary education physical literacy initiative, UK Coaching, Rugby Canada and the University of Winchester Play and Creativity festival.

Dr. Helen Clarke is a Senior Lecturer at the University of Winchester, UK, where she teaches on Initial Teacher Education programmes. She is a Senior Fellow of Learning and Teaching at the University and Senior Fellow of the Higher Education Academy. She has particular expertise in science education in the early years and primary phases. Committed to celebrating the energy and enthusiasm that children, students and teachers bring to their learning, she has researched children's early exploration and enquiry, rights respecting education, sustainability, environmental education and teacher development, both in the UK and overseas. She is currently working with a colleague to explore innovative teaching and learning ideas that connect children to environments through place attention and responsiveness (@Attention2place).

Dr. Andrew Clements is Lecturer in Organisational Psychology at the University of Bedfordshire. He is an Associate Fellow of the British Psychological Society and a Senior Fellow of the Higher Education Academy. His research interests include work commitment, employability and student engagement.

Nancy Davies is a Learning Technologist (University of Leeds, Institute of Medical Education). Nancy develops technological solutions to enrich medical education with a particular focus on supporting students to become reflective practitioners.

Dr. Tracy Dix is a Learning Development Adviser at the University of Leicester, working with academics to develop creative and inclusive teaching practices and integrated support for students' academic literacies. She developed the Harvard Referencing Game while part of the Teaching and Learning team at the University of Warwick Library.

Dr. Sarah Dyer is an Associate Professor of Human Geography at the University of Exeter in the UK. Sarah is the director of the University's Education Incubator, an initiative for developing and spreading innovative and effective educational practice. She teaches across the geography undergraduate programme and is B.A. programme director in the department. Sarah is also module convenor for the University's postgraduate academic practice module 'Creating Effective Learning in Higher Education'.

Dr. Rebecca Fisher was the Academic Projects Manager at the Institute for Advanced Teaching and Learning at the University of Warwick and is one part of The Dark Would team, along with Amy Clarke, Philip Gaydon and Naomi de la Tour (warwick.ac.uk/thedarkwould). Along with the other Dark Would-ers, she is an author of *Playfulness in Higher Education: A Playbox* (warwick.ac.uk/playbox). Her work on The Dark Would reflects her scholarly and feminist commitment to testing and dismantling unhelpful binaries within and beyond the classroom: The Dark Would disrupts accepted hierarchies of power by bringing together teachers, students and administrators to spark innovation out of challenge, friction and transgression. She is currently the Departmental Administrator for Research, Finance and Operations in Sociology at the University of Warwick.

Dr. Carey Fleiner is Senior Lecturer in Classical and Early Medieval History and Programme Leader in Classical Studies at the University of Winchester. Recent publications include '*Optima Mater*: Power, Influence, and the Maternal Bonds Between Agrippina the Younger (AD 15–59) and Nero, Emperor of Rome (AD 54–68)' in *Royal Mothers and Their Ruling Children: Wielding Political Authority from Antiquity to the Early Modern Era, Vol. 1*, ed. Ellie Woodacre and Carey Fleiner (Palgrave, 2015): 149–170; *The Kinks: A Thoroughly English Phenomenon* (Rowman, 2017); 'Doctor, Go Roman: Emperor Nero, and Historical Comedy in *Doctor Who*, 'The Romans' (1965)' in *Doctor Who and History: Critical Essays on Imagining the Past*, Carey Fleiner and Dene October, eds. (McFarland, 2017). She lives on the south coast of England.

Philip Gaydon was a sessional teacher and funding recipient at Warwick's Institute for Advanced Teaching and Learning. During his time with IATL, he constituted one-quarter of The Dark Would team and his research focused on virtue epistemology in children's literature and education. He contributed to the creation of the online resource *Playfulness in Higher Education: A Playbox* (warwick.ac.uk/playbox) and the attempt to instil a sense of playfulness in HE teachers and classrooms underpins his *The Warwick Handbook of Innovative Teaching*. He is now a teacher of philosophy at St Paul's School in London.

Dr. Natalia Gerodetti is a Senior Lecturer in Sociology and a Senior HEA Fellow. Her research has been in the wider area of gender and sexuality as well as on food and identity. She has a particular interest in developing and engaging students with games-based learning, and together with Dr. Darren Nixon, she has been involved in ongoing staff–student games design groups that address a variety of curriculum and curriculum supporting activities. The collaborative games developed as part of the Leeds Games Group are two research methods games and a transition game for first-year students.

Tim Harrison was a secondary school teacher of chemistry for 25 years, head of chemistry, deputy head of science and Science College Director before joining the University of Bristol to become its first School Teacher Fellow. He is now Director of Outreach for the Bristol ChemLabS Centre for Excellence in Teaching and Science Communicator in residence. He has won national and international awards for his contributions to science education but is most well known for his legendary talks to schools and the general public, aided by awe-inspiring demonstration experiments, which he has given on five continents.

Dr. Maxwell Hartt is a Lecturer in Spatial Planning in the School of Geography and Planning at Cardiff University. In addition to his research on game-based learning, Maxwell studies shrinking cities, economic decline, ageing and age-friendly policy. Maxwell was a SSHRC postdoctoral research fellow at the University of Toronto, a Fulbright Scholar at Tufts University, and he holds a PhD in Planning from the University of Waterloo. In 2017, Maxwell was identified by the Order of Canada and the Walrus Foundation as 1 of 50 Canadians under the age of 35 guiding the future of Canada.

Chantelle Haughton is a Senior Lecturer in Early Childhood Studies at Cardiff Metropolitan University and a Senior HEA Fellow. She is a Forest School Leader and trainer responsible for developing an Outdoor Learning Centre, which uses an ancient strip of woodland and concrete patches on the university campus. Chantelle was awarded Student Led Teaching Fellowship Award (2013) and Vice Chancellors Staff Award for Excellence (2011), and HEA CATE finalist (2017) awards were related to the live, playful, innovative community engagement projects that involve students, local children and practitioners as partners.

Bernadette Henderson is a Senior Lecturer in Child and Adult Nursing at the University of Bedfordshire. Bernadette has an M.B.A. with the Open University and an interest teaching leadership and management in nursing alongside self-disclosure as a learning technique. As a Fellow of the Higher Education Authority, Bernadette is developing the use of playful learning pedagogies in her role as a nurse educator.

Professor Clive Holtham is Professor of Information Management at Cass Business School and responsible for a significant strand of work on creativity, initially technology oriented, now focussing on educational and arts-based approaches. He co-founded the City University Centre for Creativity, with its thriving Master's in innovation, creativity and leadership. His team has refined methods for stimulating reflection within business innovation processes through visual methods for both students and executives and developed an acclaimed M.B.A. elective on 'The Art of Management'.

Dr. Hadi Hosseini is an assistant professor in the Department of Computer Science at Rochester Institute of Technology (RIT). His research interest lies at the interface of artificial intelligence, computer science and economics. More specifically, most of his research is on algorithmic game theory, matching theory, social choice and computational fair division. Beside his work in multiagent systems, he studies novel teaching approaches in higher education pedagogy. Hadi was a postdoctoral research fellow at Carnegie Mellon University. Prior to that, he received his Ph.D. in computer science from the University of Waterloo, where he also worked as an instructional developer at the Centre for Teaching Excellence. He was a recipient of several awards including the government of Canada's NSERC fellowship and UW's Exceptional Teaching Award.

John Hudson is a co-founder of Bright Sparks Theatre Company. John's ongoing work over the past five years has seen a gamut of productions with Devon-based 'Wolf and Water' and 'Get Changed'

Theatre Companies. John is member of the Patient/Carer community at University of Leeds School of Medicine.

Seth Hudson serves George Mason University as Assistant Professor of Game Writing in the Computer Game Design program. He teaches story design for computer games, criticism and research methods, and the history of computer games. Hudson's scholarship has addressed topics including international humanitarian law in games; student identity in higher education; pedagogy in game writing; portfolio-focused curriculum development and involving students' undergraduate research. Past conference engagements include Computer Game Design (CGD), the American Society for International Law, the International Society for the Scholarship of Teaching and Learning, and the East Coast Games Conference, where he organises and produces the Education Summit.

Professor Alison James is a Professor of Learning and Teaching at the University of Winchester, a National Teaching Fellow and Principal Fellow of the Higher Education Academy in the UK. She is co-author, with Stephen D. Brookfield, of *Engaging Imagination: Helping Students Become Creative and Reflective Thinkers*, published by Jossey Bass in 2014. Her long-standing interests in higher education are the use and development of creative and alternative approaches to tertiary learning. In particular, she has explored this in relation to personal development planning, reflective practice and identity and self-construction within the disciplines. Alison is an accredited LEGO® SERIOUS PLAY® Facilitator.

Dr. Debra Josephson Abrams a committed Freirean, has taught English to native and non-native English users for decades. A frequent conference presenter, Abrams publishes often and is a monthly columnist for Multibriefs Education, with articles in TESOL's *English Language Bulletin* and other publications. She is Assistant Professor of English at Seoul National University of Science and Technology (Korea) and was the U.S. Department of State 2016–2017 English Language Fellow at the Higher School of Economics in Moscow. Abrams's professional expertise includes critical pedagogy; teacher training, peer coaching and mentoring; multiple intelligences and learning styles; composition pedagogy and practice; critical and creative thinking, critical literacy and critical reflection; research and research training; course and curriculum design; formative assessment; and issues in d/Deaf education. Abrams, an endurance runner, photographer, avid cook and ASL user, operates Parts of Speech Educational Creativity, www.partsofspeechec.com.

Emma King is the Director of Instructional Design at Keypath Education UK, where she works with a team of Instructional Designers and Developers to partner with academic colleagues to deliver world-class, accessible online learning. Emma's expertise in approaches to online learning has been central to her previous role at the University of Warwick, supporting colleagues to develop their skills and knowledge to deliver high-quality learning opportunities. Emma has worked across all phases of education and draws on her experiences as a school teacher to inform a range of innovative approaches to teaching and learning, including effective use of space and the potential of game-based learning.

Dr. Ann Marie Klein teaches literature at the University of St. Thomas in MN. Previously, and she taught in Dallas at SMU and UD where she obtained her Ph.D. Before doctoral studies, she helped found a competitive bilingual high school in Finland. Her publications include an article in the forthcoming G. M. Hopkins anniversary edition of *Religion and the Arts* and two articles in *Hopkins Quarterly*: one on Duns Scotus's influence on Hopkins and the other on Hopkins's friendship with poet Robert Bridges. Her examinations of parallels between Eliot's *Romola* and Carlyle's *Sartor Resartus* were published in the *Victorian Institute Journal* and between More's *Utopia* and Plato's *Phaedrus* in *Liberal Arts and Core Texts*. She is finishing a book on work's dignity in Hopkins's prose and poetry.

Professor Roger Kneebone is a clinician and educationalist who leads the Centre for Engagement and Simulation Science at Imperial College London and the Royal College of Music–Imperial Centre for Performance Science. His multidisciplinary research into contextualised simulation builds on his personal experience as a surgeon and a general practitioner and his interest in domains of expertise beyond medicine. Roger has built an unorthodox and creative team of clinicians, computer scientists, design engineers, social scientists, historians, artists, craftsmen and performers.

Roger has an international profile as an academic and innovator. He is a Wellcome Trust Engagement Fellow and in 2011 became a National Teaching Fellow. He is passionate about engagement, which he sees as a translational resource bridging the worlds of clinical practice, biomedical science, patients and society.

Dr. Alexander Kofinas is the Head of Department of Strategy and Management at the University of Bedfordshire Business School. His recent publications have focused on two main areas; one is on the impact of gamification on HE education, and the second area of interest is on marketing strategy, especially online social media marketing. Alexander has a B.Sc. and M.Sc. from Sussex University, an M.B.A. from the International University of Japan and an M.Res. and a Ph.D. from Manchester Metropolitan University. He is an HE fellow and currently involved in a HEFCE-funded student experience project with research implications on the use of playful pedagogies in higher education.

Dr. Bruce Kothmann is a Senior Lecturer in Mechanical Engineering and Applied Mechanics (MEAM) at the University of Pennsylvania's School of Engineering and Applied Science. He received the 2012 Provost's Award for Teaching Excellence. He is an avid user of laboratory and interactive teaching spaces. Before coming to Penn, Dr. Kothmann designed fly-by-wire flight controls for Boeing Rotorcraft. He is a regular invited lecturer at the US Navy Test Pilot School and earned his Ph.D. from Princeton University. Dr. Kothmann loves to modify the rules of games and is the co-inventor of the Staccabees adaptation of the traditional Chanukah dreidel game.

Rob Lakin is the Creative Director of the Fashion Business School at the London College of Fashion. He has an interest in enhancing the student experience through the development of a creative, multidisciplinary curriculum, with a variety of live industry collaborative projects.

He makes a major contribution to the creative identity of the Fashion Business School and the London College of Fashion through the design, development and implementation of a number of innovative curriculum interventions.

Dr. Daphne Loads is an academic developer in the Institute for Academic Development at the University of Edinburgh where she leads a developmental pathway for university teachers and a scheme which awards funds for teaching research and innovation. She teaches on a Postgraduate Certificate in Academic Practice and contributes to other continuing professional development opportunities related to learning and teaching. Her first degree was in English, and she has professional qualifications in social work, counselling and teaching in higher education. Daphne has an Ed.D. (Doctorate of Education) and is a Senior Fellow of the HEA. Her research interests include academic identities and arts-enriched development practice. She loves gardening and travelling with her partner.

Professor Gareth Loudon is a Professor of Creativity at the Cardiff School of Art and Design, Cardiff Metropolitan University, and Director (and co-founder) of the Centre for Creativity. Gareth's research interests focus on understanding the factors and processes affecting creativity, combining ideas from anthropology and psychology, engineering and design. Gareth has been active in academic and industrial research for almost 30 years and has taken several research ideas all the way through to commercial products for companies such as Apple. Gareth is a Fellow of the Institution of Engineering and Technology and the Higher Education Academy.

Tanya Lubicz-Nawrocka is a Ph.D. student in higher education research at the Moray House School of Education, University of Edinburgh. Her work focuses on student/staff partnerships in co-creating the undergraduate curriculum. At the time of writing, Tanya worked as the Academic Engagement Coordinator at Edinburgh University Students' Association.

Dr. Judith McCullouch has a lifelong passion for joy within mathematics and is deeply frustrated by the persistent acceptability of not being able to do and not liking mathematics. She came to teaching as a second career (having being a fighter controller in the RAF—wonderful, dynamic three-dimensional moving geometry) and then moved into HE. Her research has encompassed many aspects of mathematics, its teaching and learning and each time, rising to the top, has been the potential of accessibility achieved through engagement in the subject, not the children having it done to them and the deep gratification of the 'ah!' moments.

Dr. Jennie Mills is a Learning and Development Adviser at the University of Warwick, where she leads professional development for new academic staff. Her previous role with the Higher Education Academy as a Consultant in Academic Practice focussed on Innovative Pedagogies, particularly within the Arts and Humanities. Jennie is currently researching the role of wonderment in HE teaching and learning, and how arts-inspired methodologies and creative play can be used to enhance academic practice, academic development and to challenge what constitutes knowledge in educational research.

Dr. Chrissi Nerantzi (@chrissinerantzi) is a Principal Lecturer within the Centre for Excellence in Learning and Teaching at Manchester Metropolitan University in the UK. She is passionate about creativity, play, learning through making and openness and has initiated a wide range of professional development opportunities that bring these three elements together in her practice and research. Chrissi is a certified LEGO® SERIOUS PLAY® facilitator with experience using the method and variations of it in a wide range of higher education context. Chrissi is a Principal Fellow of the Higher Education Academy, a Fellow of the Staff and Educational Development Association, a National Teaching Fellow, the Learning Technologist of the Year 2017 and received the Award for Best Open Research Practice in 2018 by the Global OER Graduate Network.

Dr. Darren Nixon is a Senior Lecturer in Sociology and a Senior Fellow of the HEA. He is the co-author of a key textbook in the sociology of work. His research explores the impact of de-industrialisation on working-class men, with a particular focus on the meaning of work and unemployment and the exploration of how class and gender intersect to produce particular kinds of work orientations. Dr. Nixon is interested in the 'Students as Producers' critical pedagogy and is currently involved in applying it within an ongoing collaboration with Dr. Natalia Gerodetti and students at Leeds Beckett University to develop games-based learning resources. He is particularly interested in how student intelligence can be incorporated into teaching practices and curriculum development.

Dr. Michael Palmer is the Director of the University of Virginia's Center for Teaching Excellence. His educational development research centres on teaching consultation techniques, graduate student professional development, course design initiatives and the impact intense professional development activities have on teacher beliefs and practices. His work has won one national research and two innovation awards from the POD Network, North America's largest educational development community. His pedagogical interests include course design, active learning, student motivation, creative thinking and teaching large-enrolment courses, particularly in STEM disciplines. He teaches a highly interdisciplinary course on infinity, a seminar on the science of learning and a large-enrolment, inquiry-based laboratory course for first-year chemistry students.

Dr. Caroline Pelletier is Reader in Culture, and Communication at UCL's Institute of Education, whose research focuses on subjectivity, games, simulation and new media. She has carried out ethnographic research projects in NHS hospitals across London, focusing on the representation of work in simulation centres. More generally, she is interested in the relationship between new media technologies in workplaces and reconfigurations of knowledge practices and subjectivity.

Mélanie Péron is a Senior Lecturer in the French and Francophone Studies department at the University of Pennsylvania. She is the Associate Director of the Penn-in-Tours summer programme. On campus, she teaches courses on French history and culture. During the summer, she teaches a writing course in Tours, France, where she encourages students to « write on walls ».

Dr. Martin E. Purcell is a Senior Lecturer in the School of Education at the University of Huddersfield, where he is Course Leader for the undergraduate Youth and Community Work programme. Having worked in community development and youth work settings across the UK for over thirty years, Martin continues to be involved in managing and delivering services for young people (particularly marginalized groups and those experiencing mental health issues) in West Yorkshire. Martin's research explores the translation of professional youth work and community development values into practice, focusing particularly on the demonstration of 'professional love' in work with children and young people.

Suzanne Rankin-Dia has been working with international students at University of the Arts London since 2001 and currently leads the Academic Language and Communication pathway on the International Preparation for Fashion at the London College of Fashion. She has a particular interest in implementing innovative and creative approaches into an EAP classroom and to empower international students to reach their full potential.

Julia Reeve is a Creative Learning Designer and DMU Teacher Fellow within Library and Learning Services at De Montfort University. She co-ordinates the East Midlands Centre for Writing PAD: http://writingpad.our.dmu.ac.uk/. Julia's pedagogic practice involves applying creative, arts-based methods to the teaching of theory in order to deepen learning and increase engagement. Her role involves the design, development and delivery of innovative workshops for students and staff, to foster confidence, self-reflection and creative thinking for writing and research, with a particular focus on researcher development. Julia previously worked as a designer in the fashion industry, a lecturer in Further Education and a Senior Lecturer in Contextual Studies for fashion programmes.

Dr. Scott Roberts is a faculty member in the Department of Psychology and the Director of Instructional Excellence and Innovation at the University of Maryland's Teaching and Learning Transformation Center. He completed his Bachelor's at Denison University, where he conducted research with chimpanzee at Ohio State, and then spent three years as a dolphin trainer and research assistant in Honolulu. Scott came to Maryland in 2003 to pursue his Ph.D. in Social Psychology, focusing on research related to deception detection and interrogation. He served as a Research Psychologist for the Federal Government before returning to Maryland in 2011 as Psychology's Director of Undergraduate Studies. In addition to his administrative work, Scott teaches graduate and undergraduate courses including introduction to psychology, persuasion and the psychology of evil.

Dr. Louise Robinson is a lecturer in Forensic Biology at the University of Derby. She is an advocate of gamification and has introduced numerous examples throughout her undergraduate teaching within both forensic science and bioscience. Louise has given talks on the use of gamification in higher education at multiple conferences and also led workshops at universities around the UK. Recently, she has designed and produced her first educational board game for use within a level 6 Wildlife Conservation module at University of Derby. The game, called 'Park Life', utilises the content of the module to draw topics together and demonstrate interaction of themes as well as provide a method of revision for the module. Park Life is presented within the text as a successful case study example.

Andrea Roe is an artist whose work examines the nature of human and animal biology, behaviour, communication and interaction within specific ecological contexts. She has undertaken residencies in a number of institutions—ranging from the Wellcome Trust to the Crichton Royal Hospital, to the National Museums of Scotland—where she has learned about and responded to research projects and collections. Her current research explores how visual art might add its voice to debates around complex cultural traditions which impact on the lives of other species. This research brings her into conversation with scientists at the Royal (Dick) School of Veterinary Studies and Scotland's Rural College who share her interests in representing animal sentience and telling animal life stories from a non-human perspective.

Siân Sarwar is a Lecturer in Early Childhood Studies at Cardiff Metropolitan University and HEA Fellow. Her research interests include music education, creativity and child participation in education, informal learning and curriculum design. Having worked as a performer, composer, orchestra administrator and secondary school music teacher, Siân then taught on the B.A. Secondary Music ITET Programme at Cardiff Metropolitan University and was the Project Officer for Musical Futures Wales.

Professor Dr. Tobias Seidl (@drseidlt) is professor for key competencies and vice-dean (learning and teaching) at Stuttgart Media University, Germany. He is a trained business coach and LEGO® SERIOUS PLAY® facilitator. His research interests are serious gaming, creativity, coaching and faculty development.

Professor Dudley Shallcross was the first National Teaching Fellow in chemistry in the UK and has been a co-Director of the Bristol ChemLabS Centre for Excellence in Teaching and Learning and is currently CEO of the Primary Science Teaching Trust. He has won national and international awards for his contributions to science education, and his interests include transition from primary to secondary and secondary to tertiary education, the use of appropriate contexts, e-enhanced learning and the use of practicals in learning. In his spare time, he is an expert of the Earth's atmosphere.

Dr. Nicola Simmons is a faculty member in Graduate and Undergraduate Studies in Education at Brock University. Past roles include regional Vice-President, Canada, for the International Society for the Scholarship of Teaching and Learning, board member for the Society for Teaching and Learning in Higher Education, including Vice-President, SoTL, Founding Chair of SoTL Canada and past chair of the Canadian Educational Developers Caucus. Her teaching and research interests are in higher and adult education, including scholarship of teaching and learning, participatory pedagogy and creative activities, educational development, and adult personal and professional lifelong learning, development and meaning-making. In 2017, she was awarded a 3M National Teaching Fellowship and the Educational Developers' Caucus inaugural Distinguished Educational Development Career Award.

Sandra Sinfield is co-author of *Teaching, Learning and Study Skills: A Guide for Tutors* and *Essential Study Skills: The Complete Guide to Success at University* (4th Edn.), a co-founder of the Association for Learning Development in Higher Education and a Senior Lecturer in the Centre for Professional and Educational Development at London Metropolitan University. Sandra has worked as a laboratory technician, a freelance copywriter, an Executive Editor (*Medicine Digest*, circulation 80,000 doctors) and with the Islington Green School Community Play written by Alan Clarke, *Whose Life Is It Anyway?*, and produced at Saddlers Wells. With Tom Burns, she has developed theatre and film in unusual places—and is interested in creativity as emancipatory practice in HE.

Juliette Smeed is the Study Co-ordinator in the Business School at the University of Buckingham. She has previously held academic skills, research teaching and student support roles in the UK and New Zealand. Juliette is interested in the social and cognitive processes of learning. In addition, her experience in business schools, teacher training and humanities departments has fostered an interest in the disciplinary nature of learning in higher education.

Professor Sophy Smith is Professor of Creative Technologies Practice at the Institute of Creative Technologies, DeMontfort University, Leicester. Sophy is a practice-based researcher whose focus includes creative collaboration and inter/multi/transdisciplinary practice, and she works extensively as a composer and performer on professional collaborative arts projects. As Programme Leader for the IOCT's innovative transdisciplinary master's in creative technologies (M.A./M.Sc.) and digital arts (M.A.), Sophy works with students at the convergence of the e-sciences and digital arts and humanities and this is reflected in her pedagogic research interests.

Rachel Stead is a Learning Development Adviser at the University of Surrey and Senior Fellow of the HEA. Since gaining fellowship, her research has focused on the potential contribution of play to learning in a variety of disciplines and areas ranging from veterinary medicine and health sciences to personal and professional development. Her most recent work has involved collaborating with faculties to develop engaging, playful learning activities using both Play-Doh and LEGO® to aid critical reflection and revision.

Jools Symons is Patient and Public Involvement Manager (University of Leeds, Institute of Medical Education). Jools is a pioneer in the involvement of patients and carers in medical education. Her focus is the empowerment of patients to be part of the educational world and recognition of the unique perspective they bring.

Kaye Towlson SFHEA, is Academic Team Manager (Information Literacy and Teaching), DMU Teacher Fellow, De Montfort University. Kaye has worked as a Librarian for many years; she ran the business information service at DMU and has worked as a subject librarian with responsibility for humanities. Her work in visual and creative learning with Julia Reeve led to the establishment of a Writing PAD centre at DMU. She has experimented with visual learning techniques within library/information literacy, employability and other contexts. She is interested in using visual and creative techniques to overcome textual barriers for visual learners and disciplines.

Dr. Ian Turner is an Associate Professor in the Centre for Excellence in Learning and Teaching at the University of Derby. Ian was previously head of forensic science and lectured in molecular biology, genetics, science communication as forensic document and handwriting analysis. Ian was named as a National Teaching Fellow in 2014 and in Royal Society of Biology Higher Education Lecturer of the year in 2017. Ian is known for a more creative form of teaching called lecture theatre 'pantomime' and has research interests in the areas of creative and innovative learning, teaching and assessment and gamification.

Marc Walton is a co-founder of Bright Sparks Theatre Company. Marc has been Stage Manager for 'The Beautiful Octopus Club' (a nightclub run by and for Learning Disabled adults) since it began at the Wardrobe Club in Leeds over 15 years ago. Marc is member of the Patient/Carer community at University of Leeds School of Medicine.

Dr. Hoda Wassif is a Principal Lecturer in Medical and Dental Education at the University of Bedfordshire (UoB) and Director of

Teaching and Learning across the School of Healthcare Practice. With a background in dentistry, Hoda achieved her Master's in clinical dentistry in 2000, her Ph.D. in 2008, and in 2016, she completed her M.A. Education. Hoda is passionate about the teaching and learning of postgraduate students in health care context. Currently, she leads M.A. dental law and ethics as well as M.A. medical education courses at UoB. Her research interests focus on innovation in teaching and learning, ethical practice and continuous professional development.

Dr. Lindsay Wheeler is Assistant Director of STEM Education Initiatives of the University of Virginia's Center for Teaching Excellence. Her research focuses on how educational development programmes for instructors impact teaching practices and ultimately student learning outcomes across STEM disciplines. She has redesigned and taught general chemistry courses and developed cross-departmental teaching courses to support graduate teaching assistants in their teaching. Her pedagogical interests include emphasising inclusive teaching practices to promote diversity in STEM disciplines, integrating student reflection on learning and utilising inquiry-based instruction. In 2015, Dr. Wheeler and Dr. Palmer received the *Robert J. Menges Award for Outstanding Research in Educational Development* for research examining student perceptions of course syllabi. Dr. Wheeler presents at conferences and runs workshops related to STEM education.

Melanie Webb (Mel) is a Senior Lecturer at the University of Bedfordshire in the Department of Health and Social Sciences specialising in children's nursing. Mel has two B.Scs from the Open University and a M.Sc. from the University of Bedfordshire. Mel gained her HEA Senior Fellow through her use of games within education and mentoring.

Sarah Williamson is a Senior Lecturer in the School of Education and Professional Development, University of Huddersfield. She specialises in the training of creative arts professionals and graduates to be art, design and music lecturers in the lifelong learning sector (FE, HE, adult education and training). Her research explores the value and transformative impact of arts-based approaches in professional education.

Boris Willis is the founder of Black Russian Games, Chief Artistic Officer of Boris Willis Moves and an Associate Professor of Experimental Game Design at George Mason University. He has performed with Liz Lerman, Elizabeth Streb, Jacob's Pillow's Men Dancers and is founder of the dance video blog danceaday.com. Willis has an MFA in Dance and Technology from The Ohio State University, a BFA in Dance from George Mason University and is a graduate of The NC School of the Arts. He is the recipient of fellowships from the Kennedy Center Local Dance Commission and Virginia Commission for the Arts Choreography.

Sharon Witt is Senior Lecturer in Education at the University of Winchester. Her research interests include playful, experiential approaches to primary school geography and place responsive learning. She is an active member of the Geographical Association sitting on the Early Years and Primary Phase Committee, and she is a Fellow of the Royal Geographical Society. With a colleague, she is currently exploring innovative teaching and learning ideas that connect children to environments through place attention and responsiveness (@Attention2place). Sharon is currently studying for a professional doctorate at the University of Exeter.

Dr. Maged Zakher is a Lecturer in Cross-Cultural Management at The University of Northampton. He obtained a Master's degree in intercultural communication from the University of Bedfordshire and a Ph.D. in social sciences research methodology with a thesis titled 'The Use of Sacred Texts as Tools to Enhance Social Research Interviews'. He has taught intercultural competence and communication in business, and he also wrote on 'Post-Revolution Egyptians' Perception of Selected Human Rights' as part of his studies in international relations. Maged is a Fellow of the Higher Education Academy, and he is involved in cultural training, English/Arabic translation and blogging.

List of Figures

Fig. 1.1	Writing with gall ink	5
Fig. 4.1	Musical chairs without chairs	47
Fig. 4.2	Balloon waterfalls	49
Fig. 8.1	Entrance to The Dark Would	84
Fig. 9.1	We roamed through animate landscapes noticing the familiar and extraordinary	98
Fig. 9.2	We meandered in the water of a stream of ideas	99
Fig. 12.1	Some items in two culture shoe boxes	118
Fig. 13.1	Fossilized animal tracks	125
Fig. 14.1	Student playing with arch blocks in mechanics laboratory	133
Fig. 14.2	A hexagonal "rep-tile"	136
Fig. 16.1	The 'Granny' model of climate	151
Fig. 19.1	LEGO® lifting bridge—full instructions	168
Fig. 19.2	LEGO® lifting bridge—no instructions	169
Fig. 20.1	The project plan	173
Fig. 20.2	A group making reflections in the mylar wall covering and reflecting on the question posted beneath it	176
Fig. 22.1	Atypical classroom: a circus warehouse	189
Fig. 22.2	Blog post turned into poster	191
Fig. 27.1	Theatrical props for medical education	214
Fig. 27.2	Manikin with pink bra	215

Fig. 29.1	Metaphorical models of barriers to trust, advocacy and death in Play-Doh®	231
Fig. 35.1	Wardopoly preparation, play and debriefing cycle	275
Fig. 35.2	Wardopoly player action and team response	276
Fig. 35.3	Wardopoly	276
Fig. 37.1	The current version of Park Life including the main board, player boards, breeding pair pieces, and resources used within the game (Photograph courtesy of David Bryson)	292
Fig. 38.1	Harvard Referencing Game	296
Fig. 39.1	Co-design of a module as a board game	301
Fig. 40.1	Extract from a game rubric for English as a Second Language students (Created by the Author)	304
Fig. A. 1	The playground model and its theoretical positioning	328

Welcome to Play!

Whoever wants to understand much, must play much
Gottfried Benn, German Poet and Essayist, 1886–1956

As you have picked up this collection, we venture that you are either already a play convert or at least open to becoming one. You might be wondering why you are not in this book, or perhaps you are feeling unsure or sceptical? Wherever you find yourself on the play spectrum, we hope that as you read on you too will agree that attitudes are changing towards play in HE. Not everywhere, and not all at once, but, as we will show, academics across continents are integrating playful practices into university teaching.

As our contributions will show, the term play is not as easy to explain as one might first think. Our offerings give a multitude of perspectives on play, and we share these as they are, for you to decide which ones resonate. One perspective is that play is free, unfettered activity intended to bring joy, relaxation and liberation to the player. The second argues that it is rule-bound and structured and has a particular purpose. The third argues that it is an immersive experience which frees us up to make mistakes, new discoveries, go beyond convention and learn through moments of discomfort. Twenty-one years ago, Brian Sutton-Smith (1997: 1) noted that there is little agreement and much ambiguity as to what play is and he is still right. Just how varied interpretations of, and contexts for, play can be is made visible in our 'How to Read This Book' section.

Before we explore the nature of play further, however, let us rewind our professional play clocks, to let you know how we came to believe in the power of play in higher education.

Our own play practices began a while ago. Chrissi first started playing to learn in 2006, at a time when she was unusual in pioneering play in her teaching; Alison started—accidentally—in 2009, making emergency use of some LEGO® bricks to explain a project visually in a presentation (James 2015). While we were lucky to find supportive colleagues, we also encountered resistance to the idea of play in HE, a pattern that seems to play out in the sector. In 2012 when Alison and Stephen Brookfield were writing *Engaging Imagination: Helping Students Become Creative and Reflective Thinkers* (2014), they originally wanted to call it creativity, imagination and play. They were advised against this, on the grounds that the word play in the title of an academic text would put readers off. Three years later, when we first mooted this book we encountered similar qualms. However, through our collaboration in 2015 with Professor Norman Jackson on Creative Academic (www.creativeacademic.uk), we could see a counter movement emerging.

Norman had set up Creative Academic as an online magazine offering a creative and alternative outlet for presenting practice in learning, teaching and research. We co-edited the second issue of the magazine, entitled *Exploring Play in HE*, and sent out an open invitation for contributions. We published 37 stories of play in HE from the UK, Canada, America, Australia, Greece and Finland and had to produce two volumes to include them all (Nerantzi and James 2015a, b).

Content ranged from the use of games during geography field trips, Friday afternoon experiments in biochemistry in response to 'what will happen if I do this?', the integration of dance and movement into business courses and the creation of animated vegetables as a form of assessment. They were lively, empirically informed and reflective accounts which confirmed for us that play in tertiary learning has been largely unpublicised or unexplored. The interest they generated prompted us to look more deeply and widely into play in HE, inspired also by our own work with LEGO® SERIOUS PLAY® techniques within and outside the university. Supporting our views were the results of a survey of academics' beliefs about play, conducted by Jenny Willis for Creative Academic. This revealed that tutors do not play simply for fun. They play in order to have greater freedom, more personal involvement and less structure, to be instinctive, open and explore without having a fixed outcome in mind. The survey underscored that its respondents were already using play in teaching to engender deeper learning and even 'undo the lack of play from A' levels'—i.e. forms of study and assessment dominant in compulsory education—bewailed by one contributor. There is a sense therefore that play is regenerative and repairing, as well as enjoyable.

A year after Creative Academic, we could see interest in play effervesce in the UK and internationally; more people seem prepared to try play or perhaps are more public in their use of play for learning—in art galleries, civic initiatives, universities, in social networks and online communities. We can see the evidence for this in a few examples from 2016.

In March 2016 in Birmingham, over eighty of the UK's top educators attended the Association of National Teaching Fellows annual symposium, dedicated to playing and researching involving all the senses. Workshop topics included using play to harness the mind and will (including to snap arrows!); creating novel, messy spaces in which learning, subject and identity are all reconfigured; encouraging responsible sexual health in students; using the Bloodhound sports car for teaching maths; and creating identity jam jars. Outside HE, in the April, The Tate Modern gallery in London housed *PLAYING UP*, an artwork by Sibylle Peter of the Theatre of Research in Germany, exploring the potential of Live Art to bridge generations. Drawing on key Live Art themes and seminal works, *PLAYING UP* took the form of a game played by adults and children together (www.playingup.thisisliveart.co.uk).

By May 2016, the Counterplay community in Aarhus, Denmark, had become a non-governmental organisation with a growing reputation and influence. Its remit? Running yearly festivals in Aarhus,

Denmark, dedicated to playful living, working and learning. Its events offered hundreds of different workshops to even greater numbers of participants. Such has been its success that from 2017 satellite events have started to take place in other countries. In July 2017, the 7th *Serious Play Conference,* which explores all aspects of game-based education, was hosted by George Mason University, with speakers from commercial companies, military organisations and universities.

In July 2016, Chrissi, who has been instrumental in galvanising enthusiasm for play, was invited to speak about play at Digifest (Nerantzi 2016a). This invitation arose out of interest in the Creative Academic issues on play, her #creativeHE course, and her work in the open access community. She had also set up The Greenhouse in 2014 (Nerantzi 2016b), an institution-wide initiative by the Centre for Excellence in Learning and Teaching at Manchester Metropolitan University to bring creative practitioners across disciplines together, nurture them and empower them to grow and innovate in their teaching. #creativeHE started as the Creativity for Learning in HE module that she turned into an open course and open community, offered in collaboration with the Creative Academic. The interest this generated has informed or been shared by a range of subsequent activities, including increased overall interest in play, and formal events, conferences and publications.

Also in July 2016, Manchester Metropolitan University inaugurated what has become their annual *Playful Learning* conference, with three days of play underpinned by research and supported by high profile 'players'. One of their first keynotes, Karen Lawson, Collaborative Learning Lead with the Scottish Government's Ingage Team, spoke about her *Emporium of Dangerous Ideas*. A two-week festival first held in Scotland in 2014 aimed at shifting thinking in education, *The Emporium* aimed to 're-establish the importance of dangerous ideas as agents of change in education'. It hosted 18 events and attracted more than 1000 delegates including those from colleges and universities. The Hidden Door Festival explored using disused public spaces as learning environments, while the Open Door initiative invited people to swap their normal working environment for an unusual setting (in one case to a brewery). Just these two examples show how playing with spaces as potential learning environments opens up new opportunities. In creating these, *The Emporium* helped forge links between education and community through play.

These examples confirm our belief that academics, researchers, students and managers can all benefit from play. In its limitless forms, it is a means of freeing up thinking, opening new channels, confronting obstacles and reframing persistent challenges. This is essential at a time when universities around the world are struggling with increased numbers and reduced resources. The identity of the university and its purpose is under siege; the climate is uncertain and unstable. We are all tasked with coming up with new, bright, motivating, resourceful and efficient solutions to support diverse learners to attain, while juggling bureaucratic and regulatory demands. We argue that play offers a response to these challenges in terms not simply of pedagogic value, but also of well-being.

The network of academics who believe in the value of play to break ice, enthuse, shake up thinking, build connections, bond people, stimulate, relax and cheer is growing. Playful communities are springing up, within and across universities and the wider world. The benefits of play are expressed in the voices of those concerned with the need to re-energise pedagogy, revive a love of enquiry, study, nurture and provoke curiosity. Academics are magpies who are constantly on the lookout for something new to bring into their repertoire, to help them bring learning alive for and with their students in the face of tests, measurements, money, uncertainty and stress.

Three years ago, when few people were writing about play in HE, we felt we could fill that gap, or would perhaps need to persuade people to play. One of the wonderful revelations of writing and editing this has been finding so many colleagues who are already playing or open to try. We have, of course, met colleagues who are less keen, or who fear they will be derided or accused of 'dumbing down' the curriculum by their peers. It may simply be that they can't remember what play is for or what it might achieve. Or perhaps it is that their conceptions of play and of the function of the academy are very particular. They may say 'my job is to educate my students, not entertain them'. We respond 'why can't you do both?'. Informed by evidence and backed by science, theory, pedagogy and practice, we hope this collection shows how you can.

References

James, A. (2015). Innovating in the Creative Arts with LEGO®. Available at https://www.heacademy.ac.uk/knowledge-hub/innovating-creative-arts-lego. Accessed May 30, 2018.

James, A., & Brookfield, S. D. (2014). *Engaging Imagination: Helping Students Become Creative and Reflective Thinkers*. San Francisco: Jossey Bass.

Nerantzi, C., & James, A. (Eds.). (2015a, June). Exploring Play in Higher Education. *Creative Academic Magazine* (Issue 2b). Available at http://www.creativeacademic.uk/uploads/1/3/5/4/13542890/cam_2a.pdf. Accessed May 30, 2018.

Nerantzi, C., & James, A. (Eds.). (2015b, June). *Exploring Play in Higher Education. Creative Academic Magazine* (Issue 2a). Available at http://www.creativeacademic.uk/uploads/1/3/5/4/13542890/cam2_part_b.pdf. Accessed May 30, 2018.

Nerantzi, C. (2016a). *Learning to Play, Playing to Learn: The Rise of Playful Learning in Higher Education – Digifest 2016*, 25 February 2016. Available at https://www.jisc.ac.uk/inform-qa/learning-to-play-playing-to-learn-the-rise-of-playful-learning-in-he-25-feb-2016.

Nerantzi, C. (2016b). Using Ecological Metaphors to Represent Professional Growth: Our Extraordinary 'Greenhouse', Its Creative Academic Gardeners and the Growing of Pedagogical Ideas. *Exploring Creative Ecologies, Creative Academic Magazine, 5,* 64–70. Available at http://www.creativeacademic.uk/magazine.html. Accessed May 30, 2018.

Sutton-Smith, B. (1997). *The Ambiguity of Play*. Cambridge, MA and London: Harvard University Press.

How to Read This book

As if you need telling! You will do it in whatever way suits. You might wish to dip in and out, or choose a theme, author or section or read from start to finish. It is up to you. However, we thought it would be worth letting you know what you are in for, in case you are expecting a certain kind of collection, or a certain homogeneity of writing.

First of all, our material does not divide neatly and evenly into chapters, nor is there a linear narrative which builds up over the different contributions. There is a holding structure, if you like: the collection is book-ended by an opening section setting the scene for play, and a closing one which offers a model for pedagogic thinking about play. However, the start and finish are not there to corral your thinking or provide a tidy framework, but rather to create a net to enclose a varied catch of 'fish'. In a gesture towards harmony, we have grouped the contents of our net into six thematic clusters, with names evoking the natures and common interests of our writers. Inevitably, we have found it impossible to create neat boundaries around each one, and didn't want to, as deep connecting strands run between all of them and naturally blur their edges. Our thoughts, ideas and practices are interwoven in so many ways. *Trainers and Developers* are also *Wordsmiths* and *Communicators*. *Gamers and Puzzlers* are also *Experimenters and Engagers*. *Wanderers and Wonderers* even mentally or metaphorically may be the architects of other kinds of play forays—including those undertaken by our *Builders and Simulators*. So expect and forgive messiness, and don't allow our attempts at organisation constrain your desire to imagine, explore and enjoy.

Our voices and writing styles are all our own and also diverse. Some are recognisable for their traditional academic format, while others are playful in form and flavour; one or two may use terminology that is unfamiliar. There are sketches (short accounts) and explorations (longer, more theorised considerations), framed by pieces by us as editors. Expect a certain eclecticism in terms of the sounds of the words on the page, as well as their subjects. It may jar you, or it may stimulate you. Whatever the effect, the variation is deliberate.

With so many contributors, we have stood back to allow for their views and experiences to be heard and respected. We have sought to represent as many disciplines as possible, to be inclusive and to give a little insight into different approaches to play considerations, aims, priorities and contexts. We are delighted to have authors from different countries and professional areas to join us in this task. However, what you have here is selected illustrations of play in HE and inevitably not the whole picture. Perspectives, opinions and experiences differ; there may be gaps or variances across cultures and disciplines; some parts will resonate with you more than others. We have allowed for US and UK spelling conventions while aiming for consistency within contributions. Where we are all united, however, is in our belief in the importance of play in higher education. This belief is expressed in different forms: the lyrical, poetic, scientific, thoughtful and practical, in contexts ranging from art to zoology. The wealth of examples gives the lie to the suggestion that play is inappropriate for higher level study. We hope they will prompt you to consider how you might draw on, integrate or amend such forms of play in your own fields of activity. Don't hold back. The time to play is now.

What's in Here? Our Contents at a Glance
While some readers will have been drawn to the book from the abstracts on the Palgrave website, other readers might find this 'headlines' section useful.

Welcome to Play—admittedly, you have just read this bit but we hope it makes clear the activities that have led up to the production of this book. A scene setter.

How to Read This Book—an explanation of our magazine style, non-linear mixture of contributions.

Section 1

Making a Case for the Playful University is a rallying cry for play in HE, introducing themes, interpretations and theoretical perspectives which will recur throughout the book. It argues for the importance of play in HE to be better understood, and for its international and interdisciplinary value.

Trainers and Developers
…stories about enabling the potential of others through curriculum and activity design, teacher training and coaching…

Becoming Playful: The Power of a Ludic Module shows how playful practices allow students to find and develop their academic identity and 'be with' each other.

ESCAPE! Puzzling Out Learning Theories Through Play. This escape game (in which participants are locked in a room and work collaboratively to make their escape) presents an opportunity for new teaching staff to experiment with unfamiliar pedagogic concepts through play.

'I learned to Play Again' shows how reconnecting with play is essential for adult sports coaches and helps broaden a student's view of actual 'life situations' and the skills required.

The Training Game introduces psychology students to the power of play to recognise, shape and steer behaviour in learning.

Play in Practice counters the assumption that play-based learning is of value only to early years teaching and learning by outlining how it has been used to develop and carry out research within a higher education postgraduate programme.

Experience of Running a 'Play and Creativity' Module in a School of Art and Design shares the author's motivation for and experience of running the module to inspire others.

Wanderers and Wonderers
…Stories about place, space and mystery…

The Dark Would is a project which creates mysterious and unusual environments within which participants can play, feel safe, stimulated, and engage as whole people with fundamental epistemic questions of the nature, creation and exploration of knowledge.

Playing with Place: Responding to Invitations tells stories of play and place-based education with students studying to be primary school teachers.

Playful Pedagogies: Collaborations Between Undergraduates and School Pupils in the Outdoor Learning Centre and the Pop-Up 'Playscape'. This sketch outlines how playful, creative practice can help students develop their understanding of challenging concepts and/or encourage them to make clearer links between theory and practice.

Cabinets of Curiosities: Playing with Artefacts in Professional Teacher Education.
This case study describes playful object-oriented pedagogy in professional teacher education, using a Cabinet of Curiosities theme rooted in the 'wunderkammer' or 'wonder rooms' of the sixteenth and seventeenth centuries.

Teaching and Learning Inside the Culture Shoe Box shows how such a box, filled with cultural objects, can be used to enhance students' learning experiences especially in teaching culture, ethics and communication.

Experimenters and Engagers
…Stories about enquiry, exploration, outreach, magic, method and madness…

Dopamine and the Hard Work of Learning Science describes the role of play in science, the importance of play in science pedagogy, and ways play in teaching helps create engaging learning environments.

Play in Engineering Education explores play as a process of discovery in engineering education which inspires and provokes wonder.

Experiencing the Necessity of Project Management Through the Egg-Dropping-Challenge takes a well-known game to enable students to experience and reflect on the challenges of project work.

Public Engagement Activities for Chemistry Students demonstrates an outreach programme which provides opportunities to 'play' which stimulate public interest in chemistry and also benefits the postgraduate student facilitators.

Playful Maths argues that Maths is a highly creative subject, whose playfulness can be detected in a vast range of games and pattern spotting, revealed in even the most mundane daily activities.

Connecting People and Places Using Worms and Waste outlines two playful workshops which address key concepts of environmental care, sustainability and animal welfare.

Maths, Meccano® and Motivation uses playful building to enable learners to thrive within mathematics, not be on the outside while mathematics teaching is 'done to them'—knowledge is not passively received but is actively built through participation.

Playful Urban Learning Space is based on an unusual collaboration between a business school and a fine art practitioner, supported by a Creative Entrepreneur in Residence funding scheme.

Novelty Shakes Things Up in the History Classroom. This sketch reveals the possibilities when desperation drives you to play in order to enable students to grapple with difficult and complicated events in history.

Wordsmiths and Communicators
…Stories about spoken, written and visual words…

Don't Write on Walls! is a project built around the notions of imagination and play, which invites participants on a 'study abroad' visit to engage in a narrative with their host city.

Poetry as Play shows how 'riskless' poetry-writing helps students 'see' more clearly both the natural world and the spiritual realm, while learning to contemplate and exchange insights.

On Word Play in Support of Academic Development shows how university lecturers are encouraged to play with language to discover new meanings and make connections with teaching practice and teacher identity.

The Communications Factory uses playful workshops to put students at ease with intercultural communication in a global classroom.

Playful Writing with Writing PAD discusses playful techniques from the arts to enhance engagement with academic writing and research across disciplines and levels.

Builders and Simulators
…Stories about theatres, bricks and modelling dough…

Wigs, Brown Sauce and Theatrical Dames examines how clinical simulation, performed in hospitals as a form of training, can be understood as play, involving creating and maintaining fictions, role-playing theatrical characters and erecting satisfying narrative structures.

Using Play to Bridge the Communication Divide uses theatrical collaboration to enable students to understand how doctors need to communicate challenging concepts and procedures to a diverse population.

Building the Abstract: Metaphorical Play-Doh® Modelling in Health Sciences. This piece explores the potential of metaphorical model making using Play-Doh® as a multi-sensory approach to learning development in higher education.

Our Learning Journey with LEGO® summarises ten years of activity working with LEGO® and LEGO® SERIOUS PLAY® for academic, educational and staff development.

Using LEGO® to Explore 'Professional Love' as an Element of Youth Work Practice:
This sketch details how dialogical and transformational learning is enhanced when LEGO® is used to facilitate classroom-based discussions with undergraduate students about critical aspects of their professional practice.

Creating LEGO® Representations of Theory shows how play-based activities, such as 'building' academic papers in progress, can help students break existing thinking patterns to uncover their implicit thinking and connections.

Gamers and Puzzlers
…Stories about rule making and breaking…

A Dancer and a Writer Walk into a Classroom examines how play can enhance teaching in game design and game writing courses.

From the Players Point of View assesses how game-based teaching techniques in both hard (computer science) and soft (urban planning) sciences show improvements in student perception of engagement, creativity, teamwork and enjoyment.

Wardopoly is a bespoke in-house practice-based board game adopting clinical simulation principles and game mechanics adapted from the monopoly genre to empower students to voluntarily adopt actively engaged, self-determining learning behaviours.

Using Play to Design Play demonstrates the benefits of working with students to design and produce games for use in sociology teaching.

Table Top Gaming in Wildlife Conservation: 'Park Life' uses a game strategy to create a sustainable wildlife park through decisions regarding investment of their limited funds.

'Frogger It, I'd Rather Be Playing Computer Games Than Referencing My Assignment' discusses an approach adapted from the classic 'Frogger' game to inspire learning about correct referencing.

Using Play to Facilitate Faculty–Student Partnership describes how play can be used to facilitate academic faculty–student partnership for module design.

Imagination Needs Moodling describes and evaluates games that have been successfully implemented in pre-college ESL courses and college English composition courses.

It's a Serious Business Learning How to Reference—Playfully showcases approaches which help to capture students' attention and lighten the learning experience in a business and management context.

In the Playground

The Playground Model Revisited is a new exploration into a framework to encourage playfulness and experimentation for academic staff and further professionals who teach or support learning in higher education.

Coda. Here, the editors bring together key messages from this highly diverse text, ending with a question and an invitation to the reader.

1

Making a Case for the Playful University

Alison James

California Dreaming

7.30 a.m. Saturday, 16 February 2018. I am on the 24th floor of the luxurious Fairmont Hotel, in their Crown Room, placing brown paper bags on tables more fit for a wedding reception than a workshop. The occasion is the 49th *Learning and the Brain Conference*, co-hosted with Stanford University, and I have come to talk about play. The huge windows offer a near 360° panorama of the city—its buildings glowing under a fresh morning sun and their outlines imprinted against a flawless blue sky. San Francisco Bay is littered with sailboats and a toy Alcatraz and tiny Golden Gate Bridge are iconic and crisp against the water. I tell myself if no one wants to play this morning, at least they have something fabulous to look at.

7.45 a.m. Slides are up, mikes are checked, and props are ready. I prowl around the space, juggling coffee and nerves. The conference is

A. James (✉)
University of Winchester, Winchester, UK
e-mail: alison.james@winchester.ac.uk

© The Author(s) 2019
A. James and C. Nerantzi (eds.), *The Power of Play in Higher Education*,
https://doi.org/10.1007/978-3-319-95780-7_1

dedicated to the relationship between neuroscience and learning. While I know where play comes into this, I wonder how many people will want to forego a weekend lie-into think about it?

Concern about participant numbers (or rather the lack thereof) had made planning a hands-on session challenging. First of all, at a time of heightened airport security I was not sure what I could bring from the UK? Were paper clips too sharp? Could Play-Doh® conceal something dangerous? Would sand make me look like a drug smuggler? (I may have been overthinking.) How much stuff should I bring? Enough for 3? 30? I felt a weight of responsibility too; my friend and dear colleague Stephen Brookfield was flying in from Tucson to co-host. What if it was not worth his while? How would we justify sitting in a room with wonderful scenery and some crazy stuff in brown lunch bags from the CVS store, if no one came?

There is a point to this preamble and to my articulation of apprehension. Worrying about who might attend your conference session is magnified when you are involving play. Play divides tertiary educators. Responses can be polarised, with colleagues open, fired up and energised by the prospect of playing, or suspicious, dismissive and uncomfortable. In San Francisco, I was confident teachers from the primary and secondary sectors would understand the importance of play for their age group of learners. However, the people I really wanted to convince were university colleagues, my target context university learning. The words of my host when I had spoken at a major UK university in January 2018 rang in my ears: 'My job is to educate my students, not entertain them. Can you persuade me why I should bring play into my teaching?'.

The short answer is, of course, that you can educate while entertaining; the longer one is to explore with people where, how and why play might fit in their given context. My goal in the States was to make the case for play in HE by actually playing, by drawing on eminent play theorists and by sharing stories of the ever-increasing engagement with play in HE. And this is what I will do here too, to lay the ground for the explorations and sketches which follow in this collection.

But—briefly—back to San Francisco. You can tell a lot about workshop participants by how they position themselves in rooms and how they relate to the things they find in them. Brown bags, sticks, peas and marshmallows, building bricks, soft items or shiny images can all attract or repel participants. For anyone curious enough to shake the bags that fine Saturday morning, they concealed a mysterious miscellany. They rattled or clicked, or emitted ruffly, soft sounds. Participants gravitated towards them, intrigued or sat as far away as possible. They lifted them, heads cocked at a jaunty enquiring angle (perhaps hoping they were breakfast?). Or left them alone, as they gazed out over the Pacific, perhaps wondering why they were up quite so early and what else they could be doing.

I will now fast-forward 90 minutes and summarise what happened. To my joy, participants arrived well before our start time of 8.15 and they kept on coming. The tables filled up; they lined the sides of the room and stood at the back. About 150 of us explored perceptions and definitions of play through building brick puzzles and responding to the contents of the brown bags. We fed views through the online backdrop of Todaysmeet.com (a virtual classroom) curated by Stephen, to gather responses and questions throughout the session. Feedback was fantastic, with many participants telling us they felt freed, inspired, energised, cheered, surprised and much more. One or two were honest about not being convinced—finding engaging in playful activity of the kind we had offered 'silly'. The different kinds of emotions, ideas, responses and convictions about play from this event are ones which I have seen recur in all kinds of educational contexts and conversations. For this reason, the San Francisco workshop summarises and symbolises many of the points which I will explore more fully now.

The Play Times They Are a Changin'

(with apologies to Bob Dylan)

Chrissi and I have already indicated that the tide is turning with regard to play in higher education. Our fellow players in the sector also know this, however there are still important developmental conversations to be had. These are about expanding our conceptions of what play is (and isn't), learning about how play is already enhancing the university experience and why play it is important, and appreciating the tensions and constraints that can mar our ability to play.

With this in mind, our San Francisco workshop opened with stimuli to prompt a conversation about play, enclosed in those brown paper bags. A scroll of tasks curled and tightly tied with coloured ribbon guided participants through. In pairs or small groups, they investigated textures, drew analogies, created patterns, played guessing games and made meaningful arrangements. They expressed their responses on their paper bags and on luggage labels; these were collated and arrayed on a table, providing an instant and powerful picture of feelings about play. This activity was inspired by UK National Teaching Fellow Giskin Day's Cupsule Conversation, which she designed to prompt thoughtful and different exchanges. Having experienced her activity, which had been surprisingly powerful and pleasurable, I have since modified it to explore a range of topics, including assessment. The creativity and credit belong to Giskin, however.

404 Einsteins and Forest School

In March 2017, 404 Einsteins walked through the streets of Toronto to get into the Guinness Book of Records for the largest gathering of people dressed as Albert Einstein (Siekierska 2017). Not only were they successful, but they were marking the beginning of the 2017 Next Einstein Competition, an annual event which looks for 'ideas that make the world a better place' (Blackwelder 2017). Setting aside the twin goals they wished to achieve (and any financial prize incentive), why else might participants have wanted to dress as Einstein? What must it have felt like? Was it expressly for a purpose, or just for the heck of it? Did it feel like sheer fun? Was there a sense of connection and camaraderie, so often experienced by those who come together in a mass and common experience? I cannot answer these without stepping into the minds of 404 participants, each of whom will have had a different response. This is because experiences of playful activity are personal and subjective.

I can, however, answer such questions after spending the day at Forest School. In April 2018, 12 of us gathered at a woodland dell in the South of England for a meeting of an accreditation network. The sound of such a group suggests we really should have been in a boardroom. Instead, we were wrapped up in our most sensible outdoor clothing, the day bright but damp, with a vestige of March chilling the air. Guided by our expert leaders, we spent the day integrating our formal business with forest activities. We collected water in storm kettles, made fire to boil them for coffee, cooked lunch over a camp fire, foraged for items to create something from nature embodying five steps, made gall ink and wrote on paper with quills. I summarise drastically. All of us agreed it was an incredibly special experience, with the clear sky and tree tops overhead and the feel and the smells of soil and vegetation all around (Fig. 1.1).

Conducting our academic practice in such surroundings had an indefinable and yet powerful impact on us all. It was liberating and exciting and did indeed create subtle bonds between us through a shared and

Fig. 1.1 Writing with gall ink

glorious experience. Our leader shared stories of the children whose teachers bring them (weekly) to Forest School and of the positive impact this has on their overall attainment. This raises important questions about the ways and spaces in which we expect learning to occur, and the enduring place of play in both of these.

What Does Play Mean? What Does Play Mean to Us?

> Where does the play of imagination come from? When are sounds music? When are patterns and colors art? When are words literature? When is instruction teaching? (Nachmanovitch 1990: 5)

I love this quote for its evocation of the blurriness between boundaries and of how difficult it can be to say something is precisely this, but not that. So it is with our definitions of play.

Play is such a small word, and yet it is wide open to application and interpretation. We can see this by scanning and selecting definitions from a range of sources. Better still, ask a large room full of people what play means to them. Both they and the dictionaries may come up with something familiar or succinct; play as the opposite of work; voluntary and intrinsically driven activity without serious purpose. (It is the same with the adjective 'ludic' (from the Latin 'ludere' to play) which some of our contributors adopt; definitions vary from pertaining to play, to more specific references to liveliness, fun or spontaneity.)

A quick browser search adds a little to this baseline; 'physical or mental leisure activity that is undertaken purely for enjoyment or amusement and has no other objective' (Playtherapy.org.uk). These basic meanings are often the ones with which people content themselves, however there are many more to be found.

Use play as a verb and the possibilities are multiplied; playing can involve performance, roles, deception and trickery. Combine play with another linguistic component—such as 'wordplay' and this conjures verbal dexterity, wit, mental agility, linguistic duelling and experimentation (all complex qualities). Horseplay suggests something else—the rough and tumble of energetic youth, physicality, liveliness, contact, abandon (no equine required).

In *Deep Play*, the author and naturalist Diane Ackerman defines ideas rather beautifully as 'the playful reverberations of the mind' (2000: 4). The notion is poetic and has an innocence or neutrality to it, whereas Brian Sutton-Smith (1997) argued that play has darker or ambivalent connotations in terms of human behaviour.

The words 'play' and 'games' are also often used interchangeably, and yet they are not synonyms. Games are largely structured activities with rules and conventions, while play can be any permutation of freedom and openness, as well as having its own particular facets (think theatre or make believe, as well as fantasy conventions). Games are one of the more popular and accepted play forms, and the creation of the term gamification (akin to what Helen Sword describes playfully as Zombie Nouns) seems to validate the practice further. The popularity of gamification in the university is clearly evidenced by our *Gamers and Puzzlers*.

Similarly, play and creativity are often conflated, and yet they are not identical in meaning; play is not necessarily creative, nor is creativity always playful. They have much in common, being experiences all can enjoy, being stimulating, energising and freeing; ones which can take you beyond yourself. For us as editors where they sometimes differ is that play can be about exploring possibilities through games and simulation, and about experience and behaviour, while creativity is about the making of newness in the form of an outcome. However, even these differentiations are too crude, as you will see in the contributions which follow, and the subtle differences between the two well worth exploring in future research.

How and Why Do We Play?

The American psychologist Peter Gray, writing for Psychology Today (n.d.), brings in the dimension of *how*—rather than *what*—we play by asserting that 'the characteristics of play all have to do with motivation and mental attitude, not with the overt form of the behavior'. This also relates to playfulness, or the manner in which we engage in an activity, rather than the activity itself. If we turn to renowned play writers and theoreticians however, we discover deeper social and existential facets of our subject.

The Dutch historian Johann Huizinga asserted that play is fundamental to the successful navigation of human existence. He argued that all play is meaningful and a cultural phenomenon; although it is actually pre-cultural, animals play without having to learn how from humans (Huizinga 1938).

In *The Play Ethic*, Pat Kane, author and one half of the 1980s singing duo Hue and Cry, offers a manifesto for play as a driver for radical social change. He argues that play is not 'merely the stuff of recreation or leisure, idleness or diversion' (2004: 6), but defines it across his publications and social media as 'taking reality lightly'. This is not to trivialise it, but rather to echo reality in a more sardonic form—perhaps as a way of making peace with life's difficulties, oddities and threats. We only have to think of the gallows humour of medics, the material of observational comedians, the sarcasm of frustrated commuters or the acid interplay of MPs jousting in political arenas to see this at work. Humans play as part of learning to survive, in establishing social order and relationships, as sanctuary from routine, when taking risks.

The psychoanalyst D. W. Winnicott (2005) saw play as an essential means of exploring identity and making sense of experiences. Kane and Winnicott's positions are both supported by the NGO Counterplay whose website proclaims that

> Games, play and being playful are means of cultural, societal, educational and commercial development and transformations as well as sources of joy. In a complex world of constant change and uncertainty, play is a way to cope, navigate, create and exist. (http://www.counterplay.org/this-is-counterplay/)

The societal and collaborative are not, of course, the only kinds of play, although I have found in group discussions the solitary, quiet kinds are sometimes overlooked. We play quietly, alone, peacefully, in our heads, or through interests we pursue alone, (jigsaw puzzles, crosswords, fantasies and imaginings), not simply by tearing around with others.

Play is also more sophisticated than it is given credit for, often being an unsung element of high-order thinking. For Chris Budd, Professor of Mathematics at the Royal Institution of Great Britain and the University of Bath, and contributor to this collection, play is inherent in maths, uniting creativity with pattern-finding, wonder and mystery—crossing boundaries between artistic and scientific thinking. The value of a university education is often evoked as furthering knowledge and expanding the capacity of individuals to contribute to and shape their world. With this in mind, how can play not figure in the tertiary experience?

The Science of Play

In his extensive research, play theorist and psychiatrist Stuart Brown discusses plasticity of the brain and how it can change in response to stimuli, for example, through play (2009). Marian Diamond, one of the founders of neuroscience, established a correlation between play and brain size in rats. In her paper The Significance of Enrichment, she reported structural differences in the cerebral cortices of animals of any age through exposure to environmental stimuli. Sergio Pellis, professor of neuroscience, stresses the importance of peer-to-peer interactions in shaping the connections of the pre-frontal cortex in the brain for healthy motor, cognitive and emotional processes (cited in Parr 2014).

The Dangers of Play Deprivation

The risks of not playing—particularly in childhood and formative years—are described by Parr (2014) as 'criminality, obesity and declining creativity'. Stuart Brown (2009) describes how play deprivation can lead individuals to anti-social or highly pathological behaviours, even murder. I do not for a moment suggest that an absence of play will render academics psychotic. However, it is clear there is an important socialising aspect to play that is integral to the present-day models of learning. A less cheerful reason given by the late & revered play theorist

Brian Sutton-Smith (1997: 198) as to the importance of play is that its opposite is depression, not work. (With an increase in mental health issues experienced by staff and students in universities due to anxiety, uncertainty and stress, it is not impossible to make this leap.)

How Do We Play?

We play in an infinitely greater variety of ways than is sometimes realised: solo or team, material and object-based, three dimensional, written, performative, structured, unstructured, rule-based, competitive, outdoor, virtual, free, purposeful, game-based, linguistic, silent, quiet, noisy, introvert and extrovert. A challenge in creating typologies of play, identified by writers such as Sutton-Smith (1997), is that there are more kinds of play than we can ever fully list. The latter also elaborates this point with illustrations from different kinds of fields—military, scientific, mathematical, anthropological and so on. His examples are helpful as some assume that play is more natural in some disciplines (dance, drama, sport and arts) than others (criminology and STEM subjects) and yet this is inaccurate, as this collection shows. Play can belong in any part of the tertiary curriculum, as long as there is imagination, openness and receptivity to support the practice.

Brown goes further and resists defining play due to the personal and subjective nature of play preferences. What is one person's idea of blissful play can be another's worst nightmare. (If play is performance, how do you feel about karaoke? Do you long to belt out tunes and release your inner diva? Or make a sprint getaway, so you neither have to sing nor listen?) Equally, what seems superficial, time-wasting play to a bystander may be deeply invested activity for the player. Watch any child negotiating life in an imaginary world, immersed in their alternative roles. Attend a Star Trek convention or observe sports fans at events: their engagement is tribal, genuine, passionate, absorbed and committed.

Feelings about play are complicated as we may reject some forms of play but be happy to try others. Similarly, there are certain types of play which organisations including universities are prepared to entertain and others which they are much more reluctant to support. The most popular forms of play in organisations are often those with pre-stated goals and end points, e.g. for developing team spirit and behaviour. They have structure, outcomes and rules, and are collaborative or competitive; they often have win/lose, selective, hierarchical or judgemental elements or a behaviourist system of reward or punishment. In short, for those that need one, they have enough of a rationale to justify spending time and energy on them.

Examples of purposeful organisational play include musical activities where entire companies are taught to sing in harmony, an obvious metaphor for working towards a common goal. Adventure-based challenges which are physically and mentally demanding (e.g. building rafts and navigating rivers) test resilience and group cohesion. Military-style exercises, where the contents of two crammed trucks have to be decanted into one, test logistical and problem-solving capabilities. Other outdoor activities include animal-handling days spent with animals such as sheep dogs. There are more radical forms of play exploration, such as developing leadership skills through learning to tango. The aims of these days are constructionist in educational philosophy and twofold in intention. Participants learn how to complete a range of activities while expanding their understanding of themselves in undertaking these.

All of the above are forms of playful learning, where either a form of play has been integrated into the exploration of a subject or activity, or the manner in which learning has been stimulated has been playful in nature. While these examples have been of organisational learning, the same principles underpin forms of playful pedagogy. As we have already noted, playful pedagogy or play-based learning may be designed to achieve a purpose or outcome, or is competitive in nature, where success is celebrated by winning. What divides academics and their students who engage in playful learning is often the matter of purpose versus freedom. We have been told firmly by colleagues that unless play is being used to achieve a clear outcome, stated from the outset, or is not really an appropriate form of pedagogy in higher education. We ask the question why we are so afraid of allowing a free space in which a purpose that is currently unknown to us may or may not reveal itself?

Fear of Free Play?

Comfort levels and questions of legitimacy seem to arise with play when an organisation cannot find a business case for it, or a 'good enough reason' to allow it. However, the basis on which this judgement is made is often a narrow one, often about avoiding threats to credibility, seniority or authority. Free play is the most challenging form of play for institutions which need to emphasise value for money and financial accountability. And yet free play is at the heart of the most groundbreaking practices. Brown is among those who claim that for play to be truly played it should have *no* predetermined purpose, a definition which would exclude a vast number of playful activities that are used for bonding or developmental purposes. Furthermore, agenda-free play does not appear to be a luxury that universities are disposed to 'allow' although variants of Google's 80:20 time allocation model have been experimented with.

As an improvising musician, Nachmanovitch writes that he is not in the music or creativity businesses but in the surrender business—about 'cultivating a comfortable attitude toward not-knowing, being nurtured by the mystery of moments that are dependably surprising, ever fresh' (1990: 21–22). In free play, the players give themselves up to the moment and to the encounter, and the need to prepare students for an uncertain future is often proclaimed as one that is met through a tertiary education. And yet for many tutors allowing any loss of control, goal or structure runs counter to their professional sense of identity and to offering a well-designed, high-quality learning experience. Somehow the idea that play is consonant with, and not anathema to, the values inherent in being a committed, responsible educator needs to be transmitted and believed. Fear of the freedom of play needs to be faced head on and examined forensically for fact or fiction; play must not become the fall guy for our nervousness concerning risk taking and experimentation in teaching and learning. In my professorial inaugural on play on 9 May 2018, I placed small envelopes under certain chairs in the auditorium. They were marked 'this is for you', or 'this is not for you'. I invited the audience to open them and tell me what was inside. The literal answer was 'nothing'. One of the answers I received was 'plenty of space for thinking'. Through the simple symbol of the envelope, I sought to question how we feel able to have the space to play; whether we believe it can and should be ours, or whether we feel pressurised by views that it is neither right nor proper activity in a university. We need to give ourselves and others permission to have this freedom and this time.

Challenges of Play

A couple of years ago, I attended an (excellent) international conference on open badges at the University of Southampton. (For those unfamiliar with them, open badges (https://openbadges.org) are described by the Mozilla Foundation as 'visual tokens of achievement, affiliation, authorisation, or other trust relationship sharable across the web'). I had gone along feeling I knew little about them and really needed to find out more. I was not disappointed. The event was characterised by passionate debate and considered experimentation as to how such badges might incentivise learning. Some of the ways they were being designed, used and shared were imaginative, colourful, thoughtful and playful. I was impressed by examples which were both fit for purpose (however defined) and amusing, while inspiring potential recipients to achieve them.

Not everyone felt the same. On Twitter, halfway through the day, a participant asserted vigorously that open badges had no place in a university education. This really struck me. Why on earth, I wondered, would anyone bother attending an event on open badges if they were convinced they were inappropriate? To reinforce negative preconceptions? This is just as easily achieved by staying at home and Googling. Surely if the tweeter had been open to change the language might have been more temperate? Perhaps they felt that badges were babyish and demeaning of higher learning? Whatever the reason, it made me think of similar unnuanced reactions I have encountered with regard to play.

Resistance to play is often due to assumptions about 'appropriate' techniques and the 'right kinds of academic knowledge' that should be engaged with at university. For some naysayers, this might also be down to an attachment to a dividing line between mind and body, academic study and vocational training, work and play. Play is the marginalised stuff you do when all the grown-up business has been attended to. Some HE teachers planning to use play have spoken of being mocked for wanting to engage in something they should have grown beyond. Play, in the eyes of their critics, was associated with the childish, the frivolous and the lightweight. The challenge therefore is often to persuade those who are anti-play that it brings something significant to study and exploration of deep and complex subjects at an advanced level. It is also about finding a way for everyone to play comfortably—or at least within a comfortable arena of challenge; rejection of play is often due to fears of feeling awkward or of being humiliated or exposed.

There are often prejudices about the props for play. Sometimes highly structured play is deemed preferable or more appropriate for serious enquiry than arts-based play, which may be seen as a softer option (although this is misleading). At others, there may be openness to creative play but with reservations. A Dean I once worked with was happy for me to run play and creativity workshops for his staff as long as I didn't bring any Play-Doh®. He made the assumption (without consultation and erroneously) that they would feel awkward using fragrant, squishy modelling dough associated with kindergarten. (Rachel Stead turns this assumption on its head later in this book.)

Discussion of play within a university setting provokes strong emotions, often tightly tied to a sense of professional credibility, our academic identity and what we consider our role in higher education to be. Therefore, if we assail one of these by presenting an approach or an activity that runs counter to them, we may meet with misunderstanding or resistance. The LEGO® group gave the moniker LEGO® SERIOUS PLAY® to its creative thinking system to reassure users of the worthiness of the approach. Often, the word 'serious' is attached to play in other contexts to ensure we appreciate its purpose or credibility. The need to accompany the word 'play' with 'serious' to make it valid in an HE context perturbs me. It implies that play cannot function as a worthy activity in its own right, without a qualifier. This I think highlights a lack of understanding of what a wide variety of play types are and what they might contribute. One of the attractions of this book, I hope, and to the credit of the contributors, is that they provide evidence of many ways this misconception can be overcome.

The Play and Creativity Festival at the University of Winchester

We drew the workshop in San Francisco to a close by showing a film of the 2017 Play and Creativity Festival a group of us hosted at the University of Winchester (https://playandcreativityfestival.wordpress.com). Now an annual event, the Festival was first created to make time for staff and students across the University to come together and play in a whole variety of ways. Our intentions were fourfold; to

- celebrate and re-energise teaching and learning
- find alternative ways of communicating complex ideas and important messages
- generate fresh perspectives and new ideas
- build connections and community.

We held it in the last taught week of semester 2—a time when teachers and students alike are tired, fraught and panicking about deadlines. Although we had similar concerns to mine in San Francisco about participation, this was not a bad choice. With playful activities running all week across campus participants could step away from the tensions, relax, switch their heads off or switch them onto other subjects entirely.

In 2017, activities included voice and performance workshops; making sessions with LEGO®, no sew bunting, collage, sensory drawing, ceramic painting; puzzles which ranged from jigsaws to code breaking to digital maze navigation; outdoor explorations and contemplative walks and many more. The Secret Life of Campus combined a mystery tour with insights into biodiversity and sustainability. Maggot racing showed the invaluable contribution blow fly larvae make to calculating rates of decomposition on Forensic Studies. A pop-up museum combined toys and kitsch social and political memorabilia gathered on a trip to the States with consideration of equality issues. Participants grappled with the challenges of running a complex organisation through digital games. They learned about eighteenth-century drama through performing stylised hand gestures and I ruined perfectly good trousers playing sitting volleyball. The quality of all of these sessions was exceptional, as was the commitment and connectedness of leaders and participants taking part.

The festival was a gamble, but we saw an extraordinary shift in reactions in the weeks leading up to it. Initial suspicion or bemusement gradually changed to interest and curiosity, as well as enthusiasm. Feedback during and after the week revealed that people loved the fact that it brought them together, and talked about feeling both energised and calmer in a frenetic week. They repeatedly said that they were having conversations with people they wouldn't usually talk to about things they wouldn't usually talk about. They met colleagues for the first time and looked at educational challenges with fresh eyes. It proved a great way to exchange ideas between teachers and between people in different departments. It was felt to offer radical, rich and unexpected opportunities for professional learning. Students were surprised by the fun they had in class by taking a different tack to a subject. A member of professional services staff wrote after attending a session: 'I see now the reasoning behind your team's endeavours this week. Play is 'accepted' as something that which is only done as, or with, a child, it seems as though as people age they 'forget' that play is a valuable learning tool'.

More than 350 people took part in festival events across a week of activity. They included the Vice Chancellor, Deputy Vice Chancellor, Assistant Vice Chancellor, those in academic roles, RKE, Marketing, Business Development, Library, Estates and AQD, Administrators, PAs and cleaners. We won an award for learning and teaching innovation and were praised for providing 'a forum for imaginative, challenging and fun pedagogic practice which, in turn, inspired colleagues to review their own pedagogic practice and open themselves to the possibility of incorporating elements of play' (testimonial; Professor Elizabeth Stuart, First Deputy Vice Chancellor).

In April 2018, we ran the festival again, this time with two Play Tents, guest players, musical activities, a student-designed play logo and 8 student Play Champions. The main Play Tent was set out on the playing field, village-fete style, and our first activity of the week was a morning of communal decorating; setting out creative corners, providing a 'lounging with LEGO®' area with deck chairs and bright orange bean bags, home-made bunting making and the creation of 50 paper pompoms. At our opening ceremony, we had a drummer, student singers, paper plate decorating (while they were balanced on our heads) and presented an award to our student logo designer. Then, the week unfolded, with music, creativity, student-led workshops, games and the evolution of three collaborative art works. These started with three blank canvases, each dedicated to one of our university values: individual matter, compassion and spirituality. By the Friday, these had become rich, colourful intricate paintings where students and staff of all kinds had all made their mark. Just as with Forest School, we had come together in companionship to explore our ideas about why we do what we do. Over the days, the Play Tent took on a special character, partly through the artefacts that began to populate it, but by the mood, activity and presence of those who spent time in it. Classes were even held in it, because it was recognised that the space allowed for a different, freer, intriguing kind of learning. We all agreed we needed a permanent tent!

Conclusion

I hope that these tales of play have pointed towards the complexities, benefits and challenges of play, and cleared the path for those which follow. In my experience and in this collection, there are many academics voicing frustration that our current models of education are stifling alternative and innovative ways of thinking and acting. Robinson (2011) is one who has long questioned rigid and unchallenged conceptions of education, asserting that schools are killing creativity in the young. We know that universities are becoming increasingly marketised and reshaped by mechanisms of measurement such as the Teaching Excellence and Student Outcomes Framework (TEF) in the UK. Financial and economic factors are making some institutions unconfident about what they should legitimately support or pursue. As a result, the space and resource to play may seem like a luxury to some who work within them.

Play spaces and resources are not luxuries, however. An obituary in The Guardian newspaper for the futurist Alvin Toffler cited his telling prediction: 'The illiterate of the 21st century will not be those who cannot read and write, but those who cannot learn, unlearn, and relearn' (Associated Press 2016). Constrained modes of education which, through a fear of risk or failure, adhere to conformity over curiosity or the unconventional are not the answer. Routine and monotony have never been the progenitors of genius. We need to play, not just to relieve our stresses, but because play makes us better at the complex, challenging, horizon-stretching work that a university needs to do.

References

Ackerman, D. (2000). *Deep Play*. New York: Vintage.
Associated Press. (2016, June 30, Thursday). Alvin Toffler Dies Aged 87. *The Guardian*. Available at https://www.theguardian.com/books/2016/jun/30/alvin-toffler-author-of-future-shock-dies-aged-87. Accessed May 30, 2018.
Association of National Teaching Fellows Annual Symposium. (2016, March). *Programme*. Available at http://ntf-association.com/wp-content/uploads/2015/06/ANTF-Symposium-2016-abstracts-v3.pdf. Accessed May 30, 2018.
Blackwelder, C. (2017, March 29). *These 404 People Dressed Like Albert Einstein to Break a World Record—And All for a Good Cause*. Available at http://aplus.com/a/guinness-world-record-albert-einstein-next-einstein-competition?no_monetization=true. Accessed May 30, 2018.
Brown, S. (2009). *Play: How It Shapes the Brain, Opens the Imagination and Invigorates the Soul*. New York: Avery.
Counterplay. http://www.counterplay.org.
Diamond, M. (n.d.). *The Significance of Enrichment*. Available at http://www.cerebromente.org.br/n11/mente/diamond1.html. Accessed May 30, 2018.
Gray, P. (n.d.). *The Value of Play*. BlogpostforPsychologytoday.com. Available at https://www.psychologytoday.com/blog/freedom-learn/200811/the-value-play-i-the-definition-play-gives-insights. Accessed May 30, 2018.
Huizinga, J. (1938). *Homo Ludens*. First ed. Later publication in 1971. Boston: The Beacon Press.
James, A., & Brookfield, S. D. (2014). *Engaging Imagination: Helping Student Become Creative and Reflective Thinkers*. San Francisco: Jossey-Bass.
Kane, P. (2004). *The Play Ethic: A Manifesto for a Different Way of Living*. New York: Macmillan.

Nachmanovitch, S. (1990). *Free Play: Improvisation in Life and Art*. New York: Tarcher/Penguin.

Parr, R. (2014, May 1). The Importance of Play. *Times Higher Education Supplement*. Retrieved from https://www.timeshighereducation.com/features/the-importance-of-play/2012937.article.

Pellis, S. Cited in Parr (2014) Above.

Playtherapy.org.uk. http://playtherapy.org.uk/ChildrensEmotionalWellBeing/AboutPlayTherapy/MainPrinciples/PlayDefinition. Accessed May 30, 2018.

Robinson, K. (2011). *Out of Our Minds: Learning to Be Creative*. Chichester, UK: Capstone.

Serious Play Conference Website. http://seriousplayconf.com.

Siekierska, A. (2017, March 28, Tuesday). World Record Set in Toronto for Largest Crowd Dressed as Einstein. *The Star, Toronto*. Available at https://www.thestar.com/news/gta/2017/03/28/world-record-set-in-toronto-for-largest-crowd-dressed-as-einstein.html. Accessed May 30, 2018.

Sutton-Smith, B. (1997). *The Ambiguity of Play*. Cambridge, MA and London: Harvard University Press.

Sword, H. (n.d.). *Zombie Nouns Ted-Ed Talk*. Available at https://ed.ted.com/lessons/beware-of-nominalizations-aka-zombie-nouns-helen-sword. Accessed May 30, 2018.

The Telegraph. (2015). University of Cambridge to Hire 'Professor of Lego'. Available at http://www.telegraph.co.uk/news/uknews/11670591/University-of-Cambridge-to-hire-professor-of-Lego.html. Accessed May 30, 2018.

University of Berkeley Obituary of Marian Diamond. Available at http://news.berkeley.edu/2017/07/28/marian-diamond-known-for-studies-of-einsteins-brain-dies-at-90/. Accessed at May 30, 2018.

Winnicott, D. W. (2005). *Playing and Reality* (2nd ed.). New York: Routledge.

Part I

Trainers and Developers

2

Exploration: Becoming Playful—The Power of a Ludic Module

Sandra Sinfield, Tom Burns and Sandra Abegglen

> What resources do you want for your 'Performance'?
> Nothing special… The usual scissors, glue, magazines, sugar paper…

Introduction

Our context is the academic skills or Higher Education Orientation (HEO) module that all our BA Hons Education Studies undergraduate students have to take. Our Widening Participation (WP) students and our inner city post-1992 University are often labelled as deficit: 'They are Mickey Mouse students for whom Mickey Mouse degrees are quite

---

S. Sinfield (✉) · T. Burns · S. Abegglen
London Metropolitan University, London, UK
e-mail: s.sinfield@londonmet.ac.uk

T. Burns
e-mail: t.burns@londonmet.ac.uk

S. Abegglen
e-mail: s.abegglen@londonmet.ac.uk

appropriate' (Starkey cited in Brockes 2003). This has never been our experience. Our students are fierce and diverse; they have walked powerfully across borders, on building sites and down hospital corridors. We are not there to fix deficits, but to give space for the emergence of voice and to acknowledge the super-complexity of university life and study and for us this could only exist in a powerful, playful, fully ludic course. Only thus could we capture the whole glorious messy business of fierce, joyous learning—the intensity—the rhizomatic (Gillies 2017)—the power of being and working with others (Nancy 2000).

Here, we explore what happened when we allowed our students to take responsibility for their learning in a celebratory and playful way and gave them the options about what they wanted to learn—and how. We discuss what role 'play' played in this and make a strong case for a more ludic approach to learning and teaching. In many ways, we designed a module stripped of what people normally see as 'content' and focussed on process: role plays, simulations, projects, exhibitions, showcases and performances. In line with the idea of hybrid pedagogy (Morris 2013), we suggest that academic content is a proposal to inspect, laugh about and jump off from, rather than something to tick off and pass through. Based on our experience and the feedback provided by our students, we see great potential in our ludic module and play itself; it provides the energy, the eruptions, the poetry and the connectivity for our students to succeed. Play transforms the 'deficit-fixing' HEO to a synoptic and challenging one. That is, our *Becoming* module, rather than being 'just' about skills, is one which allows the students to make of all the other modules they are taking. It allows them to understand Higher Education (HE) overall and through that has the power to transform education and educational experiences.

The Module: *Becoming* an Educationist

We developed our one-year, first-year module *Becoming an Educationist* (*Becoming*) as a 'de-schooling' process (Illich 1971)—to get students to explore what learning feels like when it is creative and empowering. We utilised 'free writing' and 'blogging to learn' to help students develop a writing habit—such that they wrote more often—and thus became better at writing, themselves (Abegglen et al. 2016a). We asked them to put on performances and produce *Multimodal Artefacts* for an *Exhibition*—rather than an assessment point—and saw them engage purposefully, experimenting with comic books, jigsaw puzzles, board games, pack of cards, songs, poems, dances, memory envelopes, cabinet of curiosities, newspaper articles, short stories, sculptures, 3D artefacts, drawings/paintings, patchworks, collages, posters, garments and videos/films/animations (Abegglen et al. 2016b): fiercely alive and fiercely learning. PLAY is a central aspect of our learning and teaching practice.

In our ludic module, 'play' is the *process* that smooths out the reductive, transactional striations of the formal education through which our students have passed. Play is the reflection and recognition of the self. This seems particularly important as our students are 'non-traditional' with awareness that they are deemed to have less academic, social and cultural capital (Bourdieu 1984) than the mythic white, male middle-class student of the Russell Group or Oxbridge universities. We wanted to start the educational journey of our students by valuing and welcoming them into the University as they are—rather than placing them immediately as 'deficit' and 'less than'. We wanted to 'see' what they bring with them and help them explore how they can utilise that as they grapple with their new present and become the professionals they want to be.

Play Is Thirdspace, Play Is Freedom

The world we occupy has competing demands on students and tutors alike. The promotion of higher level cognitive skills competes with the imperative to deliver challenging and yet purposeful content that develops soft skills and has high pass rates. Lecturers have to design curricula that address the concerns expressed in the National Student Survey (NSS), Higher Education Academy (HEA) benchmarks and UK Professional Standard Frameworks (UKPSF), Quality Assurance Agency (QAA) descriptors and professional body standards. They also need to incorporate academic literacies, digital literacies, research skills and employability to satisfy 'consumer' and business demand, in particular when teaching academic skills modules.

We used Shields' (2004) model of Lefebvre and Soja's (1996) argument of *Thirdspace* as a way to explore the challenges that conventional HE demands. The classroom and our creative pedagogic practice were harnessed as ludic spaces for empowering practice. By addressing our students' strengths and their experiences, we gave them the opportunity to develop, playfully. Play is not 'dumbed down' learning, but 'serious business' (Parr 2014). As Winnicott (1971: 54) argues, '[i]t is in playing and only in playing that the individual child or adult is able to be creative and to use the whole personality, and it is only in being creative that the individual discovers the self'. As such play has the potential to make explicit the need for and provoke a paradigm shift in curriculum design, and in our learning and teaching practice. With Winnicott (1971), we argue that play is important in counteracting the implicit threat that occurs when we are in transitional spaces—between worlds, between social classes and in alien educational settings. Play is 'freedom' (Huizinga 1949).

The Essentials

There were some *essentials* we put forward to enable our students the space and time to learn—and play. These essentials, outlined in our Module Handbook and presented to students in the very first session of the module, are as follows:

Essential 1—Be there
You ARE the course! The course happens as we talk, listen, engage and generally do stuff together. It's important for you to attend—to be with your fellow students—to work together to create the course.

Essential 2—Get involved
We want you to talk, listen, discuss and present; to *make* notes of usefulness; to read actively and interactively; to join in with energy and enthusiasm to all the different things that you will be asked to do; and to reflect on what you have done and why; to self-test and make your learning conscious.

Essential 3—Think about it

Think about it: learning is reflective, that is, you have to think about what you have done and why. Each week, write a blog entry. You will get some guidance on this from your 2nd-year mentors. Your blogs do not always have to be written. They can be collages, drawings, photographs, etc. To remember what you have learned, you have to make the learning conscious and you have to revise what you want to keep. Hence, we ask you to keep a weekly learning log/blog, where you make your learning conscious and memorable.

Plus, we asked students to:

- Join in with energy and enthusiasm: smile—and work hard;
- Ask lots and lots of questions;
- Have fun;
- Write something each week; and
- Start their Learning Projects early.

Learning Through Play: The Projects

Rather than following a week-by-week programme where we told our students what to do, alongside our immersive and activity-based workshop sessions, we asked them to direct their learning by engaging in a range of projects. We made some suggestions, below, but were happy if students came up with their own ideas (see also Abegglen et al. 2016b):

- Writing: Blogging to learn
- Multimodal Exhibition
- Develop a Digital Me
- End of year Performance
- Reading—Make it fun
- Sketch Books
- Art and Artists
- Writers and writing
- Learning Project.

We asked students to get into *Performance Groups* to work on a *Multimodal Exhibition* and *End of Year Performance*—where each group was asked to plan, develop and deliver the outcomes of their work. The performance itself was their chance to get as creative as they wanted: devise theatre, music or dance productions; deliver a set of presentations; and set up interactive workshops or produce an interactive exhibition. They could do anything that would engage, inform and entertain their audience, their peers—as long as it somehow connected to teaching, learning and/or assessment—and challenged, stimulated or extended our/their thinking on what it means to become an inspiring, emancipatory educationist.

Examples of their work can be found here:

2014/2015: http://learning.londonmet.ac.uk/epacks/posters-digital/
2015/2016: http://learning.londonmet.ac.uk/epacks/posters-digital2/
2016/2017: https://educationandsocialpolicy.wordpress.com/2017/03/22/multi-modal-exhibition/.

Student Feedback: Focus Groups

We asked a *Becoming* graduate to run a small image-mediated focus group to explore what other students thought of the *Becoming* module. The themes that came up were as follows:

- Importance of the ability to be able work together—something which needs to be learnt—as it is challenging—but seems essential to achieve goals;
- Play helps create a sense of unity—and achievement;
- Play = enjoyment, fun—which, in turn, helps to achieve, brings success;
- Fosters development of self—helps students to build confidence—allows them to become who they want to be.

What they said:

> In the multimodal exhibition I learnt how to be creative with my work but most importantly how to make my work reflect who I am as a person and what my work means without having to explain it to others when they see it.
>
> This module has taught me unique ways of teaching such as group activities or individual research projects. I have learnt to look at things in an unusual way, and the importance of education and its meaning.
>
> Overall, this module has taught me more than what I knew at the beginning. It helped me to be confident in myself when presenting work in front of a group of people, which is something that I have struggled with. I am happy to say that these activities have benefitted me incredibly.
>
> At the end of the module, I am quite proud of myself. I feel that my knowledge is a lot more extended now and I can actually debate about education with solid arguments.

Climb Every Mountain

As the team that devised and delivered this module, we found that the main obstacles for us were those of timetabling and rooming: we needed to break out of the traditional lecture theatre and the one-hour lecture plus two-hour seminar division of our University time, class and space. Yes, we could play for short periods of time and on the lecture theatre steps, but *Becoming* worked better when we were scheduled for three hours in one adaptable classroom—with movable tables and chairs; with resources for drawing, painting and making; and where we used the three hours for an intense workshop on a particular theme or task. For our students, the 'obstacles' were opening themselves up and becoming vulnerable; the perpetual challenge of group work; and not feeling creative or artistic. The broader challenge is to get senior managers and discipline academics to realise the emancipatory impact of this ludic practice and thus to be brave in the development and delivery of their own creative modules.

And So…

Learning is social, collective and embodied, and there are different ways of learning, knowing and being—and many different arguments as to what makes a good learning and teaching environment. On television, Gareth Malone runs 'empowering' choirs to help people re-discover their confidence and their communities, and 'Strictly Come Dancing' turns novices into dancing experts via personal relationships and tailored tuition. We asked our students to come on a de-schooling, playful journey to engage with their own learning and learning spaces in powerful ways.

The HE sector is currently undergoing radical changes with a strong emphasis on measurable outcomes. We need our WP students to recognise the skills and potential they already have so they can build on their strengths. By making our classroom playful, engaging and productive, we were enabling them to begin the learning journey from where they are. We gave them 'a voice', allowed them to be with others, and place themselves and their assignments in meaningful contexts. It is play that surfaces, nurtures and develops the aptitudes, skills and knowledge to be a successful HE participant and engaged citizen. We definitely do not want to make it simple for our students—but we want to provide them with meaningful learning experiences on which they can build.

We call on all educators to explore the potential of ludic practice—making students not only reach for the stars but enabling them to build the required rocket. Classroom activities do not have to mirror the win/lose format of formal assessment or exams. Learning and teaching practice has to challenge, yes, but in ways that allow students and staff to experiment—and get it wrong, again and again, before getting it right. Playful learning is joyful yet not easy. Because of this, as Nerantzi and James (2015) argue, we cannot afford to leave it out of our practice.

References

Abegglen, S., Burns, T., & Sinfield, S. (2016a). Critical Pedagogy: Utilizing 'Critical Writing Exercises' to Foster Critical Thinking Skills in First-Year Undergraduate Students and Prepare Them for Life Outside University. *Double Helix, 4*.

Available at http://qudoublehelixjournal.org/index.php/dh/article/view/80/266. Accessed May 30, 2018.

Abegglen, S., Burns, T., & Sinfield, S. (2016b). Hacking Assignment Practice: Finding Creativity and Power in the Fissures and Cracks of Learning and Teaching. *Journal of Learning Development in Higher Education, 10*. Available at https://journal.aldinhe.ac.uk/index.php/jldhe/article/view/347. Accessed May 30, 2018.

Bourdieu, P. (1984). *Distinction: A Social Critique of the Judgment of Taste*. London: Routledge.

Brockes, E. (2003, January 15, Wednesday). Taking the Mick. *The Guardian*. Available at http://www.theguardian.com/politics/2003/jan/15/education.highereducation. Accessed May 30, 2018.

Gillies, D. (2017). *Rhizomatic Learning: A Brief Critical Dictionary of Education*. Available at http://www.dictionaryofeducation.co.uk/r/r/rhizomatic-learning. Accessed May 30, 2018.

Huizinga, J. (1949). *Homo Ludens: A Study of the Play-Element in Culture*. London: Routledge & Kegan Paul.

Illich, I. (1971). *De-schooling Society*. New York: Harper & Row.

Morris, S. M. (2013). Decoding Digital Pedagogy, Pt. 1: Beyond the LMS. *Hybrid Pedagogy*. Available at http://www.digitalpedagogylab.com/hybridped/decoding-digital-pedagogy-pt-1-beyond-the-lms/. Accessed May 30, 2018.

Nancy, J. L. (2000). *Being Singular Plural*. Stanford, CA: Stanford University Press.

Nerantzi, C., & James, A. (2015). A Waterfall of Questions—Or Can We Afford Not to Play in HE? *Creative Academic Magazine*, 2a. Available at http://www.creativeacademic.uk/magazine.html. Accessed May 30, 2018.

Parr, R. (2014, May 1). The Importance of Play. *Times Higher Education*. Available at https://www.timeshighereducation.com/features/the-importance-of-play/2012937.article. Accessed May 30, 2018.

Shields, R. (2004). *Henri Lefebvre*. Available at https://sites.ualberta.ca/~rshields/f/lefebvre.htm. Accessed May 30, 2018.

Soja, E. W. (1996). *Thirdspace: Journeys to Los Angeles and Other Real-and-Imagined Places*. Oxford: Blackwell.

Winnicott, D. W. (1971). *Playing and Reality*. London: Tavistock.

3

Exploration: ESCAPE! Puzzling Out Learning Theories Through Play

Jennie Mills and Emma King

This chapter considers how an escape room game can enhance learning about learning as part of a mandatory professional development programme for new academics in higher education, by enabling exploration of pedagogic theory through embodied experiences and active experimentation. Escape rooms are team-based games where players discover clues and solve puzzles to accomplish a specific goal (usually escaping from the room) in a limited amount of time (Nicholson 2015). The escape room provides players with a series of prompts (physical, lexical, visual and philosophical) that encourage them to investigate different approaches and possibilities as they manipulate knowledge to arrive at new understanding. Through this play, individuals both employ and challenge what they know and can do already to develop their practice and level-up.

J. Mills (✉)
University of Warwick, Coventry, UK
e-mail: J.Mills.3@warwick.ac.uk

E. King (✉)
Keypath Education, Coventry, UK
e-mail: emma.king@keypath.uk.com

© The Author(s) 2019
A. James and C. Nerantzi (eds.), *The Power of Play in Higher Education*,
https://doi.org/10.1007/978-3-319-95780-7_3

Highly structured, the escape room typifies Nicholson's (2012) definition of a game:

$$Game = Play + Goals + Structure.$$

The staged discovery of an escape room is predicated upon reward. Participants can only progress by demonstrating sanctioned knowledge/behaviours in response to pre-determined short-term goals. The escape room creates an environment analogous to the real world but which imports fictional constraints and risks, transposing a narrative which has no place in the everyday experience of higher education. Familiar story tropes (e.g. save the world and find the microfilm) combine with the immersive nature of the game and the physical reality of being locked-in to introduce perceived peril. Jeopardy is essential to create sense of adventure, motivate active participation and give players agency, but the nature of the threat in the scenario should be respectful of local context and cultural sensitivities. Our game aimed to enable individuals to gain deeper understanding of theory by making connections with their own experience through puzzles *about* particular learning theories which directly rewarded learners for reproducing knowledge. The knowledge and activities within the game space carried little, if any, explicit meaning back to the non-game world, instead meaning was created by learners reflecting upon their embodied experience of learning theory. Escape therefore embodied a purposeful purposelessness. The flexibility that this afforded created an authentic emotional response, which formed the basis for reflection—and the locus for meaningful cognitive growth and real-world learning.

The convergence of space, narrative and learning objectives can create the conditions for effective learning (Sandford and Williamson 2005) and triggers four intrinsic motivators: a sense of control, challenge, stimulated curiosity and fantasy (Barab et al. 2005). The synergy between problem solving and research skills has occasioned the use of escape room games to develop information literacy in HE (Clarke et al. 2017; Kincaid et al. 2016). Going beyond content, escape games create an ecosystem in which collaboration, communication, creativity and critical thinking thrive with the potential to enhance learning across disciplines.

Research indicates that the escape room experience is predominantly emotional and characterised by fun, pleasure and wonder (Kolar 2017: 1330). The emotional core of the escape room is narrative, which energises players to play (Gee 2003). The fictional scenario establishes a ludic circle within which real-life events and objects assume special meaning. The escape room door is a door to another world, a world which resembles and yet overlays the everyday place left behind. When players cross the physical threshold and enter the game space they become a figurative version of themselves, assuming a role which is emotionally embedded within the story. Their experience of their own emotional response to the game, their interaction with the game environment and their fellow gamers creates the game. Motivated learners are more likely to undertake challenging activities, to be actively engaged, to enjoy and adopt a deep approach to learning, and to exhibit enhanced performance, persistence and creativity (Schunk et al. 2008). Anecdotal evidence and recent research (Deaker et al. 2016; Quinn 2012) indicates that academics are frequently resistant to professional development and undertake it reluctantly. This is exacerbated as educational theory and research is alien to their own disciplinary ways of encountering the world. Academics who build their identity upon their status as experts feel disempowered by their state of unknowing (Weller 2011). The escape game has the potential to address these issues. It brings together the intrinsic motivation offered by fun theory and the affordances of the escape room game in which players are literally 'trapped' in a situation from which it is 'difficult to escape without learning what he/she is intended to learn' (Biggs 2003). Players are liberated into the game space and regain control of their experience. This offers the potential to re-engage academics who are alienated in their encounters with educational theory by enabling them to inhabit and embody those theories. As the ludic circle is always transformative, it enables players to retain a little of their new role as they return to normal life. So, although they enter the game as novices, players leave as the hero of their own pedagogic adventure.

<u>The game is on—an example</u>
<u>The date: Wednesday 5 July 2017</u>
The scenario: eminent pedagogue Stanley Yelnats (pseudonym taken from the palindromic hero of Louis Sachar's novel *Holes* 1998), disaffected by the strategic direction of his institution, has gone rogue.

Initially recruited by a new HE provider to ensure their Gold rating in the UK Teaching Excellence Framework, he is now the lynchpin of a plot to obliterate their greatest business threat, The University of Warwick. Yelnats is attending a conference at Warwick and has left in his room a laptop linked to a device which will destroy campus. Players have one hour to save the University.

The set: a standard single conference centre *en-suite* bedroom. Puzzle elements were objects that a conference-going academic might have—suitcase, gym bag, laptop, suit, laboratory coat, notebook. Two unobtrusive replacements to the normal fixtures and fittings of the room also carried clues. The verisimilitude of this site-specific set was crucial in making the physical setting co-extensive to the fictional space reinforcing the same but different game world. The laptop displayed a timer counting down the hour and inputting the correct code stopped the timer and won the game.

The puzzles: digital (mobile phone unlock patterns, computer passwords and augmented reality) and analogue (padlocks, heat activated objects and UV images). All puzzles were designed to embody different learning theories. Behaviourist puzzles engaged participants in repetitive activities, which offered rewards after each successful iteration. Constructivist puzzles required players to add new pieces of information to their current knowledge to unlock learning. Social constructivist puzzles made players work together, each receiving different pieces of information which together generated shared meaning. Gestalt puzzles encouraged learners to identify patterns in the evidence presented to solve problems. Connectivism was represented obliquely by the games master who provided clues and a link to the outside world and in this way epitomised the network.

The play: four players were briefed on the scenario and entered the room. Players were observed and could communicate with the games master via Skype. The game ran three times with three different groups, and each group had a distinctive blend of acquaintance, escape room experience and pedagogic expertise, which informed their expectations and conceptualisation of the game.

The game generated a state of 'flow' synonymous with play (Csikszentmihalyi 1990). Players lost their sense of time and became less self-conscious. Flow requires a balance between challenges and skills—and puzzles which were too hard destabilised the relationship between effort and progress. The ability of the games master as ally on the outside to give timely clues helped assuage the danger of frustration and disengagement, clarifying goals and offering immediate feedback.

Although not all players enjoyed the game, all agreed that it was an intense and exhausting experience. Time and space to decompress and reflect was essential. None of the groups successfully completed their mission, so players weren't swept back into the real world on a wave of jubilation, which impacted upon the debrief and feedback. Disappointment produced greater awareness of defeated expectations, particularly amongst group members with pedagogic expertise. Knowing that the game was designed to enable learning about learning theory distorted perceptions of its utility. Research indicates that educators (Bardon and Josserand 2009) and students (De Freitas 2007) need to recognise the potential educational benefits of a game. In this instance whilst learners were willing to suspend disbelief to realise anticipated benefits, the manner in which benefits were realised did not fit expectations. In response, one might jettison the learning-related content and depend upon the embodied experience of the different learning theories and post-escape reflective work. This would privilege the purity of the game. One might integrate reflective breaks—having a pause button—to allow learning to be unpacked as it happens. However, this could compromise the integrity of the game. The third way would be to develop puzzles which closely integrate content and the game—perhaps requiring players to prepare for the game by undertaking specific learning activities, mastering particular skills or knowledge.

Puzzles we thought straightforward were hard for players to solve. Over-familiarity with our clues may have distorted our perception of difficulty, but our guest games master (and escape room aficionado) also thought they were easy. Players who struggled to solve these initial problems offered negative feedback, highlighting the importance of making timely progress within the game (Malone 1980). It is possible that cognitive abilities are altered by entering the highly affective game space which could warrant further exploration.

Our two main challenges were interrelated. The first was creating suitable puzzles able to represent learning theories faithfully. It was difficult to create content which remained true to the ethos of the escape game, and which met our aim to embody learning theory. Behaviourism was relatively straightforward and co-extensive to the affordances of escape rooms. The others were harder, particularly given the constraints of borrowed space and limited budget. A dedicated space, which can be physically constructed, manipulated and controlled, and which could offer the ability to isolate or anchor game elements or participants, would resolve some of these issues.

To create a story-rich environment, we added written additional props to seed the story. This narrative excess created confusion, diverted focus and depleted our players' energy and appetite for discovery. Players found the lack of linearity and false clues disorienting, with one reflecting: '[T]hat we often get learning pre-packaged. When we're exposed to just a mass of potential we sometimes don't know what to do with it (or ourselves)'. These issues relate to an imbalance between effort and reward, with players calling for more 'quick wins'. Feedback indicated that more structured narrative which widened the ludic circle, immersing people within the story world before the physical game 'threshold' and extending engagement beyond it would promote reflection in a more 'game-related' way.

The need for reflection and debrief after the event was always key. Players had expected to learn something concrete in the room. Consequently, they felt that they had missed the 'wider learning' or expressed disappointment that they only superficially engaged with the 'material'. The embodied experience of these theories is only valuable after undertaking reflective work. One stated that they remembered nothing about content of posters on behaviourist theorists as they were only scanning for clues which prompted a discussion about surface and deep learning. It is possible that the impact of the escape room experience will only be realised through reflection as part of future practice, and that evaluation will need to be longitudinal.

An escape room appears to sit on the periphery of free play. It is highly structured, with no improvisational potential or possibility for players to deviate from a pre-ordained pathway. If play is freedom through imaginative agency, then locking people in a room seems its antithesis. An escape room compels players to relinquish control as all props are pre-imagined and the narrative is fixed. However, if we figure game makers, game masters *and* game players as players, then some agency is reclaimed. There may be value in a play one, watch one, make one model.

Conclusion

The escape game promises active and exploratory learning. However, inescapable time constraints demand simple problems, confining learners to the conceptual shallows. Escape is perhaps not suitable for teaching higher level concepts. The extended three-tier exposure to escape, where learners play, watch and then create, offers greatest potential. This approach supports extended reflection as they reflect on new knowledge and put it into practice. This approach is time hungry as escape rooms can be run only for small numbers of individuals simultaneously. We therefore recommend that escape elements should be integrated into broader learning experiences, such as pervasive games, flipped classroom approaches, or as small-scale learning activities within a workshop/class. Whilst this may not offer the same immersive experience time efficiencies facilitated by larger groups increase potential for high-quality feedback and scaffolded discussion to support reflection and eventual success.

References

Barab, S., Arici, A., & Jackson, C. (2005). Eat Your Vegetables and Do Your Homework: A Design-Based Investigation of Enjoyment and Meaning in Learning. *Educational Technology, 45*(1), 15–20.

Bardon, T., & Josserand, E. (2009). Why Do We Play the Game? Exploring Institutional and Political Motivations. *Educational Training, 51*(5/6), 460–475.

Biggs, J. (2003). *Aligning Teaching for Constructing Learning*. York: The Higher Education Academy. Available at https://www.heacademy.ac.uk/system/files/resources/id477_aligning_teaching_for_constructing_learning.pdf. Accessed December 1, 2017.

Clarke, S. J., Peel, D. J., Arnab, S., Morini, L., Keegan, H., & Wood, O. (2017). EscapED: A Framework for Creating Educational Escape Rooms and Interactive Games for Higher/Further Education. *International Journal of Serious Games, 4*(3), 73–86.

Csikszentmihalyi, M. (1990). *Flow: The Psychology of Optimal Experience*. New York: Harper & Row.

De Freitas, S. (2007). *Learning in Immersive Worlds: A Review of Games-Based Learning*, JISC. Available at https://www.webarchive.org.uk/wayback/archive/20140615100504/jisc.ac.uk/media/documents/programmes/elearninginnovation/gamingreport_v3.pdf. Accessed December 1, 2017.

Deaker, L., Stein, S. J., & Spiller, D. (2016). You Can't Teach Me: Exploring Academic Resistance to Teaching Development. *International Journal for Academic Development, 21*(4), 299–311.

Gee, J. P. (2003). *What Video Games Have to Teach Us About Learning and Literacy*. New York: Palgrave Macmillan.

Kincaid, J., Miller, E., & Robson, D. (2016). *Escape to the Library: Building a Library Learning Environment for Incoming Students*. Available at http://www.txla.org/sites/tla/files/groups/LIRT/UNT_EscapeRoom%20-%20LIRT.pptx.pdf. Accessed December 1, 2017.

Kolar, T. (2017). Conceptualising Tourist Experiences with New Attractions: The Case of Escape Rooms. *International Journal of Contemporary Hospitality Management, 29*(5), 1322–1339.

Malone, T. W. (1980). What Makes Things Fun to Learn? Heuristics for Designing Instructional Computer Games. In *Proceedings of the 3rd ACM SIGSMALL Symposium and the First SIGPC Symposium on Small Systems*. Palo Alto, CA, United States.

Nicholson, S. (2012). Strategies for Meaningful Gamification: Concepts Behind Transformative Play and Participatory Museums. In *Proceedings of the Meaningful Play Conference*. Lansing, MI. Available at http://scottnicholson.com/pubs/meaningfulstrategies.pdf. Accessed July 15, 2017.

Nicholson, S. (2015). *Peeking Behind the Locked Door: A Survey of Escape Room Facilities*. Available at http://scottnicholson.com/pubs/erfacwhite.pdf. Accessed July 15, 2017.

Quinn, L. (2012). Understanding Resistance: An Analysis of Discourses in Academic Staff Development. *Studies in Higher Education, 37*(1), 69–83.

Sachar, L. (1998). *Holes*. London: Bloomsbury.

Sandford, R., & Williamson, B. (2005). *Games and Learning*. Bristol: Futurelab.

Schunk, D. H., Pintrich, P. R., & Meece, J. L. (2008). *Motivation in Education* (3rd ed.). Upper Saddle River, NJ: Pearson Merrill Prentice Hall.

Weller, S. (2011). New Lecturers' Accounts of Reading Higher Education Research. *Studies in Continuing Education, 33*(1), 93–106.

4

Exploration: 'I Learned to Play Again' The Integration of Active Play as a Learning Experience for Sports Coaching Undergraduates

Richard Cheetham

At 9:30 am, along with tea and coffee informal introductions were done and then the workshop began. A ninety-minute play workshop for sports coaches with my main goal to change the 'temperature' in the room from a reserved cold blue to an expressive, freethinking red hot where adults gradually took their 'protective self-conscious armour' off and returned to that energising playground of activity, imagination, spontaneity and laughter. The session was designed to highlight the essence and value of play integrated into coaching delivery by reinforcing the transfer of learning, development of skills and the heightened levels of engagement that can be achieved. More structured instruction, an emphasis on the technical and tactical aspects as players' progress from the early stages of skill acquisition in sport comes at the expense of play. I do not believe it should be an 'either or' scenario. The 'play sales pitch' was about to begin! So after initially being met with caution and scepticism, I remember distinctly reflecting with the group afterwards that I had just seen that same group

---

R. Cheetham (✉)
University of Winchester, Winchester, UK
e-mail: richard.cheetham@winchester.ac.uk

of adults playing a game (with great intensity and engagement) which they created called butterflies or flowers! Playfulness 1, Fear 0, what a result!

A playful approach to teaching was always something I wanted to adopt more, break a few rules and move away from a more 'traditional and linear' style of delivery. My belief in its importance in teaching and coaching had become further shaped after a series of conference presentations on the subject to National Governing Bodies of Sport (NGBs). The concept of play may have been relegated to the childhood years of the delegates and now regarded as an unaffordable luxury in an increasingly formalised approach to education. Yet through their work, the NGBs were influencing the sport and physical education experiences of children with curriculum and programme development as well as delivery. This is where play content (integral to a child's physical and emotional development) is essential (Pica 2006). I felt there was a need therefore to create an authentic recreation of play and playfulness in these sessions so they could revisit the associated emotions and then be more able to connect with its importance, value and impact. It is entirely possible to 'flick this switch' by asking a group of adults to imagine something, anything and then draw it on a piece of A4 paper. Oh and one rule—that the paper is placed on their head while they draw! Then to set them the task of guessing what one another has drawn. Trust me, it is one of the simplest ideas but the wheels of playfulness have been put into motion.

Runco (2014: 62) highlighted that 'the loss of unstructured experiences is the direct result of increases in structured experiences in formalized and organised sport'. Robinson (2016: 94) endorses this view from an educational perspective where he believes 'the exile of play is one of the great tragedies of standardised education'. It is through my role at the University that I feel able to influence redressing this balance in coach education. For participants, play is a critical learning tool and not an 'end of session reward'. I want there to be more 'play advocates' as a result of the undergraduate degree programme.

I first integrated an experiential learning approach to the Coaching Children through Play element of a final year practical module for University of Winchester Sports Coaching undergraduates. Each Friday I would take the students out of the lecture room to the nearby playground where they experimented by bringing a series of children's stories to life through movement. Frogs jumping off lily pads, pirates balancing on stormy seas and witches taking off on their broomsticks became the playful way to teach fundamental movement skills. The sessions began analysing the narrative, the characters and their characteristics in order to integrate them into a moving story. It was their playful imagination and creativity which directed the teaching and learning and I felt very strongly about its inclusion. The degree course seeks to prepare students for a predominantly vocational career and 'authenticity' in the study experience is at the heart of my teaching philosophy. Rod Judkins stated 'The future belongs to those who can reconnect with play. It is the child in you that is creative not the adult' (2016: 92). I did not want those who can influence a child's early learning experience in sport and physical activity to be without some opportunity to develop their play expertise on the degree programme. I sought to unearth the dormant feelings of childlike behaviour.

From an educational perspective, the value of recreating a playful learning environment for students was an opportunity to break free from a more 'normalised' approach to studies. As many of those involved in this programme will pursue a career in teaching and coaching sport to children of all ages therefore I felt it would be invaluable to revisit play and not only try and see it through their eyes but 'experience it'.

Pritchard (2009: 115) focusses thoughts on the restructured educational setting away from 'conventional' to one where 'knowledge creation comes from personal experiences, collaborative work, active learning and movement'. It is this break from convention where the coaching module structure proved to be so worthwhile because the students generated ideas together. They compared dragons with gorillas, showed how crocodiles moved, how flamingos ate their dinner and shipwreck survivors collected treasure from the other side of a hot lava stream.

It was also important the students did not feel this was *a one-man crusade* to change the way they were taught but one that has had clear underpinning rationale. Forencich (2006: 199) referred to the inclusion of play as 'authentic engagement with the real world'. Kaufman and Gregoire (2016: 10) believe that as 'adults, cultivating a childlike sense of play can revolutionise the way we work' in an increasingly play deficient society. And Brown (2009: 207) discusses the benefits of recalling our 'play history' encouraging spending some time revisiting moments from childhood 'things that got you really excited'. Play can be an individual or shared multisensory, memorable experience and I sought to foster an environment where recollections could elicit smiles and laughter as individuals felt transported back in time. I found these play recollections were experiences full of stories, activities, the games they (the students) invented and the friends they played with. The importance of a reflection on the sessions was to highlight (by recalling these experiences) the freedom, the imagination, the lack of boundaries and adventure. This could then shape and influence their approach to coaching as an appreciation of the transfer of learning that becomes evident in purposeful developmental experiences. I believe this was one of the key outcomes—the relationship between the relevance of the play experience to the sport skills required created a realisation of its worth and its potential as a coaching approach.

The following examples are three play interventions which were developed. Included with their content, rationale is some feedback from the groups.

Musical Chairs …. Without Music and Without Chairs

The safe 'building of a scrum' in Rugby Union can be a challenge to coach and for the participant to learn the skill effectively. Posture, balance and accuracy of technique are the real building blocks required and ones that need to be reinforced. This was taught through an imagined musical chairs game. One without music, without (real) chairs and without anyone being excluded. As the coach calls out '*stop*' to the group, they sit on an 'imagined' chair (the basis for a squat position often referred to as the 'tower of power'). Select people each time to have 'lost' their chair so they have to combine (bind) with another to form an 'imagined' two seater sofa. As more chairs are taken away groups of three (a three seater sofa) are established. The one in the middle binds on to those either side (now we have a hooker—the position of the player in the middle in the front row of the scrum). They then 'sit' as they did individually at the beginning. The squat position, the stability and the posture are gradually being learnt (Fig. 4.1).

Fig. 4.1 Musical chairs without chairs

Balloon Waterfalls

As my 6-year-old daughter Kitty spotted a leftover birthday party balloon in the corner of her room, she embarked upon 'avoid going to bed syndrome' and clearly exploited her dad's softer side. *See how many times you can keep the balloon up before it hits the floor Daddy!* Thirty minutes of fun and laughter in this activity and other balloon game adaptations sowed the seeds for ideas as I observed some of those wonderful play characteristics— simplicity, creativity, skill acquisition and the chance to strengthen the parent–child bond. The bonding between coach and participant can also be enhanced by providing activities with similar characteristics. The adoption of these simple ideas has led to a series of remarkable 'eye-openers' in the world of play within teaching at the university. The first session with third-year undergraduates was akin to a noisy child's birthday party. I watched the students play with the balloons in an improvised game they called 'balloon waterfalls'—a challenging game with movement, collaboration and decision making. *'Don't let any of these raindrops* (balloons) *hit the floor'* one exclaimed as more and more were inflated and added to the melee in the sports hall. Each person could only inflate a second balloon if they kept the first in the air at all times (no holding onto it allowed). A real aerobic warm-up alongside developing fine and gross motor skills (Fig. 4.2).

My observation focussed on recognising the intensity and style of play elements—the level of enjoyment (seeing their faces, hearing their voices); the interaction and connection between one another in the group; the persistence with the game and their eagerness to play and finally the creative ways with which they approached their challenge.

Critically the teaching session allowed time for a period of reflection afterwards through a group discussion. What did we all observe, how did we all feel, what was that playful world like and *why* were they asked to play?

> Freedom, you just allowed us to play, to get on with it…..we made up the rules

> I remember how simple it all is (*play*), you just gave us a pack of balloons and we were off, I was surprised how quickly everyone felt so comfortable with the games

Fig. 4.2 Balloon waterfalls

My kids *(coaching group)* will see another side of me next week……they think I will be like one of them….hopefully! I understand this more now, at first I thought you were just sharing an idea but now you have shared a philosophy!

The Bangkok Traffic Jam

Let me share a third example of how play was introduced with the new intake of first-year coaching undergraduates who were learning the importance of enhancing physical literacy. The session required a change of behaviour and 'status' from adult to child in an environment where a scenario was set in a Bangkok traffic jam. A chaotic movement of cars seemingly driving without any adherence to rules or traffic control! A limited space was set up (10 m square), students pretended to be cars moving from a walk to a run, changing direction (agility), stopping at imagined lights (the ability to stop quickly as well as accelerate in invasion games such as rugby is an essential skill and rarely taught) and then drove under 'low bridges' (a skipping rope attached to two badminton posts) to challenge their mobility skills. Every so often an animal would escape from the zoo into the traffic, with the group copying their movement patterns. A silverback gorilla impression was used to teach the foundation of good posture, a kangaroo to jump and land softly and a flamingo on one leg a perfect example of balance. The group chose more to add to the story from frogs to crocodiles and eagles to lions. Play really did foster and fuel creative thinking. Someone called out *'a sloth has escaped'* but I think it was when they grew tired! And so they played on, learning movement skills disguised in play. The significant and interesting aspect that emerged from the students feedback was that they were willing play participants: 'Can we do this every week?'

The students and I were richer for what was learnt and what can be achieved through and understanding 'powerful play'. Children have the 'expertise' of play as they are more often immersed in it, unaffected by the constraints that accompany the 'growing up process' and are able to fully experience its freedom and joy. The distancing from play that is a consequence of moving from a child to an adult was highlighted by Brooks (2011). In his book *The Social Animal*, he describes an enthusiastic father wishing to join in with his young son's games. His inadequacy at playing was such that it was compared to an amateur basketball player trying to scrimmage with the best team in the NBA (National Basketball Association). He was no match in the play domain, needing to be instead liberated from formality and routine in order to embrace what was required.

So with this in mind, what would be the consequences of not paying attention to the role of play and its benefits through a formal educational setting learning? For those about to enter an environment where expertise in play is essential the preparation needs to be our responsibility. It requires all of us involved to develop a greater empathy to a child's view of the world and one which 'begins by recognising in ourselves the emotions that others are feeling and how we would feel in the same circumstances' (Robinson 2015: 78).

The observations from all the activities encouraged students to think about using 'play' more in their coaching. These play sessions enhanced their motivation to learn and develop creativity as the learning environment removed any perceived fear of failure and encouraged trial and error. For example, the Bangkok traffic jam had speed bumps, road works and one way street by the end of the practical coaching session! The enhancement of motor skills can be and were developed through play—balloons can be unpredictable by developing spontaneous, challenging and reactive movement patterns. Play proved to be an excellent way for the coach to connect with the group. Children are more likely to engage with a coach who provides enjoyable, fun and engaging sessions.

These findings from a pedagogical perspective with this approach to learning can be 'justified' when in the right context and vindicated when designing learning opportunities in Higher Education for undergraduates. Butcher et al. (2006) consider that the educational intent of those leading and teaching on programmes should be to develop transferable skills which are authentic, realistic and appropriate. Effective teaching can include providing 'new material as a quality learning experience' and 'changing the classroom dynamic' (2006: 87). These observations can support the opportunity for embedding 'play' into this environment which encourages students to see something in a completely different way.

The contribution of experiential learning through the inclusion of play activities offers an opportunity where a 'base for learning is broadened' (Toohey 2002: 102) as the foundations and fundamentals of sport skills begin to be developed. Knowles (1984) reflects on the '…importance of organising learning experiences around life situations rather than according to subject matter units' (cited in Toohey 2002: 59). What will the students need to be prepared best for and how can lectures provide these conditions as near as possible in their teaching.

Reflections on the integration and promotion of activities, formal or informal, which promote and develop playfulness of coaches, teachers and other educational leaders, could have a positive and profound effect on professional practice in Higher Education. Our coaching styles and approach can be a projection of how we learnt, how we were coached and what we believe is expected of us. Perhaps our experiences lacked the opportunity and outlet to play but it is not a reason why this should not be part of a more creative and broader thinking coaching philosophy. Should there ever be doubt about considering the use of play then these activities describe can provide some of the evidence to support it's worth and inclusion. Bassok et al. (2016: 1) highlight 'a focus on an academic content might crowd out other important types of learning experiences' but this is in reference to a shift in the balance primary education. If play is crowded out in these early years then there could be even more need to find a place for it in higher education teaching. So be a silverback gorilla and fill your balloons as it's not just child's play! After all, it was once said that growing up is inevitable, growing up is optional.

References

Bassok, D., Latham, S., & Rorem, A. (2016). Is Kindergarten the New First Grade? *American Educational Research Association, 1*(4), 1–31.

Brooks, D. (2011). *The Social Animal: A Story of How Success Happens*. New York: Random House.

Brown, S. (2009). *Play. How it Shapes the Brain, Opens the Imagination and Invigorates the Soul.* New York: Avery.

Butcher, C., Davies, C., & Highton, M. (2006). *Designing Learning: From Module Outline to Effective Teaching.* New York: Routledge.

Forencich, F. (2006). *Exuberant Animal: The Power of Health, Play and Joyful Movement.* Bloomington, IN: Author House.

Judkins, R. (2016). *You Are More Creative Than You Think: The Art of Creative Thinking.* London: Hodder & Stoughton.

Kaufman, S. B., & Gregoire, C. (2016). *Wired to Create.* London: Vermilion.

Knowles, M. S. (1984). *Andragogy in Action: Applying the Principles of Adult Learning.* San Francisco: Jossey-Bass.

Pica, R. (2006). *Running Start: How Play, Physical Activity and Free Time Create a Successful Child.* New York: Marlowe & Company.

Pritchard, A. (2009). *Ways of Learning: Learning Theories and Learning Styles in the Classroom.* London: Routledge.

Robinson, K. (2015). *Creative Schools.* London: Penguin.

Robinson, K. (2016). *Creative Schools: Revolutionising Education from the Ground Up.* London: Penguin.

Runco, M. (2014). *Creativity: Theories and Themes: Research Development and Practice* (2nd ed.). London: Elsevier.

Toohey, S. (2002). *Designing Courses in Higher Education.* Buckingham: Society for Research into Higher Education & Open University Press.

5

Sketch: The Training Game

Scott Roberts

One of the things that I truly enjoy about teaching Introduction to Psychology is the opportunity to engage students with aspects of the field that have played a large role in my own life. One such topic is behaviour modification—the science and art of using reinforcement to shape an animal's behaviour towards some goal. Whether you are training service dogs or your own pet, the better you understand the nuanced process of shaping behaviour the better the experience and outcome for you and the animal alike. As a former dolphin trainer, I want my students to do more than memorize the definitions of related terms; I want them to develop a deeper understanding of the process by which a trainer can communicate without language to achieve a behavioural goal.

In my experience, the best way to do that is to play. I cannot take credit for creating "The Training Game," it was popularized by Karen Pryor (visit www.clickertraining.com/karen for more information about

---

S. Roberts (✉)
University of Maryland, College Park, MD, USA
e-mail: scott@umd.edu

© The Author(s) 2019
A. James and C. Nerantzi (eds.), *The Power of Play in Higher Education*,
https://doi.org/10.1007/978-3-319-95780-7_5

her work and publications), and I first learned about it from others at the dolphin facility who used it as a way to teach visitors the basics of animal training. To play, one student volunteers to be the "animal" and leaves the room. The group decides on a target behaviour for the trainer, who will have to get the animal to do it using only the word "good." For example, the animal might need to go flick the classroom lights on and off, collect objects from desks and bring it to the teacher, or fly around the room flapping their arms like a bird. Basically, it can be anything the student wouldn't naturally do on their own that is not dangerous or embarrassing.

The trainer briefly discusses a plan for how to shape the behaviour by reinforcing very small steps in the right direction before the naïve animal returns to the room and starts behaving randomly in search of reinforcement. It might require a little patience to wait out all of the unwanted behaviours, but eventually the animal might raise its arms, even just a bit... "good!" The next time they have to go just a bit higher to earn reinforcement, and later on "good" comes when they raise the arms high enough and start to lower them. The next thing you know, you have the animal flapping around the room and students laughing and cheering.

Those who play, and the rest who observe, experience the process live and leave the classroom with a far better appreciation for the intricacies of timing and clarity than could not have been learned from simply reading about it. Long after they forget the difference between positive and negative reinforcement, they will remember watching someone learn a behaviour using only the word "good." As an added bonus, they have a good time and learn a new party game that is even more fun without all the rules.

6

Exploration: Play in Practice—Innovation Through Play in the Postgraduate Curriculum

Sophy Smith

Introduction

Play is essential for children's development, building their confidence as they learn to explore, to think about problems, and relate to others. Children learn by leading their own play and by taking part in play that is guided by adults (Department for Education 2017: 9).

Play is well-established as central to the learning processes of young children (including Anning [2015], Moyles [2015], and Wood and Attfield [2005]) and is included in UK state legislation, central to the Statutory Framework for Early Years Foundation Stage (2017), which states that children's learning and development 'must be implemented through planned, purposeful play'. However, the assumption seems to be that play is only important to learning until the age of 5, when children enter Key Stage 1. Legislation outlines how '… it is expected that the balance will gradually shift towards more activities led by adults,

---

S. Smith (✉)
Institute of Creative Technologies, De Montfort University, Leicester, UK
e-mail: ssmith05@dmu.ac.uk

to help children prepare for more formal learning, ready for Year 1' (2017: 9). This exploration will counter the assumption that play-based learning is of value only to Early Years teaching and learning by outlining how it has been used to develop and carry out research within a Higher Education postgraduate programme.

Children Doing Research and Adults at Play

Jane Murray (in Moyles 2015: 106–108) identifies links between children's epistemic play and the research process, outlining how when leading play, children display similar behaviours to adult researchers. She cites 4 behaviours that professional researchers specify as important to research—exploring, finding a solution, conceptualising and basing decisions on evidence. It is clear to see the links between these practices and those she witnessed as an Early Years teacher where she came across children '…questioning, planning, acquiring information, analysing and interpreting, solving problems, exploring and reporting novel ideas and artefacts they had created' (ibid.: 106). Murray cites Hutt et al. (1989: 222–224) who describe epistemic play as 'the acquisition of knowledge and information… problem solving… exploration… productive, as well as focused on materials and transformations, in other words knowledge construction' (2015: 109). This same knowledge construction is central to the premise of research—could these play-based learning approaches be used to facilitate the knowledge construction by adult researchers as well as Early Years learners?

The value of play is not confined to childhood, and as Chazan (2002) suggests, is in fact synonymous with life:

> Playfulness bespeaks creativity and action, change and possibility of transformation. Play activity thus reflects the very existence of the self, that part of the organism that exists both independently and interdependently, that can reflect upon itself and be aware of its own existence. (Chazan 2002: 198)

Elizabeth Wood and Jane Attfield (2005: 14) regard play as inherent in adult life, remarking how 'lifelong playing' is central to lifelong learning (ibid., 2015: 13) and listing a variety of different types of adult play including theme parks, sports, extreme sports, and computer and board games (ibid., 2015: 14). However, these are play-based activities. What is of greater interest is how the *process* of play-based learning can enable the development of new knowledge for adults undertaking research. Catharina Dyrssen (in Biggs and Karlsson 2011) describes how most scientists regard play and creativity as being central to their scientific work. In play, researchers must relinquish control, and this lack of control is, 'a necessary part of innovation and cross-disciplinary contact and therefore not only acceptable, but also needed as an ingredient in most research processes today…' (Dyrssen 2011: 238).

Play in Practice

In 2007, the Institute of Creative Technologies (IOCT), De Montfort University, launched the innovative Masters in Creative Technologies (MA/MSc), which for the following decade was led by the author. Over the 10 years, students have completed questionnaires relating to their experience as learners, which have been drawn upon in this chapter. The programme was designed to support learners in developing and strengthening their individual practice within the context of the increasingly multi/inter/trans disciplinary environments and collaborative digital world, encouraging innovation and developing new modes of collaboration in e-science and digital arts research. Working across and beyond students' home disciplinary areas is challenging and new modes of working, that incorporate play, have been explored to support students in the development of their practice. Key to this has been embedding play into the curriculum, as a way of taking the students back to basics in terms of recognising and celebrating the excitement and strength of open exploration. Following years of formal academic education, students often arrived ill-equipped to develop ideas freely, without restriction, both individually and play in groups. One particular strength of this approach is its value across disciplines. Rather than being of relevance solely to arts-based areas, play has also become central to developing new knowledge in technology and e-science practice.

Peter Gray (2013: 140) outlines 5 characteristics of play—self-chosen and self-directed; intrinsically motivated; guided by mental rules; imaginative; and conducted in an active, alert, but relatively non-stressed frame of mind. The Masters programme has drawn on these key characteristics to develop an environment conducive to play, through three main approaches across both formal and informal contexts. Work is both self-chosen and self-directed—learning is scaffolded by short taught sessions, around which students are able to explore their own learning pathways. Assessments are negotiated, enabling students to develop their individual area of interest aligned to the given module learning outcomes, and assessment formats are equally flexible, with students choosing how best to show their learning. In addition to this more formal environment, weekly whole-group sessions are run, bringing the group together to collaborate, explore and experiment in a supportive open environment. By having this time for non-credited activity, students are able to take risks and innovate in an unpressured environment, free from the threat of formal failure. One student reflected:

> … they have been an open time for discussion and play. I think serious play is a very important part of any creative activity, I feel that the less rigidly structured sessions have been very valuable. I would have liked more time to play and create with other course participants… (Response to Student Questionnaire 2011)

This reflexive and responsive approach aims to create a playful environment within which new knowledge construction can take place. As Gray (2013: 134) reflects, any pressure to perform well can interfere with new learning and pressure to be creative interferes with creativity. By creating a safe space for more risky play, we facilitate the creative mood needed to enhance creativity (Gray 2013: 136) and the more playful state of mind needed to solve logic problems (Gray 2013: 137).

After 10 years of this approach at Masters level, we are able to reflect on specific areas of impact within Higher Education teaching and learning with specific reference to the development of research. Four main areas of interest have been explored—how embedding play into the postgraduate curriculum can enable the development of supportive creative environments where learners are able to experiment and innovate, how curriculum and assessments can be designed to encourage play and experimentation, how permission to play can enhance the creative practice of learners and how play-related knowledge and skills can meet the needs of a changing workplace.

Central to the play-based approach of the IOCT Masters in Creative Technologies has been the development of a supportive creative environment where learners are able to experiment and innovate. In *Free to Learn*, Peter Gray describes the inhibitory effect of teacher-led learning—where students are shown a specific way to approach a problem they will regard this as the only way. However, though a play-based approach students explore the problem in greater detail, finding different ways to approach it and by doing so understand the full dimension of the problem and the 'full power of possibilities' (Gray 2013: 118). For students, the assurance that the result of play was valid research was liberating and validated their research practice:

> …during my time as a student on the Creative Technologies course, I have been encouraged to embed play in my research process… Being able to "play", rather than follow a set of strict guidelines, requirements and expectations, enabled every student to step forward with their personal views and employ their individual knowledge to contribute effectively for the accomplishment of projects. (Response to Student Questionnaire 2017)

For some students, this play-based approach to postgraduate study has created a transformative learning environment:

> I come home from the IOCT with a head full of ideas, inspiration and new questions. I feel that the interdisciplinary environment opens up a space for new ideas, and its nature prevents it from becoming stagnant

in a certain mindset as many institutions do by developing set norms for achievement and learning outcomes. It's been a truly remarkable environment and I have at times been overwhelmed with gratitude for being able to study there. (Response to Student Questionnaire 2011)

By placing control in the hands of the learners, students take on the responsibility of their learning, developing confidence and aspiration:

It has really impressed me that we have been given this trust [to play]… I am still surprised at what I have been able to achieve given the expectation to do so, to be allowed to float in the river, to become confident and grow in skills and knowledge. (Response to Student Questionnaire 2011)

Within this playful context, how can curriculum and assessments can be designed to encourage play and experimentation? Gray describes how where the task involves creative thought or learning a new skill, the presence of an observer/evaluator inhibits the majority of participants:

Learning, creativity and problem solving are facilitated by anything that promotes a playful state of mind, but they are inhibited by evaluation, expectation of rewards, or anything else that destroys a playful state of mind. (2015: 139)

Students are enabled to retain this 'playful state of mind' through the assessment process, with flexible approaches to both content and format. Students reflected how they '… had the freedom to do what we wanted creatively, and although given support, were left to plan the work and motivate ourselves'. Another remarked; 'I make sure that the way I interpret tasks allows me to express myself through play and creative joy, even if say I am doing a technical programming element of a course'.

Indeed, this permission to play enhances the creative practice of learners. As Henk Borsdorf (in Biggs and Karlsson 2011: 15) reflects, 'Research is more like exploration than like following a firm path' and through a play-based learning approach researchers have the skills to explore with greater confidence. Hazel Smith and Roger T. Dean

(2011: 48) suggest that one way to consider knowledge creation is to accept that it is often 'productive to explore creative possibilities that are informed by, but not captive to, existing frameworks of knowledge'. Prior knowledge they suggest can 'limit the opportunities for using things anew' (ibid.: 48) and 'creative options and new associations occur in situations where there is intense concentration, but within an open landscape of free-range possibility rather than a closed geography of well-trodden pathways' (ibid.: 48). We have found that play-based approaches can enable students to find these new knowledge pathways, one student reflecting:

> Allowing creative play within technology focused learning enables the student/researcher to find, and then push, boundaries that more traditional users of the technology may not encounter. The play encourages technological development by asking new questions. (Response to Student Questionnaire 2017)

Another commented:

> … the permission to play led to a highly beneficial, as well as enjoyable educational experience… The fact that the course offered the liberty to play motivated me to gain knowledge in multiple areas… By playing together for our research, we were able to establish that anyone's opinion and concept is as valid, as everyone else's… the process itself allowed everyone to learn something new, to look from a different point of view, it opened the door to a world of creativity with unlimited opportunities to all of us. (Response to Student Questionnaire 2017)

For many students on the programme, play is central to their research process, one computing student describing how play features in their work:

> Initially I will have a broad concept and work towards it as if I were writing functional code. Then as the development progresses I will begin to play around with the various parameters built into the code, and based upon these experiments my idea of the outcome changes. This playful mode of programming gets gradually more prominent the further

through a piece I am, becoming the dominant way of working when I have fixed the structures and processes which control the final piece. (Response to Student Questionnaire 2011)

Another computing student reflected:

While my practice was framed by existing literature and artefacts, I chose the areas I wanted to explore and play in/with. Extensive and well documented play resulted in experiments which I used in my analysis… There was no framework to work in and I didn't adhere to rules (not even self-imposed ones). To me playing was a way of transforming vague ideas into reality to test their viability followed by subjective evaluation. You set yourself up with tools and contexts and ideas emerge during playtime. (Response to Student Questionnaire 2017)

Importantly, this play-based approach to knowledge construction places graduates in a position of strength when entering the contemporary workplace. As Wood and Attfield (2005: 16) reflect, 'creating a continuum between lifelong playing and learning is perhaps even more critical in the twenty-first century as economic success becomes dependent on people who are creative, flexible, innovative, imaginative and playful in the workplace'. This is recognised by the students who regard play as vital to any workplace that strives for innovative practice:

Any workplace that does, in any serious way, want to enable innovation must be open to allowing play and free imaginative thought amongst all its employees, not only the assigned "creatives" … I think that if you want to encourage innovation you have to consciously make space for play, and recognize its value within the whole culture of the company or establishment. (Response to Student Questionnaire 2017)

Another reflecting:

We are living in a time of rapid change - social, cultural and technological… chances for a better professional realisation come easier when people have managed to develop play-related skills and knowledge, simply due to the fact that they are much more likely to find a creative solution to possible problems… The play-related knowledge and skills would also naturally lead to the ability to be flexible, and look from a different point of view. (Response to Student Questionnaire 2017)

Conclusion

Though short, this exploration has aimed to outline a number of benefits of play-based approaches to teaching, learning and wider curriculum development at postgraduate level, offering an alternative approach to knowledge construction. The value of play-based learning extends well beyond Early Years settings, as through play-based learning, postgraduate students can move away from the more 'closed' traditional models of research practice, towards a more 'open' landscape (Smith and Dean 2011: 48), enabling the emergence of new knowledge often across discipline areas. A play-based approach to postgraduate programmes can enable programme teams to create transformative learning environments that enable risk-taking and innovation, enhancing the creative practice of learners and meet the changing needs of a contemporary workplace. For this reason, play is too important not to be taken seriously by Higher Education.

References

Anning, A. (2015). Play and the Legislated Curriculum. In J. Moyles (Ed.), *The Excellence of Play*. Maidenhead: Open University Press.
Biggs, M., & Karlsson, H. (2011). *The Routledge Companion to Research in the Arts*. Abingdon: Routledge.
Chazan, S. (2002). *Profiles of Play*. London: Jessica Kingsley.
Department for Education. (2017). *Statutory Framework for Early Years Foundation Stage*. London: Department for Education.
Dyrssen, C. (2011). Navigating in Heterogeneity: Architectural Thinking and Art-Based Research. In M. Biggs & H. Karlsson (Eds.), *The Routledge Companion to Research in the Arts*. Abingdon: Routledge.

Gray, P. (2013). *Free to Learn*. New York: Basic Books.
Hutt, C., Tyler, S., Hutt, C., & Christopherson, H. (1989). *Play, Exploration and Learning*. London: Routledge.
Moyles, J. (Ed.). (2015). *The Excellence of Play*. Maidenhead: Open University Press.
Murray, J. (2015). Young Children as Researchers in Play. In J. Moyles (Ed.), *The Excellence of Play*. Maidenhead: Open University Press.
Smith, H., & Dean, R. T. (Eds.). (2011). *Practice-Led Research, Research-Led Practice in the Creative Arts*. Edinburgh: Edinburgh University Press.
Wood, E., & Attfield, J. (2005). *Play, Learning and the Early Childhood Curriculum*. London: Paul Chapman Publishing.

7

Exploration: Experiences of Running a 'Play and Creativity' Module in a School of Art & Design

Gareth Loudon

Introduction

I am a Professor of Creativity at the Cardiff School of Art & Design at Cardiff Metropolitan University. One of my areas of research is the importance of play and creativity to the economy and to personal well-being, and part of this investigation has involved running a play and creativity module for 2nd-year undergraduate art and design students at the school over the last three years. The aim of the module was to highlight what factors affect play and creativity, both positively and negatively, and to provide tools, techniques, strategies and processes to help students improve their creative practice. Here I share my motivations and experiences of running the module and include reflections from the students themselves.

G. Loudon (✉)
Cardiff Metropolitan University, Cardiff, Wales, UK
e-mail: gloudon@cardiffmet.ac.uk

Play and Creativity Research

I have undertaken research over the last few years into the factors and process affecting creativity and one of my main motivations for running the 'Play and Creativity' module was to share the key lessons I have learnt along the way. My colleague Gina Deininger defines creativity as 'the ability to come up with ideas or artefacts that are novel, valuable and substantive within a psychological or historical context' (Deininger 2013: 39) and highlights two key determinants for creativity: a person's 'state of being' and 'dynamic movement'. Gina defines 'state of being' as 'the emotional, mental and physiological condition of a person', and 'dynamic movement' as 'the continuous motion of personal experience that is of a non-linear and spontaneous nature' (Deininger 2013: 35–38). As a result, we created a new model for creativity (Loudon and Deininger 2014) called the LCD (Listen, Connect, Do) model that puts a person's state of being at the centre of the approach.

Our concept of doing relates to play as it includes elements of exploration, experimentation and making, but in a playful way, that is, it recognises the importance of a person's state of being while undertaking actions. Gwen Gordon describes play as 'highly purposeful, though usually not toward any explicit goals' and that 'play's purpose is to generate more possibilities' (Gordon 2009: 14). Play naturally encourages divergent thinking, a core component for creativity (Runco 2010). Characteristics of play include joy, freedom, safety and the absence of consequences (Lieberman 1977; Gordon 2009; Brown and Vaughan 2010). Bateson and Martin (2013: 5) argue that play is 'an evolved biological adaptation that enables the individual to escape from local optima and discover better solutions'. Gordon (2014: 241) describes exploratory play as 'the basis for learning, goal pursuit, and growth' as it gives people permission to explore ideas in a non-linear manner.

In the context of art and design, play is a very important element of the creative process. Students need to play with thoughts as well as form (through making) to help discover new unusual connections, to gain new insights and to improve their skills. However, play is often seen as something associated with childhood not adulthood and not being a serious endeavour (Bateson and Martin 2013). Consequently, in my experience, students are often reluctant to play, or to be seen playing, as they think it is not acceptable adult work behaviour.

Another important element related to play is playfulness. Bateson and Martin (2013: 2) describe playfulness as 'a positive mood state… that facilitates and accompanies playful play'. Gwen Gordon highlights that 'playfulness correlates with a number of psychological and physiological benefits, including nonlinear, divergent thinking, problem solving, physical activity, emotional regulation, and imagination' (Gordon 2014: 249). From my experience, one of the biggest challenges for students in relation to producing new ideas or artefacts of value is often their state of being. Anxiety and stress can result in 'creative block' and this can have a negative impact on their self-confidence and their resultant work. Therefore, another motivation for running the play and creativity module was to help students understand how their state of being affects their creativity and what strategies they can put in place to enhance their creativity—with a key strategy being more playful.

The Play and Creativity Module

All disciplines in the school follow the same curriculum structure of three core modules (Subject, Field and Constellation) where the Subject module covers the core skills and knowledge for the discipline; the Field module focuses on encouraging collaboration between disciplines and provides the opportunity to gain new skills and experiences; and the Constellation module underpins creative practice by exploring ideas, theories and contextual studies. The play and creativity module was an optional field module open to all students in the school and lasted five weeks in total. The module explored a range of topics including factors that affect play and creativity, different creativity models (including the LCD model) as well as useful tools, techniques and processes.

I followed a model of teaching advocated by Sir Ken Robinson that included the sharing of knowledge balanced with the freedom for students 'to inquire, question, experiment and to express their own thoughts and ideas' (NACCCE 1999: 102). During the first three weeks of the module, I ran two 5-hour sessions per week. Ideas on play and creativity were explored in the sessions through group discussions; through individual and group-based activities including idea generation challenges, problem solving puzzles, exercises on personal motivation and values, and various games including improvisation with props; and through student-led creative practice, including poetry writing, drawing and making tasks.

In terms of theory, students were introduced to the concept of flow (Csikszentmihalyi 1996) and its relationship to a person's state of being. Different aspects and types of play were studied, including the psychology of play and the relationship between play, making and divergent thinking. The module also looked at the link between play and creative insights, the fear of making mistakes, and the relationship between intrinsic motivation and creativity. In addition, the module explored how different physical and social environments affect a person's state of being and creativity.

I used a variety of exercises throughout the module to help students discover what motivated them, what made them stressed/relaxed, and how they processed information. The exercises also included reflections on when and why they might have creative block, and where and when they get their best ideas. Students were also asked to reflect on their attitudes to play and how they could explore ideas by being more playful.

At the beginning of the module, the students were briefed on the summative assignment they had to complete by the end of the module. The topic of the assignment changed from year to year, but was always kept very broad, for example, one year being about sustainability, another year being about well-being. Students were given complete freedom on how to explore the topic; however, the output from the exploration had to be a piece or pieces of art or design work that could be exhibited. They also had to record their personal reflections, thoughts, learning, ideas, experiments and creations throughout the module in a diary. Students were told explicitly to do what motivates and interests them. They could undertake the assignment as a group (with a maximum of three people) or individually, whichever was their preference. In addition to the formal sessions listed above, tutorials and peer-group discussions were held throughout the five weeks to provide support and guidance for the assignment. The art or design work created, along with their reflective diary, was assessed based on the new ideas explored in their work; the skills shown in making the work; and how they employed various strategies, techniques and processes to try and improve their creative practice.

The idea behind the assignment relates to the product-oriented learning strategy advocated by Yong Zhao (2012: 240) where the student becomes 'responsible for seeking and securing the necessary guidance, knowledge, skills, and support to make high-quality products'. A wide range of work has been created by the students over the years including videos; games; paintings; new products; illustrations; animations; sculptures; designs of creative spaces; furniture; pottery; and clothing designs. Many of the students chose to work in small groups and many chose to work on their own.

Reflections from the Students

A common reason given by students for choosing the play and creativity module was because they felt they often lack confidence in their own creative abilities and wanted to improve their creative skills and learn something new ('I was not too confident within my own work', 'I would say that my main barrier is my self-confidence which blocks me to do what I want'). Students commented that they often suffer from creative block and anxiety.

The exploration of play in the module prompted a variety of reflections from students. These included reflections that being too self-critical was harmful to their creativity and that play was a way to overcome this ('I found that not being so critical opened up my options and ideas for the benefit of my work'). Student reflections also related to their own playfulness and that they felt they were not as playful as they used to be when they were young ('I don't feel that I am as 'playful' as I was as a child… I remember being very adventurous and imaginative when I was younger'). One of the activities in the module involved improvisation with props. This was challenging for many of the students, as they struggled to be playful in front of their peers because of the fear of judgement, however, many saw benefits to breaking down those barriers ('This really put me out of my comfort zone but while doing this 'silly' show I actually had a lot of fun! I think this was the aim, to show that it is ok to be playful and not to worry about it'.). Another key reflection from the students on their assignment work was the power of playful play for experimentation and creativity and the positive affect on self-confidence.

- 'At first, I wasn't comfortable or confident in what I was creating; however, as I played with different techniques and ideas I became more confident in what I was capable of'.
- 'By just playing around I discovered an animation technique with water colour'.

Students also reflected on the link between play and their state of being ('when you are playing you are in the moment, you don't think about your problems, things that you have to do, you are really living it in the more natural way for you to be'); but didn't directly comment on how play might have helped them overcome creative block. However, they did comment on how their state of being affected creative block, and techniques they had learnt to overcome these problems.

One of the other major areas for comment and reflection by the students related to the exercise I ran on intrinsic motivation and values, based on the work by Chad Lejeune (2007). I used this exercise to help students find out what really interests them, what their passions are, and to provide some insights into topics they might want to focus on for their assignment. Generally, this exercise was very well received ('most beneficial … (was) developing a real understanding for motivation, and creativity', 'the exercises helped me … figure out what I wanted to do … about what motivates us').

There was a mixed response from the students to the broadness of the assignment brief, with some students finding it hard to know where to focus, while others commented on the freedom it gave them ('I found it really difficult to establish an opening', 'it was nice to have a topic where there wasn't so many restrictions and boundaries'). For those who embraced the freedom of the brief, they took the opportunity to try something new and created some excellent work. For those who found the openness of the brief a bit overwhelming, they struggled more with their work.

Final Reflections

Overall, the module has been a success, with most students commenting that they enjoyed the module and found it very useful, with some students suggesting that the module should have been made compulsory for all art and design students at the beginning of their studies. However, the fact that the module was optional I think worked well, as motivation is a key part of creativity.

The arts students generally found the open brief easier to cope with, as they were already used to working on topics that interested them. In contrast, some of the design students struggled more, maybe because they were used to assignment briefs from clients with clear requirements and not used to finding their own topic of interest. Moving forward, maybe a better solution would be to offer a mixture of client briefs and open briefs to the students.

At the end of the module, we had an exhibition of the work in the school, but on reflection, I think it would have been better to have a more formal public exhibition. Many of the students produced great work; however, I think a public exhibition would have encouraged more of the students to work harder and to produce higher quality work. This links to Yong Zhao's motivations for product-oriented learning referred to earlier (2012).

Overall, I think getting students to take play seriously is still a challenge, and the importance of play and creativity needs to be reinforced throughout the whole of the curriculum. It also needs to be taken more seriously in secondary schools if we want to produce creative, innovative and entrepreneurial graduates.

References

Bateson, P., & Martin, P. (2013). *Play, Playfulness, Creativity and Innovation*. Cambridge, UK: Cambridge University Press.

Brown, S., & Vaughan, C. (2010). *Play: How It Shapes the Brain, Opens the Imagination, and Invigorates the Soul*. New York: J. P. Tarcher/Penguin Putnam.

Csikszentmihalyi, M. (1996). *Creativity: Flow and the Psychology of Discovery and Invention*. New York: HarperCollins.

Deininger, G. M. (2013). *Does State of Being and Dynamic Movement Have a Relationship with Creativity?* (Unpublished Ph.D. thesis). Cardiff Metropolitan University.

Gordon, G. (2009). What Is Play? In Search of a Definition. In D. Kuschner (Ed.), *Play and Culture Studies, from Children to Red Hatters: Diverse Images and Issues of Play* (pp. 1–13). Lanham, MD: University Press of America.

Gordon, G. (2014). Well Played: The Origins and Future of Playfulness. *American Journal of Play, 6*(2), 234–266.

LeJeune, C. (2007). *The Worry Trap: How to Free Yourself from Worry & Anxiety Using Acceptance and Commitment Therapy*. Oakland: New Harbinger Publications.

Lieberman, J. N. (1977). *Playfulness: Its Relationship to Imagination and Creativity*. New York: Academic Press.

Loudon, G. H., & Deininger, G. M. (2014). A New Model for Supporting Creativity in Research Organisations. In S. Schimpf (Ed.), *Proceedings of the R&D Management Conference* (pp. 93–100). Stuttgart, Germany: Fraunhofer IAO.

NACCCE. (1999). *All Our Futures: Creativity, Culture and Education, Report of the National Advisory Committee on Creative and Cultural Education*. London: Department for Education and Employment.

Runco, M. A. (2010). Divergent Thinking, Creativity and Ideation. In J. C. Kaufman & R. J. Sternberg (Eds.), *Cambridge Handbook of Creativity* (pp. 413–446). New York: Cambridge University Press.

Zhao, Y. (2012). *World Class Learners: Educating Creative and Entrepreneurial Students*. Thousand Oaks, CA: Corwin.

Part II

Wanderers and Wonderers

8

The Dark Would: Higher Education, Play and Playfulness [i]

Rebecca Fisher and Philip Gaydon

The Dark Would (TDW) is a collaborative and transdisciplinary project which seeks to explore transformative and alternative approaches to pedagogy within higher education (HE). The interests of the diverse research team—made up of teachers, researchers and administrators—coalesced around exploring the unseen rules of HE, and so we began with the classroom, a space in which the very furniture reinforces invisible hierarchies (Lambert 2009, 2011). Part alternative classroom, part pedagogy experiment, part conceptual laboratory, we created The Dark Would Space (TDWS) to encourage learners and teachers to play with the rules of the standard HE classroom and models of knowledge formation by inverting, transforming and challenging the notion of what

---

R. Fisher (✉)
University of Leicester, Leicester, UK
e-mail: rebecca.fisher@le.ac.uk

P. Gaydon
University of Warwick, Coventry, UK
e-mail: P.K.Gaydon@warwick.ac.uk

a learning space can and should be. We hoped that participants could then explore the effect that that breaking (or following) the rules had on them and their teaching/learning.

Images and examples from TDWS can be found online and later in this chapter you'll be able to take your own first steps into TDWS through our first paper-based TDWS. We hope you find a new perspective on whatever it is you wish to explore. For now, we'd like to share some of the philosophical and thematic considerations that have arisen from our experiences.

Defining Play/Playfulness

Our working understandings (informed by but in tension with Bateson and Martin 2013):

- **Play** is an activity in which participants act in accordance with self-imposed, unnecessary rules for the sake of an end such as fun, social gain, specific learning outcomes;
- **Playfulness** is the disposition to create new, unnecessary rules or change existing ones usually in order to increase enjoyment or explore alternative possibilities.

TDWS responds to these understandings by seeking to:

- reveal traditional rules of pedagogic spaces as forms of play. As much as the spaces and people that make up a HE institution might protest, the rules by which they are governed are not necessary in any strict sense. They are derived from social, moral, political and economic beliefs. Those who operate according to them are playing by a particular set of rules;
- make visible some of the rules of this play, offering opportunities to experiment with new rules;
- allow participants to discover their own understanding of the rules by which they are governed in HE;

- heighten participant playfulness to maximise their ability to challenge and transform rules;
- support participants in translating the results of their playfulness into their everyday practice.

Participant feedback has acknowledged that TDWS prompted them to engage critically and creatively with the rules of learning spaces through safe, focused playfulness:

> I was sceptical of what I would get out of [TDW] [….] I was unprepared for the path ahead. The Dark Would has renewed my passion for teaching - or rather, exploring with students. My year of teacher training gave me a toolkit and a map covered in warnings. "Do not enter." "Here be dragons." "This way to level 7.". Two days in The Dark Would gave me a backpack with survival essentials and a map covered in doodles. "Uncharted." "Goblins (friendly?)." "Last sighting of unicorn."

Implications of These Definitions

These definitions may seem reductive and overly broad, but we're not arguing that these are the only ways of understanding play/playfulness. Instead, these definitions highlight key aspects of TDWS and offer an opportunity to contrast them with other definitions of play/playfulness we've experienced.

1. *Unnecessary rules, and so play, underpin most of human activity*

One might object that in order to define HE as play we have stretched our understanding of the 'necessary' to ridiculous proportions: anything which is non-essential to immediate survival isn't necessary. Surely, if we are to think of HE as play then we must also include politics, economics, philosophy, business, religion, etc.? We not only accept this but positively embrace it. We welcome the opportunity to extend the free and adaptable nature of play to those aspects of life that appear to be unchangeable. We open up these fields to rethinking by approaching them as play, shifting the onus of proof onto those who want to maintain the status quo: can they demonstrate that their rules are or should be the only rules?

2. *Play can be forced*

Our understanding of play/playfulness challenges the notion that if you're being forced to play then you're not really playing. We don't deny that there is a stark contrast between the actions and state of forced and free players, but we do maintain that defining play as antithetical to enforced or unconscious participation paints an idealised picture of play. Deliberate and freely chosen play *can* be liberating, and therefore A Good Thing, but to regard this as essential to play overlooks the fact that we spend our lives playing games which we may not even perceive, such as those mentioned above. Within TDWS, we chose to explore the potential for liberation that lies in the revealing of hidden or assumed rules.

3. *Play doesn't have to be collaborative*

Collaborative play has a self-perpetuating, pragmatic benefit: each player has the potential to bring or create something new as part of a game, providing their fellow players with more diverse material to use within their own playful explorations. Our positive position on collaborative play is thus an expression of an ideology concerning the treatment of others, and of the causal relationship between broadened perspectives and the challenging of established structures. However, this is a normative position, not a definitional one; many existing definitions which highlight the ability of play to heighten a sense of social cohesion do not acknowledge that in doing so they are also expressing a moral position on the value and purpose of play.

We wish to hold two opposing positions in relation to collaborative play which are productive in their tension. While we believe in and have experienced the benefits of collaboration, we also wish to recognise that play/playfulness can be entirely self-focused—even selfish—for perfectly legitimate reasons. In TDWS, we offer opportunities to draw each other down new paths, but recognise that individual reflection can also be productive and playful.

4. *Play is not carried out for its own sake*

Our definitions present play/playfulness as a means to an end. Our play always has a purpose, regardless of whether that purpose is to learn or to have fun, create social bonds or satisfy curiosity. We argue that the idea of play-for-play's-sake is not a useful one in the context of HE; as pedagogues we find little use for learning activities which are engaged in for their own sake, and incorporating play-for-play's-sake into HE appears to be counterproductive to the ends of education (but we're prepared for some playful discussion on this point! see Savin-Baden 2007: 13–15).

5. *Play does not have to be fun*

Fun can be a tool for engagement, a step towards creating a safe learning environment, a catalyst for social bonding and many other positive things. However, we argue that—just like education—play can be difficult, tiresome and risky. It can be highly taxing, taking you into unknown places and causing you to question fundamental rules which underpin your identity. But this doesn't mean you aren't playing. Saying otherwise is the expression of philosophy about the ideal outcome of play rather than the act of play itself: this moral position may be defensible, but it has to be acknowledged and made visible first.

Characteristics of TDWS' Model of Play/Playfulness

1. *Surprise, wonder and the childlike*

We argue that a childlike experience of ignorance—from the fleeting to the more profound—can develop into excitement with growing awareness. As adults, we rarely get to revisit the joy and renewal of perspective we feel when we are surprised by the world around us. While it is difficult to predict what will evoke these feelings, TDWS invites you to enter a state which allows for their potential awakening through a sudden emergence into a transformed and unexpected space via crawl spaces and curtains, encounters with materials or tasks usually associated with childhood such as paints, bubbles and crayons, as well as objects and places to be explored like boxes, drawers and dens.

Our playful disposition begins to develop as we the rules that govern us become visible and we shift into a state of possibility: if I'm given permission to draw in this book, can I also tear out a page? Our own observations in TDWS have shown that this revelation of possibility leads to excitement, which in turn transforms participants from passive to motivated, and they are much more likely to extend the lifespan of their playful approach to the world beyond TDWS.

2. *Identity*

As TDWS invites participants to reflect on themselves, they engage in a form of playfulness that can result in the challenging/changing of the most fundamental rules that surround them. They often, implicitly or explicitly, come face-to-face with questions of identity such as: Who am I? Who have I been made to be? Who do I want to be? Can I achieve that? This, as Alice found when she was pressured by the Hookah-smoking caterpillar, is an unsettling process and can even lead to a potentially Sartrean revelation of radical freedom: if everything but the most basically necessary components of my existence are playful structures, what is left to ground me and my values? Often participants intuit that it lies ahead when they are faced with a space which requires them to enter the unknown; the feeling that they are being asked to take risks is all the more palpable because they are not even certain what that risk is. The wondrous/childlike elements of TDWS help to mediate this by giving participants a sense of nostalgic or excited warmth, and the option to take part in group tasks as well as working alone allows participants to choose their preference between safety in numbers or comfortable solitude. It's important to consider how to empower participants with a autonomy over the degree of risk and the effect this has on their play.

3. Learning objectives

'*It's lovely but where's the learning?*' This was a question asked by colleagues from Warwick's Learning and Development Centre when they experienced one of the earliest—and most freely playful—iterations of TDW. The feedback captures a sense that the space was *too* open and *too* free in its play, especially as it was billed as a playful *learning* space rather than a playful retreat or play-as-therapy space.

The TDW team have always debated whether a pleasant or challenging experience can only achieve its full value in an educational setting if the participants fully understand the purpose of the activity (see Wood et al. 1976). We experimented with adding textual prompts to TDWS in the form of tasks or challenges, as well as bookending TDWS with introduction and reflection time, debrief workshops and information sheets. We found that a more directive space gave participants a greater sense of productivity and security, and offered more opportunity for focused post-space reflection. However, we did not want to sacrifice too much autonomy or subversive-potential by doing so. Spaces like TDWS, which attempt to develop playfulness as a vehicle for change, should be seen as distinct from what might be termed 'playful learning' or 'learning-through-play', experiences which aim to bring participants to a predetermined learning outcome via play/playful activities. As such, we found that we needed to signpost that the added tasks were imposing rules which could be challenged; TDWS should be as subject to playfulness as the ideas and institutions it's holding up for examination.

We have found the following question useful in our post-TDWS forays into playful pedagogic projects: Am I trying to help students learn something via play? Or am I giving them an opportunity to change their perspective through play? We suggest that it is important to articulate this distinction and which (either or both) you are aiming for in your own projects.

The next few pages invite you to reflect playfully on who you are, and how you play, learn and grow.

Take this book, a pen, a pencil and some crayons somewhere safe and comfortable (*or don't*), away from distractions (*or somewhere full of them*), and you'll get the most from the experience (*or you won't*) (Fig. 8.1).

Fig. 8.1 Entrance to The Dark Would

Your journey begins in darkness.

Blink once, again, as your eyes adjust.

Unexpected sensations: the scent of earthy coriander; feet scuffing aside drifts of whispering leaves.

Something brushes your face and you startle—eyes wide and breath quickened.

It takes a moment for your heartbeat to settle; you smile ruefully in the dimness. It's just a leaf, and this is just a classroom.

Isn't it?

Chapter One: Transformation

Draw yourself in a classroom you use frequently.

Don't even think about doing so on this page. Academic collections aren't meant for that kind of nonsense. We can just about put up with highlighting and serious notation, but no more!

Pick up a different colour and add—or delete—to make you and the space more playful. Does anything change in how you look, feel, speak or act?

This page is not intentionally left blank… That's why I'm here.

Chapter Two: Imagine

Write the story of how you became—or are becoming—playful.

Beginning

Middle

End

Is there suspense? Comedy? Tragedy? Does it end with a tidy conclusion or a cliffhanger?

Do you feel different about yourself after telling this story?

Chapter Three: Create

Choose five objects from your surroundings and build them into a sculpture that represents your playful self.

Draw it here:

What does the combination of objects reveal?

What objects did you reject? If you could include any object, what would it be?

Chapter Four: Reflect

Write a playful goal to check back on in a few weeks.

Who/what might help achieve your goal? What challenges might you face?

Did things turn out as you expected?

"I'm sorry, but we're out of time."

Clay, down.
Crayons, down.
Costumes, off
suddenly lifeless.

Curtain aside,
brick exposed,
shoes on.
Tighten.

Harsh light
face paint
cracks.
Hardens.

People are staring.
World in focus.

My phone buzzes and my email pings.

Where was I?

Acknowledgements TDW is a collaboration between four colleagues from IATL which includes the two authors, along with Amy Clarke and Naomi de la Tour. The latter two are represented here in spirit, and now in name. See warwick.ac.uk/darkwould for more information, images and resources. We would also like to acknowledge the project which inspired TDW (Robbie Foulston and Leah Egglestone's 'The Making Space') and one that has sprung from it (Conor Heany, Hollie Mackenzie and Ian MacKenzie's 'Learning, Exchange, and Play').

Inspiration

Bateson, P., & Martin, P. (2013). *Play, Playfulness, Creativity and Innovation*. Cambridge: Cambridge University Press.

Friere, P., & Shor, I. (1987). *A Pedagogy for Liberation: Dialogues on Transforming Education*. South Hadley, MA: Bergin; Basingstoke: Macmillan.

Lambert, C. (2011). Psycho Classrooms: Teaching as a Work of Art. *Social and Cultural Geography, 12*(1), 27–45.

Lambert, C., Wilding, D., Moorhouse, L., Evans, L., & Lever, H. (2009). *Project: Spaces and Stories of (Higher) Education: A Historical Investigation*. Available at www2.warwick.ac.uk/fac/cross_fac/heahistory/research/spaces_and_stories. Accessed November 27, 2017.

Monk, N., Chillington Rutter, C., Neelands, J., & Heron, J. (2011). *Open-Space Learning: A Study in Interdisciplinary Pedagogy*. London: Bloomsbury.

Ranciere, J. (1991). *The Ignorant Schoolmaster: Five Lessons in Intellectual Emancipation*. Stanford, CA: Stanford University Press.

Sartre, J.-P. (2003). *Being and Nothingness: An Essay on Phenomenological Ontology* (H. E. Barnes, Trans.). London: Routledge.

Savin-Baden, M. (2007). *Learning Spaces: Creating Opportunities for Knowledge Creation in Academic Life*. Maidenhead: McGraw Hill.

Smith, K. (2012). *Wreck This Journal*. London: Penguin.

Wood, D., Bruner, J. S., & Ross, G. (1976). The Role of Tutoring in Problem Solving. *The Journal of Child Psychology and Psychiatry, 17*(2), 89–100.

9

Exploration: Playing with Place—Responding to Invitations

Helen Clarke and Sharon Witt

> He who has kept to the highway in his pilgrimage through a country has not seen much of it; it is by detours and false paths that we learn to know a country, for they compel us to pay keen attention, to look about us on all sides, and to observe all landmarks in order to find our way … Whoever has always kept to the highway of prescribed school experiences and of acknowledged truth, without the courage to turn aside and wander, has not seen very much in the land of truth. And long wandering means long remaining young.
>
> Paulsen and Perry (1895: 208)

James and Brookfield (2014) suggest taking a 'what if' rather than a 'how to' approach to learning and teaching. In this exploration, we invite educators to adopt a more imaginative view of established curricula; a spirited 'more than' approach (Trueit and Doll 2010).

H. Clarke (✉) · S. Witt
University of Winchester, Winchester, UK
e-mail: Helen.clarke@winchester.ac.uk

S. Witt
e-mail: Sharon.witt@winchester.ac.uk

We draw on experiences with primary education students, amazing young people who are simultaneously undergraduate learners and developing professionals. These students are preparing to be primary school teachers, charged with the responsibility of nurturing children's thirst for knowledge and their dynamic fascination and curiosity with the world. Ours is a courageous adventure in teacher education, which seeks to take our students beyond the Teachers' Standards (DFE 2012), a list of minimum national professional competencies. This pedagogy encourages learners to travel differently, 'playing with and exploring differences, attending to intuition and abiding with mystery and ambiguity, happily relinquishing certainty' (Trueit and Doll 2010: 138).

A reflective theory—practice nexus is central to professional development for teachers (Pollard 2014). Our undergraduate programme themes of 'Identity', 'Perspectives' and 'Relationships' foster the development of the whole learner and frame our curriculum for student teachers, whose future profession demands that they become adept at moving between theory (on campus), practice (in schools), and appreciate the possibilities offered by the world (in between) through children's eyes. A playful response to place adds situated experience to this interaction and recognises a theory–practice–experience relationship. Experience founded in playful approaches, that values different ways of knowing, prompts emergent ontological change within students, where learning is generated by students' own activity, rather than directed by tutors (Rice 2009).

The question we address in the context of playful pedagogic strategies is not why, how or when, but *where* playful learning might occur. Places are 'rich in significance and meaning' and a 'powerful pedagogic phenomenon' (Wattchow and Brown 2011: 180). What if we think differently and consider working off-campus, with our students letting the place lead learning? What if we take up the invitations and provocations offered by place? Experiences with place can rekindle a 'child-like' wonder and spirit of playfulness and invoke tools of imaginative education that include the use of narrative, anomalies, agency, humanisation, mystery, wonder, imagery, pattern and humour (Judson 2016). This work is framed in transactional ways of knowing. Dewey (1938) proposed a relational pedagogy, where new acquaintances are made with people, places and materials in worldly encounters. We play, in place, to break down common binaries; of cognitive and emotional, of knowledge and experience, of the familiar and the extraordinary.

Playful teaching may require educators to step outside established comfort zones and do something differently, to enter the 'realm of possibility' (Seymour and Witt 2014). The following case study of student and tutor learners exemplifies playful innovations with place. The action occurred in the rural Hampshire village of Selborne, described by Mabey (1986: 15) as a place of 'responses and echoes'. This example is rooted in place-based nature education (Sobel 2008), place narrative (Payne 2010) and pedagogy of place (Wattchow and Brown 2011). We worked with the premise that an ecological imagination emerges out of students' playful participation with the world through activities and learning opportunities in which bodies, emotions and imaginations are actively engaged '… and takes us to the new, the unusual and the extraordinary' (Judson 2010: 4). Imagination is central to the process of becoming a teacher and requires students to use senses beyond the visible world (Fettes 2005).

This exploration is also written playfully; it is rich in descriptive verbs, as an account of a living enquiry, a journey based on relational encounters in place, where students were action-oriented, worked with ideas of openness, and were responsive and receptive (Kind 2006). We prepared ourselves for place encounters with ceremony; we wore stickers, face paint and magic dust. We travelled in, through and with the place. We drew on literature from subject disciplines of education, and of science and geography, yet we viewed possibilities through multiple lenses. We all became students of Selborne. Through deep journeying, we opened doorways to new disciplinary and pedagogical knowledge. As reported by a Professor of 'Promenadology', the science of walking involves 'more than putting one foot in front of the other', and is rather, 'the concentrated and conscious perception of our environment' (Deutsche Welle). We travelled as a community of explorers, in dialogue with each other and with the place (Witt and Clarke 2012). Moreover, we were alert to possibilities, a world of 'doorways' (MacFarlane 2014: 316), which might open at our arrival.

And so,

- We slowly ambled from the village centre, stopping to challenge notions of pace in education. The students were immersed in a slow eco-pedagogy, which encouraged the travellers to, 'pause or dwell in spaces for more than a fleeting moment', to recognise place attachments and to make meaning within the landscapes they inhabit (Payne and Wattchow 2009: 16). We offered opportunities to 'rediscover our own sense of joy, excitement, and mystery' (Louv 2005: 164), because '…it takes time – loose, unstructured dreamtime – to experience nature in a meaningful way' (117).
- We climbed the 'Zigzag Path', where, from increasing altitude, the village revealed itself to us as if opening minds with every step taken. The possibilities within the site invited different thinking about the world and education, as through our actions we subverted notions of linearity and embraced uncertainty, and by engaging in the complex systems of education in a playful manner we found 'modes of resistance which allow us – to exist in the between spaces of one AND another in order not only to survive but thrive' (Kidd 2015: 22).
- We wandered in the woods with a 'wand of enquiry' (Buckley 1879: 231), we posed ideas of subject disciplines and notions of curriculum. We acknowledged the complexity, and perhaps impossibility, 'of truly knowing nature - nature's epistemological mystery … that which can never be fully known, intellectually possessed' (Bonnett 2007: 713). One participant commented, '*I like to question things. I know the physical place will not tell you the answers but it might show you or lead you. It may also leave unanswered questions*'.
- We navigated between haptic relational encounters (Rodaway 2011) in an active, transformative, meaningful exchange of messages between the world and humans in co-relation, where invitations were accepted to slide, to climb, to drift, to build in a childlike wonder and spirit of playfulness. Participants found, '*a place to … hide… think…explore…and discover*', '*echoes of the past*', and '*enough space*

to stop and look'. Students responded to place and opportunity; they saw trees and they climbed them, they came across a river and they splashed in the water, they found leaves and they threw them into the air, and they played on tree swings.

- We entered clearings in the wood and noticed opportunities for placemaking. Emotional engagement not only nurtured possibilities for the development of more traditional ways of knowing, but also fostered openings to the students' imaginative responses (Payne 2010). A participant commented, '*As tutors you allowed us the opportunity to be independent, imaginative and reflective learners which, in turn, allowed us, even as adults, to play and interact with nature in a variety of contexts and ways*'.
- We roamed through animate landscapes noticing the familiar and extraordinary, working with macro- and micro-scales, valuing the cognitive and the emotional, and embracing both the planned and the spontaneous. '*The idea of a small-world enquiry unsettled my notion of curriculum experiences. I found I had to become more open to a new creative teaching method which made me engage more with the task*' (Fig. 9.1). Our journey, planned and emergent, ranged from hill to woodland, meadow to river and garden to house:
- We meandered in the water of a stream of ideas and waded in the flow of possible futures (Hicks 2014). We raced toy ducks along the channel and become 'giddy' (Tovey 2007) with excitement as we engaged with, and appreciated, the wonder of a river. We flew pigeon puppets across the meadow, with new and embodied perspectives. We transitioned between the wildness of the beech woodland, to open parkland and across a ha-ha to the formality of the cultivated space to shape and inspire our thinking. We tortoised around the garden, recalling stories of different places, cultures and times, whilst dreaming in the footsteps of others. We tiptoed through the house, in bright socks, having removed our boots and lined them up along the corridor as if a class of children had arrived. *One participant concluded that, 'real life is a completely interrelated journey with boundaries constantly being crossed and mixed'* (Fig. 9.2).

Fig. 9.1 We roamed through animate landscapes noticing the familiar and extraordinary

This exploration has shared playful attention in and with place, underpinned by a belief in a philosophy of action where knowing itself is positioned as a relational activity. Paying attention is an integral part of travelling and employs all the senses to reveal the familiar, the less often noticed, and the 'more than human'. How we travel determines what we see and how we engage. Where we educate determines what tutors and students notice and how they interact in relation to each other and to place. As Huebner (1999: 405) suggests, learning is, 'a journey into the land of the unknown, taken by ourselves, but with others'. Such collaborative engagements foster a 'wide-awakeness' … an 'awareness of what it is to be in the world' (Greene 2000: 35). In communities of playful learning, resonant moments involve multisensory responses, produced in collaborations, which organically guide discussions, storied encounters, wonder and meaning-making (Somerville 2008).

Fig. 9.2 We meandered in the water of a stream of ideas

Our aim is for playful place responsive pedagogies to foster personal and professional development within our teacher education programmes. These are '… deeply serious in intent (and critically considered), yet are rendered with a lightness of touch, engaging and playful in their execution' (Ward 2016).

References

Bonnett, M. (2007). Environmental Education and the Issue of Nature. *Journal of Curriculum Studies, 39*(6), 707–721.
Buckley, A. (1879). *The Fairyland of Science*. Chapel Hill, NC: Republished by Yesterday's Classics.
Deutsche Welle. http://www.dw.com/en/the-sciencce-of-taking-a-walk/a-2374179. Accessed June 30, 2017.

Department for Education. (2012). *Teachers' Standards*. Available at https://www.gov.uk/government/publications/teachers-standards. Accessed June 30, 2017.
Dewey, J. (1938). *Experience and Education*. New York: Kappa Delta Pi.
Fettes, M. (2005). Imaginative Transformation in Teacher Education. *Teaching Education, 16*(1), 3–11.
Greene, M. (2000). *Releasing the Imagination: Essays on Education, the Arts, and Social Change*. San Francisco: Jossey-Bass.
Hicks, D. (2014). *Educating for Hope in Troubled Times: Climate Change and the Transition to a Post-carbon Future*. Stoke-on-Trent: Trentham Books.
Huebner, D. (1999). *The Lure of the Transcendent*. London: Routledge.
James, A., & Brookfield, S. D. (2014). *Engaging Imagination: Helping Students Become Creative and Reflective Thinkers*. San Francisco: Jossey-Bass.
Judson, G. (2010). *A New Approach to Ecological Education. Engaging Students' Imaginations in Their World*. New York: Peter Lang.
Judson, G. (2016). *Three Toolkits to Help Maximize Student Learning & Engagement*. Available at http://gettingsmart.com/2016/07/nurture-heart-learning/. Accessed October 27, 2016.
Kidd, D. (2015). *Becoming Mobius. The Complex Matter of Education*. Carmarthen: Crown House Publishing.
Kind, S. (2006). *Of Stones and Silences: Storying the Trace of the Other in the Autobiographical and Textile Text of Art/Teaching* (Unpublished doctoral dissertation). University of British Columbia, Canada.
Louv, R. (2005). *Last Child in the Woods*. Chapel Hill, NC: Algonquin Books.
Mabey, R. (1986). *Gilbert White—A Biography*. London: Century Hutchinson.
MacFarlane, R. (2014). *Landmarks*. London: Penguin.
Paulsen, F., & Perry, E. D. (1895). *The German Universities: Their Character and Historical Development*. New York and London: Macmillan.
Payne, P. G. (2010). Remarkable-Tracking, Experiential Education of the Ecological Imagination. *Environmental Education Research, 16*(3–4), 295–310.
Payne, P. G., & Wattchow, B. (2009). Phenomenological Deconstruction, Slow Pedagogy, and the Corporeal Turn in Wild Environmental/Outdoor Education. *Canadian Journal of Environmental Education, 14*, 15–32.
Pollard, A. (2014). *Reflective Teaching in Schools*. London: Bloomsbury.
Rice, L. (2009). Playful Learning. *Journal for Education in the Built Environment, 4*(2), 94–108.
Rodaway, P. (2011). *Sensuous Geographies*. London: Routledge.

Seymour, M., & Witt, S. (2014, Spring). La Chasse à l'Ours: A Journey Exploring Teacher Trainees. Attitudes to Primary Foreign Language Teaching. *Francophonie*. Available at http://journals.all-languages.org.uk/2014/05/la-chasse-a-lours-a-journey-exploring-teacher-trainees-attitudes-to-primary-foreign-language-teaching/. Accessed September 3, 2016.

Sobel, D. (2008). *Childhood and Nature: Design Principles for Educators*. Portland, ME: Stenhouse Publishers.

Somerville, M. J. (2008). 'Waiting in the Chaotic Place of Unknowing': Articulating Postmodern Emergence. *International Journal of Qualitative Studies in Education, 21*(3), 209–220.

Tovey, H. (2007). *Playing Outdoors*. Maidenhead: Open University Press.

Trueit, D., & Doll, W. E. (2010). Thinking Complexly, Being-in-Relation. In D. Osberg & G. Biesta (Eds.), *Complexity Theory and the Politics of Education*. Rotterdam: Sense Publishers.

Ward, E. (2016). *Playful in Execution, Serious in Intent. Developing a Research Culture in Learning and Engagement at the Whitworth and Manchester Museum*. Available at http://bit.ly/1Swf82O. Accessed October 24, 2016.

Wattchow, B., & Brown, M. (2011). *A Pedagogy of Place*. Clayton: Monash University Publishing.

Witt, S., & Clarke, H. (2012, July 12). Selborne: A Place of Responses; a Cross-Curricular Opportunity for ITE Students to 'Watch Narrowly'. In *The UK TE Network for Education Sustainable Development/Global Citizenship Fifth Annual Conference*. London South Bank University.

10

Exploration: Cabinets of Curiosities—Playing with Artefacts in Professional Teacher Education

Sarah Williamson

Introduction

This case discusses an example of playful object-oriented pedagogy in professional education and how a collection of objects and artefacts was curated for students to explore through play. The aim was to inspire a creative and critical approach to the development of both teaching and learning strategies and resource development in PGCE students training to be teachers and lecturers for the lifelong learning sector. The highly prescriptive approaches of current standards-based teacher training programmes in the UK reflect a general move towards instrumentalist teaching, learning and assessment in higher education (Williamson 2017). However, the use of play as a creative pedagogic strategy can present an alternative to this instrumentalism, offering richer, deeper learning experiences and the potential for critical thinking and new insights.

S. Williamson (✉)
School of Education and Professional Development,
University of Huddersfield, Huddersfield, UK
e-mail: S.M.Williamson@hud.ac.uk

The Classroom Cabinet of Curiosities

Using a 'cabinet of curiosities' concept, the '*Wunderkammer*' or 'wonder rooms' of the sixteenth and seventeenth centuries inspired a lesson on 'resource development' staged as a wonder room. These cabinets of curiosity, 'devices of wonder' (Stafford 2004), were collections of antiquities and rarities, the fantastical and the exotic, all elaborately organised and displayed. 'Ideally', state Kasworm and Bowles (2012: 389), 'higher education offers an invitation to think, to be, and to act in new and enhanced ways', and the student teachers were given real invitations prior to this lesson, which hinted at what was to come: 'Consider the scene: a collector in the 17th century, probably noble, definitely male, ushers an erudite friend into his "cabinet". It is in fact a whole room – for viewing of certain curiosities…' (Dillon 2013: 14). Many of the students said the invitation had been intriguing and built the anticipation that something, 'out of the ordinary' and exciting was imminent. They entered a room filled with a mass of objects displayed and arranged attractively. The lights were dim, fairy lights twinkled on some objects or in containers, and visual imagery was projected onto a screen. Rhythmic, repetitive Indian music was playing. The classroom was almost a magical space to enter, a wonder room inviting engagement and play.

The student teachers were encouraged to play, handle and tinker with 'a sense of wonder' as they carouselled in groups around a wide variety of artefacts and 'curiosities'. Some were traditionally associated with play such as vintage games, dolls, puppets, models, musical instruments, hats, dressing-up clothes, a doll's house and things in miniature. Others were unusual or unexpected in their playful juxtaposition, curated and arranged in a spirit of art 'assemblage' to create unanticipated associations. Many of the objects had 'playful affordances' (Frissen et al. 2015: 22) and ludic qualities, in other words characteristics which invited play. Compartmentalisation, concealment and play were features of many historical 'cabinets of curiosity', with contents often nested, sometimes hidden, in cabinets within cabinets, shelves, niches, drawers within drawers and boxes within boxes. This inspired the placing of many things in envelopes, boxes, bags, tins and small suitcases so that the exploration, 'opening' and 'unfastening' aspects of play were noticed. Some objects offered obvious provocation, for example, a blue-eyed blonde-haired Barbie doll dressed in pink satin and an Action Man doll dressed in camouflage instantly invited comment and discussion about gender and stereotyping. As a result, the student teachers started to realise the educational possibilities of such artefacts to provide a 'dialogic and visual platform to encourage critical consciousness' (Clover et al. 2016: ix).

The student teachers were introduced to artists, designers and musicians whose work, exhibitions and performances could be linked to curiosity cabinets, objects and play. For example, movements such as Dada and Surrealism, and individuals such as Alexander McQueen, Susan Philipsz, Armand Fernandez, Susan Hillier and Paul Neagu. Boxes and contents designed to be explored through tactile play were a feature of Neagu's work and students' attention, and the implications for education, was drawn to his 'Palpable Art Manifesto!' of 1969, which stated that 'you can take things in better, more completely, with your ten fingers…than with only two eyes'. Object play in educational research was also introduced through the work of Loi and her use of playful triggers, eccentric objects and anomalous artefacts (2006).

In some ways, the classroom became a 3-dimensional version of the artist's studio wall described by Malbert (2013: 9) as a place of pinned 'miscellaneous ephemera' where 'diverse categories and objects co-exist', and which can be regarded as a 'single physical and epistemological space'.

Curiosity and Play

The contents of a Wunderkammer can encourage 'inquisitive voyaging' (Stafford 2004: 2) and engage students in 'the inquisitive medium of curiosità' (Yurtkuran and Taneli 2013: 73). The principle of 'curiosità' is one of 'Seven da Vincian Principles' which Gelb (2004: 9) has used to describe the intense curiosity of Leonardo da Vinci. Referring to da Vinci's childlike sense of wonder and inquisitiveness, 'curiosità' is described as 'an insatiably curious approach to life'. The Wunderkammer of this case study promoted curiosity through play, allowing a childlike sense of wonder to return to a higher education classroom. The seven principles which Gelb has identified as underpinning da Vinci's genius and creativity, in addition to curiosità, include 'dimostrazione, sensazione, sfumato, arte/scienza, corporalita and connessione' (2004: 9). Some of these can also be helpful when considering the pedagogic potential of object play. For example, the principle of 'sensazione', or continual refinement of senses to enliven experience, has direct application due to the physicality of object handling and play; 'sfumato', or the willingness to embrace paradox and ambiguity, has relevance when asking students to consider how objects can inspire possibilities by having alternative purposes or meanings. The principle of 'connessione', which Gelb (2004: 220) describes as 'the recognition of and appreciation for the interconnectedness of all things', refers to da Vinci's practice of combining and connecting disparate elements to create new and different forms. Playing with objects can allow and promote 'connessione', and Gelb (ibid.: 224) states that many of da Vinci's inventions and designs arose from his playfulness as an adult allowing him to make unprecedented, original connections.

The Cabinet of Curiosities Classroom as a Higher Education Playground

In his classic work on play, Huizinga (1938: 10) states that the spaces where play takes place are 'play-grounds' which can take many different forms, and these are 'marked off beforehand either materially or ideally'. They are 'temporary worlds within ordinary world'. The university classroom described in this case study was physically separate, 'marked off', and a 'temporary world' from the rest of the university world. It became an 'imaginative play-space' which Norgard et al. (2016: 1) associate with the concept of the 'magic circle'. Huizinga (ibid.) referred to the 'magic circle' as a space for play, and this has since acquired a metaphoric meaning in the field of game studies and play culture. Playful teaching and learning in the magic circle can promote imagination, participation and critical thinking as it allows a place for open exploration and experimentation (Norgard et al. 2016: 1). Frissen et al. (2015: 19) suggest that even when engaging in playful activity, and the magic circle of the play-world has been stepped into from the everyday world, there is actually yet another play—the play of a double existence and double experience. A player is aware of being 'simultaneously in the ordinary world and in the play-world'. In this lesson the students, all future teachers, engaged in this double play, continually stepping in and out of the classroom play-world back into the real world of the teacher, reflecting on how they could transfer their learning and experience into their future teaching and lessons. The wonder classroom also created an intensification of experience, a 'kind of exhilaration of the senses', where 'learning, fascination, enchantment' were 'caught up with each other' (MacLure 2006: 737). Play can sometimes have a 'magical condensation' and a 'reach towards otherness' that MacLure (ibid.) suggests were also characteristics of wonder cabinets.

Play and playfulness with materials and objects through which to learn and think also relate to ideas of embodied cognition. Chatterjee (2008: 269) states that, with reference to learning with objects, the implication of Winnicott's 'playing is doing' (1971: 41) is 'an active need to "do" things with objects', as it is '*active* touching that is integral to the creative exploration of objects and therefore of "learning" itself'. Tactile play with an object often involves a physical 'turning round' and 'turning over' of the object, and students explored how this could facilitate a cognitive 'turning' (linking to Dewey's description of reflective thinking as 'turning over a subject in the mind' 1933). This can also be associated with Jarvis and Graham's view (2015: 13) that play with physical materials can give space for the making of connections and ideas through 'mind wandering', offering a way of thinking beyond stereotypical articulations based on language.

The Student Experience

This lesson was vividly remembered by the student teachers, supporting the view of Romanek and Lynch (2008: 284) 'that object-handling has a long-lasting effect and relationship with memory, more so than text-based learning often has'. Prown (1982: 9) states that objects allow sensory, intellectual and emotional engagement, and this was evident, recognised and referred to by the students: 'an immersive, all-senses experience' was a typical comment. While the sensory pleasure of being able to touch, handle and play with artefacts in education was realised by the future teachers, there were other outcomes. One student teacher significantly reflected with regard to inclusion and equality that 'there was a lot of power in that session, because it can make all people equal if everyone can touch something'. One statement that 'it was a safe way to talk about yourself because you're not really talking about yourself, you're talking about the object in front of you' also revealed developing reflection about inclusive classroom practices. Another student commented on how any teacher could create a cabinet of curiosity, making their classroom a Wunderkammer, and again with reference to equality said, 'I realised that anyone can collect, it's not to do with wealth now, it doesn't haven't to be precious, I like that'. One student referred to the development of empathy, reflecting on the powerful impact upon him of learning about a collection of shoes and how they symbolised the stories of their refugee owners. The lesson 'made me think about trust' reflected one student, and how being allowed to play with the objects sent the message of 'I'm trusting you with my things'. As a result, she had taken a collection of her own personal objects into a college class she was teaching, and reported how positive this had been in building the teacher–group relationship.

The students all realised the value of play, discovery and exploration and the implications of this for them as potential teachers and lecturers in the lifelong learning sector: 'I realised there's still that same desire to discover in adults that children have'. Anticipation, suspense and intrigue were words used with reference to the items which needed to be opened, unfolded and unfastened, an example comment being: 'the opening, you don't know what's in there do you…and no matter what age you are, it's that discovery, it's that seeing a box and not knowing what's in it'. It was recognised by the students that playful behaviour with objects and artefacts can be intrinsically motivating, encouraging curiosity, stimulating thinking, questioning and reflection and that playful states can spark creativity, innovation and new ideas (Norgard et al. 2016). The object play, had in the words of one student, 'opened up imagination, opened up conversation, opened up ways of teaching'.

With regard to critical reflection and personal change, the following demonstrates the transformative impact of the lesson for one student teacher:

> I think it helped me to remember who I was as a person actually, and it was after that, that I started to think about how I could present myself… because before doing that I think I was trying really hard to fit into my preconceived idea of a teacher. But then that kind of playfulness, it was like a kind of light switch…I think after that time I felt I had more freedom to have my personality in my teaching

The notion of a magic circle allows the 'imagining of a different type of learning environment' according to Norgard et al. (2016: 1), and in this lesson the student teachers experienced and noticed the positive impact of a learning environment which invited play and engagement. The learning environment as a magic circle associated with play, in this case a cabinet of curiosity, can be linked to Tutchell's (2014) triangular concept which includes the environment as the third teacher in the relationship between learner, teacher and the space for learning.

Conclusion

This lesson, staged as a wunderkammer, encouraged students to act and think through play with objects and artefacts; a principle which can be transferred to many other disciplines. Playful object-oriented pedagogy in higher education has the capacity to promote critical curiosity and imagination in many subjects, and lead to critical reflection and new insights. In the 'magic circle' of a classroom cabinet of curiosity, objects and artefacts which invite tactile play and playful connections in any subject offer not only vivid and memorable learning experiences, but many 'provocative pedagogical possibilities' (Clover et al. 2016: viii).

References

Chatterjee, H. (2008). *Touch in Museums*. Oxford: Berg.
Clover, D., Sanford, K., Bell, L., & Johnson, K. (2016). *Adult Education, Museums and Art Galleries: Animating Social, Cultural and Institutional Change*. Rotterdam: Sense.
Dewey, J. (1933). *How We Think: A Restatement of the Relation of Reflective Thinking*. New York: D. C. Heath.
Dillon, B. (2013). Essays at Curiosity. In *Curiosity*. London: Hayward Publishing.
Frissen, V., Lammes, S., De Lange, M., Mul, J., & Raessens, J. (2015). *Playful Identities: The Ludification of Digital Media Cultures*. Amsterdam: AU Press.
Gelb, M. (2004). *How to Think Like Leonardo da Vinci*. New York: Delta.
Huizinga, J. (1938/1970). *Homo Ludens: A Study of the Play Element in Culture*. London: Maurice Temple Smith Ltd.
Jarvis, J., & Graham, S. (2015). *It's All About the Shoes*. York: Higher Education Academy.
Kasworm, C. E., & Bowles, T. A. (2012). Fostering Transformative Learning in Higher Education Settings. In *The Handbook of Transformative Learning*. San Francisco: Jossey-Bass.
Loi, D., & Dillon, P. (2006). Adaptive Educational Environments as Creative Spaces. *Cambridge Journal of Education, 36*(3), 363–381.
MacLure, M. (2006). The Bone in the Throat: Some Uncertain Thoughts on Baroque Method. *International Journal of Qualitative Studies in Education, 19*(6), 729–745.
Malbert, R. (2013). *Curiosity*. London: Hayward Publishing.
Neagu, P. (1969). *Palpable Art Manifesto!* In Bottinelli, G. (2002). Available at http://www.tate.org.uk/art/artworks/neagu-palpable-object-mosaic.
Norgard, R., Toft-Neilson, C., & Whitton, R. (2016). *Playful Teaching Between Freedom and Control*. SRHE Conference 2016.
Prown, J. (1982). Mind in Matter: An Introduction to Material Culture Theory and Method. *Winterthur Portfolio, 17*(1), 1–19.
Romanek, D., & Lynch, B. (2008). Touch and the Value of Object Handling. In *Touch in Museums: Policy and Practice in Object Handling*. Oxford: Berg.
Stafford, B. (2004). *Devices of Wonder: From the World in a Box to Images on a Screen*. Los Angeles: Getty Research Institute.

Tutchell, S. (2014). *Young Children as Artists*. Abingdon: Routledge.
Williamson, S. (2017). Pop-Up Art Schools and the 'Carnivalesque'. In *Informal Learning: Perspectives, Challenges and Opportunities*. New York: Nova Publishers.
Winnicott, D. (1971). *Playing and Reality*. London: Tavistock Publications.
Yurtkuran, S., & Taneli, Y. (2013). Medium of Curiosita. *Art, Design and Communication in Higher Education, 12*(1), 65–90.

11

Sketch: Playful Pedagogies— Collaborations Between Undergraduates and School Pupils in the Outdoor Learning Centre and the Pop-Up "Playscape"

Chantelle Haughton and Siân Sarwar

A playful approach within Higher Education sometimes involves asking students to literally play or, alternatively, adopt a creative, practical approach, thus supporting them towards developing their understanding of challenging concepts and/or encouraging them to make clearer links between theory and practice. On Early Childhood Studies (ECS) within Cardiff Metropolitan University, the serious business of play is often at the heart of our practice. As such, Early Years practice represents the bedrock of our pedagogy, providing scope for students to explore, interpret, adapt and transfer what they experience within Higher Education into their own practice (cf. Kleiman 2008). Both creativity and playfulness are fundamental to the design of many modules, thus forming a catalyst for creating communities of practice (Lave and Wenger 1991;

C. Haughton (✉) · S. Sarwar
Early Childhood Studies, Cardiff Metropolitan University,
Cardiff, Wales, UK
e-mail: chaughton@cardiffmet.ac.uk

S. Sarwar
e-mail: ssarwar@cardiffmet.ac.uk

Wenger 1998) involving a number of stakeholders which include students, staff, local children and practitioners, all of whom then engage in a process of reciprocal learning (O'Meara and Jaeger 2016).

Moreover, community engagement has been pivotal to the university's outdoor learning centre which has been developed, using a previously unused strip of ancient woodland on campus to introduce a suite of log circle classrooms and a log cabin, both of which are now used on a regular basis across a range of programmes. The OLC has facilitated a number of community projects involving a range of stakeholders, such as local children, students, practitioners, lecturers, families (Benneworth et al. 2008 cited in Wood 2012) which have, in turn, influenced and been integrated within our curriculum and extra-curricular activities. For example, an outdoor play project in which reception-age children from a local primary school visited campus weekly over a period of seven weeks not only provided opportunities for local children to engage in free play in a natural woodland environment but also enabled students to be involved in an action research project which utilised action cameras and camera classes as a means of data collection, thus developing their knowledge and understanding of research methods and the challenges surrounding data collection as well as their knowledge and understanding of outdoor play. Whilst the practitioners accompanying the children were not involved directly in the research, the woodland play sessions provided opportunities for them to see how the children responded to the woodland environment in comparison with the formal school environment.

In fact, involving student volunteers in the re-energising of previously unused outdoor spaces on campus is becoming a playful habit within Cardiff Metropolitan University: design and education students recently transformed a barren concrete patch into a colourful installation which is now used as an outdoor play, learning and teaching space. The 'Forest of Plinths' project emerged from a brief, which called for the creative design of storage of loose parts to support children's play and the 'new' space is now used in weekly workshops by students studying BA (Hons) Early Childhood Studies (ECS) and BA (Hons) Primary Education Studies, teachers, children and the local community. The concrete patch extends students' experience of learning outdoors as they explore issues, such as the value and challenges of play, learning and space.

Playfulness and creativity are not, however, reserved for the outdoor environment. For example, in order to support their' engagement in and understanding of their academic reading, ECS students have used graffiti art to, for example, conceptualise different constructions of childhood. This approach adopts a creative platform to encourage students to discuss what they have read in relation to a particular subject and to identify ways to interpret meaning. The output, whilst a creative, visual representation, adopts the same skills used in paraphrasing and therefore, represents a strategy to support their essay and report writing. Differentiating between policy and legislation represented an area of ambiguity identified by a number of students. Therefore, creating (and decorating!) policy and legislation flowerboxes represented a strategy to support students in learning to differentiate between the two, doing so in way which not only addressed the gap in their knowledge regarding the distinction between policy and legislation but did so in a way in which learning became entwined with time, place and context, thus committing the experience to memory along with the knowledge and understanding gained (Ewing and Gibson 2015).

Such approaches encourage all our stakeholders, be they students, staff, practitioners, children and so on, to take risks as they construct and take ownership of their learning, whether it be independent and/or collaborative, curricular or extra-curricular, formal or informal.

References

Ewing, R., & Gibson, R. (2015). Creative Teaching or Teaching Creatively? Using Creative Arts Strategies in Preservice Teacher Education. *Waikato Journal of Education (2382-0373), 20*(3), 77–91.

Kleiman, P. (2008). Towards Transformation: Conceptions of Creativity in Higher Education. *Innovations in Education & Teaching International, 45*(3), 209–217.

Lave, E., & Wenger, E. (1991). *Situated Learning: Legitimate Peripheral Participation*. Cambridge: Cambridge University Press.

O'Meara, K., & Jaeger, A. (2016). Preparing Future Faculty for Community Engagement: Barriers, Facilitators, Models, and Recommendations. *Journal of Higher Education Outreach & Engagement, 20*(1), 127–150.

Wenger, E. (1998). *Communities of Practice: Learning, Meaning and Identity.* Cambridge: Cambridge University Press.

Wood, J. (2012). The University as a Public Good: Active Citizenship and University Community Engagement. *International Journal of Progressive Education, 8*(3), 15–31.

12

Sketch: Teaching and Learning Inside the Culture Shoe Box

Hoda Wassif and Maged Zakher

With the fast development of technology, engaging students within higher education has shifted towards the use of more classroom technology (Dey et al. 2009). However, when it comes to teaching some challenging topics such as ethics, business values and cultural communication, there is a belief that adult learners need to engage with these subjects differently (Wassif 2016).

The Culture Shoe Box is an inexpensive, hands-on educational resource that was introduced to facilitate workshops and enhance students' learning experience in a higher-education setting. The authors started using this resource to teach ethics to postgraduate dental students and cultural communication to undergraduate business management students. The resource is simply an empty shoe box that was filled

---

H. Wassif (✉)
University of Bedfordshire (UoB), Bedford, UK
e-mail: hoda.wassif@beds.ac.uk

M. Zakher
University of Northampton, Northampton, UK
e-mail: Maged.Zakher@northampton.ac.uk

© The Author(s) 2019
A. James and C. Nerantzi (eds.), *The Power of Play in Higher Education*,
https://doi.org/10.1007/978-3-319-95780-7_12

Fig. 12.1 Some items in two culture shoe boxes

with cultural items (such as a papyrus bookmark, an African t-shirt, a miniature Indian elephant and similar items) (Fig. 12.1). The idea was to provide students with some real items that would trigger and sustain a discussion around the topic. It also facilitated discussion about abstract topics (such as values, ethics and culture) through tangible items that can partly reflect some facets of those notions. The fun of opening the box and selecting an item to discuss at each table added to a positive environment needed for some otherwise challenging topics. Shoe boxes in general have some positive connotations whether they are used by charities or in an educational setting. Moreover, visual aids and realia have been extensively used in language teaching to enhance learners' engagement.

Postgraduate as well as undergraduate students who used the resource welcomed it and were positively involved in discussions that were sparked around the items they selected from the box to talk about. Dental professionals studying law and ethics found the box to be intriguing and inviting to deeper discussions and more interesting angles, especially in class discussions around ethical issues. For educators, this teaching tool adds an element of versatility and excitement through engagement and play, especially when teaching the same topics to different groups of learners. The authors have used the resource with postgraduate dental students, intercultural communication students as well as undergraduate business management students; however, the flexibility offered by the resource makes it also usable with other disciplines within the social sciences. The reusability of the Culture Shoe Box (via using it with different classes at different levels) and also its renewability (through adding more items) promotes an always-interesting feel in the classrooms not only for learners but also for teachers. Teachers using such a tool need to be open for discussions that could be novel, student-centred, and usually outside the box!

References

Dey, E. L., Burn, H. E., & Gerdes, D. (2009). Bringing the Classroom to the Web: Effects of Using New Technologies to Capture and Deliver Lectures. *Research in Higher Education, 50*(4), 377–393.

Wassif, H. S. (2016). *Perception of Using Culture Shoebox as an Educational Tool in Teaching Ethics and Culture Among Postgraduate Students Studying Dental Law and Ethics* (MA). University of Bedfordshire, 1–65.

Part III

Experimenters and Engagers

13

Exploration: Dopamine and the Hard Work of Learning Science

Lindsay Wheeler and Michael Palmer

> People are naturally curious, but we are not naturally good thinkers; unless the cognitive conditions are right, we will avoid thinking.
> Daniel T. Willingham (2009: 3)

Learning science is hard (Brown et al. 2014). Meaningful learning—the kind of learning that lasts well beyond the course—is really hard. To successfully "learn" science, we must accumulate vast stores of foundational knowledge, struggle through complex ideas, identify and reconcile misconceptions, take risks, persevere through failure, continually practice and rehearse, manage feedback and monitor our own learning. In other words, we must make a significant, non-trivial investment. Yet, despite the odds against it, we learn.

So what are the right cognitive conditions for meaningful learning?

L. Wheeler (✉) · M. Palmer
University of Virginia, Charlottesville, VA, USA
e-mail: lsb4u@virginia.edu

M. Palmer
e-mail: mp6h@virginia.edu

At the most basic, primitive level, our brains are wired to respond to fear and pleasure. Fear makes us hide from things, run from them, and avoid them. It makes us anxious, stressed and distrustful. Fear is counterproductive to learning. Pleasure, on the other hand, makes us curious, want to come closer, and seek out. It makes us happy, content and trusting. Neuroscientists know that learning produces pleasure in the form of small doses of dopamine (Zull 2002). It is this biological candy that helps us and our students do the hard work of thinking and learning. It is triggered when we are curious, solve complex problems, discover something new, novel, unexpected or intriguing, believe we have choice, control and autonomy, or imagine a creative solution.

Unfortunately, students often experience science as a set of incontrovertible facts and concepts to be memorized and regurgitated during exams. They fear bad grades rather than taking pleasure in learning about and doing science. They miss out on the beautiful, underlying questions, the imaginative, creative solutions, the small steps that lead to giant discoveries, and the pure joy of solving problems no one even dreamed existed. They miss out on the playfulness of science, how Einstein chased a beam of light, how Hilbert imagined an infinite hotel, how Kekulé dreamed of snakes biting their tails and how Schrödinger killed (or did not kill) his cat. They miss out on the dopamine.

Educational play shares many of the qualities of science and scientific inquiry. Play involves creativity, imagination and freedom. Play requires an active, alert mind receptive to questions, observations and answers. Play is tolerant of false starts and dead ends. Play's value derives from the means more so than the ends. Play does not have prescribed goals or outcomes. Play is pleasurable. Play produces dopamine (Previc 2009). Thus, if we believe pleasure is an important component of learning about science, then play must also be an important—maybe essential—component of learning about science.

With this guiding premise, we outline two case studies describing the use of educational play in our science classrooms. The first example involves using play as an instructional approach in a Science Teaching Methods course. Play allows students—science department teaching assistants (TAs)—to explore their own common misconceptions about science in a safe, enjoyable learning environment. The second example outlines a series of play-based assignments in a large-enrolment, first-year, undergraduate chemistry laboratory course, where the play experiences are designed to help students discover value in learning chemistry (and maybe even learn to love the discipline).

Play and the Nature of Science. On the first day of my Science Teaching Methods course, I (Wheeler) ask my TAs, "What is science?" This simple but important question gets them thinking about: how science is different from other disciplines, the ways in which we gain scientific knowledge, and what science can tell us about our reality. The discussion helps shape the course as a place where we will explore challenging epistemological questions that do not always have nice, tidy, incontrovertible answers.

The first play experience TAs have centres around the nature of science or the ways scientific knowledge is developed. The *fossil tracks* activity (Bell 2008) requires them to assume the role of a geologist on a field expedition. As a class, students first make observations about fossilized tracks shown in Fig. 13.1a, without knowledge of parts b and c.

"They're footprints," or "two animals are walking toward each other," the TAs say. Neither of these are observations, though. An observation might be: there are two types of symbols, 12 of one kind and 13 of another. This initial exercise helps the TAs develop an accurate definition of a scientific observation: a non-judgmental statement made with one of the five senses. We then contrast this definition with the one for inference: a logical conclusion drawn from observations.

I then reveal the next piece of the geological excavation (Fig. 13.1b) and ask for more observations and inferences. Now with some practice under their belts, the TAs begin to consider more advanced things, such

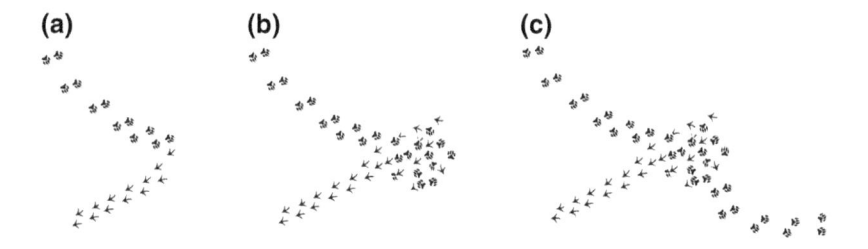

Fig. 13.1 Fossilized animal tracks

as counting the tracks and taking measurements of them. But, the real play is in their inferences. TAs infer the tracks are made from, for example, two animals fighting or greeting each other. Sometimes a TA thinks out-of-the-box and asks, "Do we even know whether the tracks were made at the same time?" The answer of course is no, we don't know that, which leads to another engaging conversation about how our own preconceived notions and prior experiences shape our interpretations. These whole class conversations are filled with back and forth banter, debates and even laughter.

The final piece of the excavation is then revealed (Fig. 13.1c). The TAs typically assume there was a fight between two animals and only one survived. But there are always others in the room with alternative explanations, for example, maybe one of the animals is a bird and it flew away. After examining the most plausible inferences, the TAs reflect on how the activity emulates the process of acquiring scientific knowledge. Some TAs recognize that different people had different inferences based on the same observations, demonstrating the collaborative, subjective and culturally embedded nature of science. We end the activity by discussing ways to integrate nature of science instruction into their own teaching. TAs brainstorm various ideas, such as asking students how their lab course experience is similar to or different from what scientists do.

Another common misconception about the nature of science is the relationship between theories and laws. I use a play activity, known as the *mystery tube* (Bell 2008), to help TAs understand that theories explain relationships while laws describe relationships. The mystery tube activity is thought-provoking/promoting and creates an element of productive frustration.

To start the activity, I ask TAs to individually write down how they define a scientific theory and a law. They often write, "Theories are educated guesses. When there is enough evidence to make them irrefutable, theories become laws." This definition is inaccurate and a misrepresentation of scientific knowledge, but this step of articulating the misconception is an important part of the activity. I then provide examples of theories and laws across science disciplines to create cognitive dissonance between their initial idea and the actual relationship between theories and laws. For example, we talk about Kinetic Molecular

Theory, which explains how gas particles move, and how it is fundamentally different from the Ideal Gas Law, which describes the relationship between temperature, pressure and volume of a gas. At this point, the TAs begin to recognize that theories and laws are two different types of scientific knowledge. Then comes the fun part: the mystery tube.

The mystery tube is a hollow, enclosed cylindrical tube that has four protruding strings on opposite sides and at each end of the tube. A knot is tied at the end of each string. Like the fossil tracks activity, TAs are first asked to make observations about the mystery tube. They often mention four strings, four knots, the location of each hole, the length of each string, distances between things, and so on. I then ask them to predict what will happen when I pull on one of the strings. I then demonstrate that when one string is pulled all of the other strings are pulled inside the tube. As I continue to pull on different strings, I ask the TAs to continue making observations. I invariably have to remind them to focus on observations rather than inferences, since their tendency is to attempt to figure out what is inside the tube that is resulting in the mysterious pulling of the strings.

Once students have a list of observations, they come up with a hypothesis to describe what happens when I pull on a string. We then discuss how we could confirm this relationship. The TAs brainstorm and share ideas with each other. We discuss how these ideas, or explanations for the observations, could be tested. Then they make their own mystery tubes. Playing with the mystery tube helps drive home the relationship between laws (the observation of the strings on the outside of the tube) and theories (the explanation for how the strings are connected inside).

I then ask, "Which explanation is right?" and inevitably, they say, "Open the tube so we can find out." Despite protestations, I never open the tube. Upon reflection, they realize that in science we never really know the "Truth" with a capital T, only our best explanation based on the evidence we have. The TAs then go back to their original definitions of theories and laws and revise them. TAs enjoy this activity so much that some share this activity with their students.

In both examples, play allows me to address common misconceptions TAs have about the nature of science that might otherwise lead to contentious conversations. Play also provides a way for TAs to learn about the nature of science, a topic that they can easily integrate into their own teaching. Our research shows that TAs do indeed better understand and intend to teach nature of science following these activities (Wheeler et al. 2018). Finally, I use play to model ways TAs can create a classroom environment that is conducive to grappling with difficult topics and helping students do the difficult work of learning.

Play and the Discovery of Value. When in social settings, I (Palmer) am often asked what it is I do for a living. When I mention I'm a chemist, there is often a collective moan and comments to the effect, "Uh, I took chemistry in college and *hated* it!" Yet, when I meet my first-year undergraduate students, they are excited about chemistry and the possibilities it offers for solving problems that matter to them. This special pedagogical challenge, of getting students out the door as excited about chemistry as when they entered, prompted me to explore ways to help students *discover* value in the things they were learning, since value leads to interest, leads to curiosity, leads to learning.

This value-discovery process, which is different for every student, happens through a variety of play opportunities. Some of the opportunities occur in class, others out of class; some are short-lived and others extended. Some help students understand key concepts; e.g. students act out the forces on electrons and protons in class to discover the intricacies of the Schrödinger Equation (HuffPost, n.d.). Some help them appreciate how chemistry intersects and shapes their lives; e.g. students explore the chemistry of sunscreens to help them decide whether it's worth buying an SPF-50 sunscreen or whether a SPF-30 is adequate.

One structural mechanism that helps me incorporate play throughout the course is a "scavenger hunt." This optional checklist of activities invites and encourages students to engage with course material beyond the traditional boundaries of the classroom. One item on the scavenger hunt is the *Molecule of the Week* competition, where students solve chemical puzzles and riddles by searching, identifying, researching and reflecting on a mystery chemical or chemistry. Here's an example of one of these puzzles: This molecule [image presented to students] is often added to dog foods. Identify it and decide whether you would buy foods for your pup that contain it.

Another scavenger hunt item is the *Our Chemical World* challenge. For this activity, students capture everyday chemical processes or products of chemistry with their cameras and then explore the science behind the photos. As one example, a student took a photo of a bicycle sprocket and chain and researched how grease works and how it's different from other lubricants. Weekly winners of both the *Molecule of the Week* and *Our Chemical World* challenges are announced in class and displayed publically on the class website (http://faculty.virginia.edu/chem1811/). They also win chocolate!

If students complete enough of the scavenger hunt items they can replace some of the low-stakes, formative assignments they may have missed during the semester and even earn a slight boost to their final grade. This turns out to be one reason about 85% of the 110 students participate in the hunt, but it's not the only one. In an end-of-semester survey, a majority of students claim they complete the activities because they are "enjoyable," and they are able to "learn new things about chemistry." Over 90% of the students agree or strongly agree that the scavenger hunt is a positive component of the course.

A more substantive play experience is built into one of the major course assignments: a digital media project. The digital media project offers students an opportunity to explore their interests and questions about any chemistry topic and present it in a fun, creative way using video. While they certainly learn something new about chemistry, they also gain experience in several areas critical to scientific success, namely literature research, material and idea synthesis, documentation and presentation of technical material, collaborative work and effective use of digital media. More importantly, though, the project allows students to be curious and to wonder. A sample of student projects include the chemistry of violins, chocolate and vampirism. Their projects often include original songs, sophisticated animations and creative film techniques, such as green-screen technology.

The vast majority of students believe the digital media project is a positive component of the course. They describe it with words like awesome, enjoyable, fun, creative, meaningful, rewarding and "very cool." One student wrote, "The digital media project was a great and fun opportunity to research a topic in chemistry. It definitely taught me a lot of chemistry, and gave us a chance to be creative as well."

Summary. Each of the play opportunities we've described is unique, closely aligned with our content and learning objectives, and engages students in meaningful ways. They are little dopamine moments that successfully capture students' attention and curiosity just long enough that they are willing to do the hard work of learning science.

References

Bell, R. L. (2008). *Teaching the Nature of Science Through Process Skills*. Boston, MA: Pearson Education.

Brown, P. C., Roediger, H. L., & McDaniel, M. A. (2014). *Make It Stick: The Science of Successful Learning*. Cambridge, MA: Harvard University Press.

HuffPost. (n.d.). *How Can You Explain Schrödinger's Equation to Someone Who Doesn't Understand Quantum Physics?* Available at https://www.huffingtonpost.com/entry/how-can-you-explain-schr%C3%B6dingers-equation-to-someone_us_59b0c546e4b0bef3378cddb9. Accessed December 4, 2017.

Previc, F. H. (2009). *The Dopaminergic Mind in Human Evolution and History*. Cambridge, MA: Cambridge University Press.

Wheeler, L. B., Mulvey, B. K., Maeng, J. L., Librea-Carden, M. R., & Bell, R. L. (2018, in review). *Teaching the Teacher: Exploring STEM Graduate Students' Nature of Science Conceptions in a Teaching Methods Course*.

Zull, J. E. (2002). *The Art of Changing the Brain: Enriching the Practice of Teaching by Exploring the Biology of Learning*. Sterling, VA: Stylus.

14

Exploration: Play in Engineering Education

Bruce Kothmann

Over the past 5 years, I have transformed all of my undergraduate and masters-level engineering lectures at the University of Pennsylvania in to Structured Active In-Class Learning (SAIL) environments. I hope this exploration will provide some feeling of the spirit and purpose of play that animates these sessions.

Each spring, about three weeks into my *Feedback Control Systems* course, I bound into the classroom carrying a large paper grocery bag, heavy with a surprise for the students. "Somebody tell me something we have learned in the class so far." Students look down, dutifully flip through their notes or nervously giggle, until a student tentatively offers, "You can model a dynamic system using differential equations."

"Excellent!" I reach into the bag, pull out a pomegranate and—*whoosh!*—toss it across the room to the unsuspecting student. "Who else can tell me something we have learned?" With some urgency now,

---

B. Kothmann (✉)
School of Engineering and Applied Science,
University of Pennsylvania, Philadelphia, PA, USA
e-mail: kothmann@seas.upenn.edu

the answers come pouring in: "We can make block diagrams of a control system." *Whoosh!* "Transfer functions." *Whoosh!* As we work our way to the bottom of the bag, the room is filled with quizzical energy: "Why is the professor throwing pomegranates at us?"

Demonstratively holding the last pomegranate while pacing about, I explain that the pomegranates are connected to modern observance of the winter Jewish holiday *Tu B'Shevat*. After a few short remarks on agriculture and astronomy, I conclude by explaining that the traditional Jewish teaching "do first, then understand"—derived from an interpretive translation of *na'aseh v'nishma* (Exodus 24:7)—is especially relevant to the study of controls, because most students find that the abstruse mathematics (Brockett 2001) only make sense *after* they have been used to solve some real problems.

I very much value the interfaith understanding that I hope will come from a discussion of solar and lunar calendars (MFC 2018). And I genuinely believe in the pedagogic value of integrating the laboratory experiments (*doing*), with the ideas discussed in lecture (*understanding*). But my real motivation for the pomegranate party is to communicate a clear message: in this class, we are going to *play*!

How do students know when they are playing? Rather than endorse or defend any one of the many formal definitions of play in the education literature (e.g. Henderson and Atencio 2007), I want to highlight three widely accepted characteristics of play that I focus on when developing classroom activities or presenting new ideas: play is imperfect, imaginative and intrinsically motivated. The following elaboration on these aspects will also include discussion of the pedagogic values they engender.

Play is imperfect. Many cognitive scientists posit that learning is best fuelled by failure (Schank 1998), in particular when we encounter a conflict between observations and the expectations derived from our existing conceptual models. Impatience, or even outright intolerance, of failure is among the greatest weaknesses in much of modern formal education. In STEM fields, this often leads to what Dan Meyer (2010) dubbed an "Eagerness for Formula," in which students expect to quickly learn how to match a given set of facts and figures to the relevant equations. Worst of all, students often mistake this rote activity for real understanding or accomplishment. Play, with ample room for mistakes or even outright failures, is a potent antidote to the narrow conception of what classroom learning looks like.

A canonical proverb for students learning the ancient game of Go is to "lose 100 games as quickly as possible (American Go Foundation 2011)." When we take this maxim into the classroom, we discover that after some initial reluctance, most students find it profoundly liberating to try things that don't work, with no care for immediate consequences or judgement (Fig. 14.1).

In the mechanical engineering sophomore laboratory course, we challenge students to use custom-made wooden blocks to build towers and arches that maximize a scoring metric, subject to simple construction

Fig. 14.1 Student playing with arch blocks in mechanics laboratory

constraints (Stokes 2005). Of course, such arches and towers often tumble suddenly and catastrophically, but this sort of "failure" is easily recognized by the students as a natural—even essential—part of learning how block stacking works.

On the heels of their many tangible failures with toy blocks, students are reminded that they will face similar challenges when they turn to the analytical and numerical treatment of masonry structures. Drawing a proper free-body diagram, or modifying the software program that computes the thrust lines running through their novel arches, is arduous and often frustrating work. But the play mindset helps the students appreciate that the struggles are neither a sign of poor performance nor of poor instruction, but rather reflect the difficult work of expanding their conceptual understanding.

Play Is Imaginative. In *An Imaginative Approach to Teaching*, Kieran Egan (2005) asserts that "In the imaginative classroom, we will expect to see much more play…" In STEM, a playful imagination begets a natural and repetitive cycle of discovery and inquiry (Firestein 2013): students emerge from play with more, and much better, questions than they started with! After a vigorous session with the building blocks, a student might ask, "Why does a short, wide arch fail by sliding sideways at the base, while a tall narrow arch fails by collapsing?" That is a much better question than "why does an arch fall down?" Note that if the instructor poses the questions at the outset, the process of developing the question from personal experience is lost, and with it much of the essential intellectual growth. The analysis and computation that follows the physical experiments provides new discoveries, leading to increasingly deeper and more profound questions: "if the analysis shows that multiple possible thrust lines exist for any given arch, how does the real arch choose the actual thrust line?" (Heyman 1997).

Play Is Intrinsically Motivated. Posing interesting and complex questions only results in learning when students avidly pursue answers, which hinges on personal initiative. With so much rich and diverse information available online, one essential job of the modern professor might be stated as "make the students want to Google something." In a seminal paper, Deci (1972) defines intrinsic motivation as performing an activity when "there is no apparent reward except the activity itself or the feelings which result from the activity." Intrinsic motivation is the antithesis of the dreaded "what do I have to do to get an A" mentality that so many educators recognize as a substantial obstacle to the kind of deep learning that we aspire to help our students achieve (Bain 2004).

In a classroom exercise in *Performance and Design of UAV's*, students are asked to stand at their seats and repeatedly toss their mobile phones into the air, so that the phone spins rapidly about one of its 3 axes. Many students require several minutes of playful experimentation before they discover the surprising results (Plasma Ben 2009). Inspired by their own sense of wonder, the students emerge eager to fully understand and numerically model what they observe. Obviously, the direct results of these investigations are not practically important, so the strong motivation to succeed is primarily intrinsic—a critical asset for persevering with the difficult mathematics of inertia tensors and advanced representations of attitude dynamics.

How Is Play Integrated into an Engineering Classroom? The types of activities and exercises that are typically used in interactive learning spaces very naturally accommodate a playful approach. But there is also ample opportunity for play in the more traditional settings of a lecture, a design laboratory or even an exam.

I often use short exercises or videos at the beginning of class to regularly reinvigorate the playful atmosphere and energy. In *Feedback Control Systems*, we start every meeting with a short math problem that is almost never applicable to controls, nor obviously solvable by any of the techniques that are covered in the core engineering math curriculum. For example, I show students an irregular hexagon, noting that 4 copies of the figure fit inside and ask them to find a pentagon with the same property (Stewart 2010). Only a few students attempt to solve the puzzles, but many comment that they do enjoy the ritual (Fig. 14.2).

In-class demonstrations can also be more effective and memorable when they playfully engage the students. For maximum effect, demonstrations should be conducted *before* the lecture, in the hope that the lecture will contain the answers to newly formed questions that the students now care very much about. In fluid dynamics, the concept of vorticity is essential to understanding everything from airplane wingtip vortices to the mixing of cream in a cup of coffee. In my *Aerodynamics*

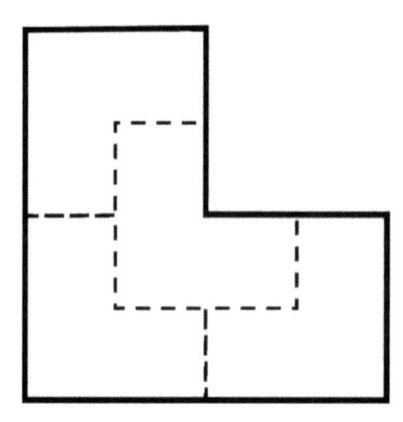

Fig. 14.2 A hexagonal "rep-tile"

course, we start with a playful alternative to the usual mathematical introduction to vorticity, beginning with a simple question: "How far away can you stand and still blow out a birthday candle?" While the class sings *Happy Birthday*, a student volunteer with a proximate birthday then uses a toy "vortex gun" to blow out a candle from across the room! "How is that possible?" The playful mood is further promoted using online videos (Evasius 2010; Physics Girl 2014) showing vortices in a variety of contexts. Generating excitement about vorticity is far more likely to have a lasting impact on students than any particular insights about the finer points of Helmholtz's theorems (Panton 2013) that I might share in a lecture.

Most engineering curricula include student projects, often culminating in a public demonstration. These events are a perfect time for play. Many projects draw motivation from a final competition, which is usually naturally playful. But we also frequently include some element of playful violation of institutional rules or norms in the venue or procedures, which helps to keep spirits high during the inevitable delays and malfunctions that a complex project will engender. For example, in the *Junior Design Laboratory* course, the vertical-axis wind turbine final demonstration requires students to maximize the useful power generated when the turbine is mounted on a cart that the students themselves push down the hall outside of the engineering library (Kothmann 2012).

Even exams can be playful, with the goal of reminding students that exams are mostly intended to help them assess their own progress and that short-term failure is often a necessary step on the journey to long-term success. In the sophomore laboratory course, the final exam included a playful cooperative exercise: "What is the most fun way to break a piece of chalk"? My intended answer (torsion or twisting) was upstaged by a student who forcefully threw the chalk at the board, causing an explosive failure that brilliantly illustrated the fracture mechanics of brittle materials. My exams also often feature photographs of cool applications of relevant technology, with a light-hearted caption, such as "No questions about the SpaceX Falcon-9 rocket."

What Are the Challenges of Incorporating Play in the Curriculum? We have seen that play has many attributes that organically promote a positive learning environment, as understood by modern learning science. And the foregoing examples and anecdotes illustrated the spirit of a playful approach to engineering instruction. But by themselves, these exercises don't necessarily teach the students anything—that is still the job of dedicated faculty working in close partnership with students. In particular, we must be vigilant in our deployment of play, or any other pedagogical tool, to avoid what Bereiter calls a "reduction to activities" in which the methods become self-justifying virtues in and of themselves:

> In simple terms, teaching means taking responsibility for someone else's learning and carrying through the actual problem solving required to bring that learning about….(Bereiter, 2009: 289) The effect of reductive practices is to remove this problem-solving element, reducing teaching to something that can just be carried out or that presents problems of a more manageable sort. (idem: 286)

A second common pitfall for play arises from the educational path that secures a student a seat at a competitive college, which typically includes a strong record of performance on traditional assessments. The upshot is that many students arrive on campus with a highly optimized internal algorithm for allocation of time and effort to maximize grades. Many experienced faculties recognize that this approach is frequently at odds with the goal of maximizing engagement and learning, our efforts to align learning and assessment notwithstanding. In an environment that is often crowded with voluminous compulsory assignments and strictly enforced arbitrary deadlines, it is all too easy for the more intrinsically motivated approaches, including play, to be pushed aside. Explicitly, enlisting students in assessing their own educational outcomes, using "portfolios" at the end of the term, has been somewhat successful in addressing this concern, but the challenge persists.

At many colleges, a shift in emphasis towards rewards that are harder to quantify but educationally much richer may require commitment at the departmental or school level. Advocates of play and other novel pedagogies must patiently and persistently pursue such commitments.

Play Is Also About Fun! We have argued that play can be an effective pedagogic tool in a variety of conventional settings, including lectures, laboratories and exams. But even if that were not the case, wouldn't we still want to find time and place for play in our classrooms? Willingham (2009) notes that even if an activity is used "simply because the students find it fun and interesting," it can still have an important role in cultivating confidence and interest. The most important reason for me to include play in my teaching is aptly summarized by DiCarlo (2009):

> Inspiring and motivating students is far more important for long-term success than delivering information. Therefore, we must create a joy, an excitement, and a love for learning. We must make learning fun, because if we are successful, our students will be impatient to run home, study, and contemplate–to really learn.

References

American Go Foundation. (2011). *Step 2: Lose 100 Games as Quickly as Possible*. Available at http://agfgo.org/pages/learn2.php. Accessed December 18, 2017.

Bain, K. (2004). *What the Best College Teachers Do*. Cambridge, MA: Harvard University Press.

Bereiter, C. (2009). *Education and Mind in the Knowledge Age*. New York: Routledge.

Brockett, R. (2001). New Issues in the Mathematics of Control. In B. Engquist & W. Schmid (Eds.), *Mathematics Unlimited—2001 and Beyond* (pp. 189–220). Berlin: Springer. Available at https://www.cds.caltech.edu/~murray/cdspanel/brockett00-springer.pdf. Accessed April 1, 2018.

Deci, E. L. (1972). The Effects of Contingent and Noncontingent Rewards and Controls on Intrinsic Motivation. *Organizational Behavior and Human Performance, 8,* 217–229.

DiCarlo, S. E. (2009). Too Much Content, Not Enough Thinking, and Too Little FUN!, Claude Bernard Distinguished Lecture. *Advances in Physiology Education, 33,* 4. Available at http://www.physiology.org/doi/abs/10.1152/advan.00075.2009. Accessed May 30, 2018.

Egan, K. (2005). *An Imaginative Approach to Teaching.* San Francisco: Wiley.

Evasius. (2010). *Extraordinary Toroidal Vortices.* Available at https://www.youtube.com/watch?v=mHyTOcfF99o&t=225s. Accessed December 18, 2017.

Exodus, *The Hebrew Bible.*

Firestein, S. (2013). *Pursuit of Ignorance.* Available at https://www.ted.com/talks/stuart_firestein_the_pursuit_of_ignorance. Accessed December 18, 2017.

Henderson, T. Z., & Atencio, D. J. (2007). Integration of Play, Learning, and Experience: What Museums Afford Young Visitors. *Early Childhood Education Journal, 35,* 245–251.

Heyman, J. (1997). *The Stone Skeleton: Structural Engineering of Masonry Architecture.* Cambridge: Cambridge University Press.

Kothmann, B. (2012). *MEAM 347 VAWT Demo Highlights.* Available at https://www.youtube.com/watch?v=k9B8h-e7LZM. Accessed December 18, 2017.

Meyer, D. (2010). *Math Class Needs a Makeover.* Available at https://www.ted.com/talks/dan_meyer_math_curriculum_makeover. Accessed December 18, 2017.

MFC. (2018). *Multifaith Calendar.* Available at http://multifaithcalendar.org/index.php. Accessed April 1, 2018.

Panton, R. (2013). *Incompressible Flow.* Hoboken: Wiley.

Physics Girl. (2014). *Crazy Pool Vortex.* Available at https://www.youtube.com/watch?v=pnbJEg9r1o8. Accessed December 18, 2017.

Plasma Ben. (2009). *The Same Physics Are Evident in Dancing T-handle in Zero-g* [Online]. Available at https://www.youtube.com/watch?v=1n-HM-SCDYtM. Accessed December 18, 2017.

Schank, R. (1998). Roger Schank Talks Training. *Technical Training*, as cited by Patrick Crispen. Available at http://www.moline-consulting.com/Reinventando/Pagines/TenemosCitasSobre.htm. Accessed December 18, 2017. See also http://www.rogerschank.com/.

Stewart, I. (2010). *Professor Stewart's Hoard of Mathematical Treasures* (pp. 133–134). London: Basic Books.

Stokes, P. D. (2005). *Creativity from Constraints, the Psychology of Breakthrough*. New York: Springer.

Willingham, D. (2009). *Why Students Don't Like School*. San Francisco: Jossey-Bass.

15

Experiencing the Necessity of Project Management Through the Egg-Dropping-Challenge

Tobias Seidl

I am teaching a class on Project Management (PM), which focuses on methods and tools of project planning and controlling. Theoretical inputs are combined with students work on a project planning assignment. After finishing their assignment, students are proficient at using project planning tools but do not necessarily understand the total flow of projects and the overall need for PM. Therefore, following Kolb's (1984) "experiential learning cycle" model, a simulation-game was included in the course to allow students to experience and reflect on the challenges of project work in self-formed groups. The game is a modified version of the popular egg-dropping-challenge (create a structure for a raw egg that protects it from cracking at a specific height of a fall).

Simulation-games model a section of reality and simulate real processes in a reduced complexity. Therefore, playing such games is suitable for the promotion of general competence in dealing with complex systems as

---

T. Seidl (✉)
Stuttgart Media University, Stuttgart, Germany
e-mail: seidl@hdm-stuttgart.de

well as for the support of competence acquisition in area-specific contexts (Kriz 2004: 363). In addition, the playing of simulation-games in class has from my own experience practical advantages:

- high motivation of the learner
- high vividness of the content
- promotion of communication and teamwork.

For these reasons, I regularly integrate (simulation-)games in different courses I teach (e.g. leadership, communication, change management).

The original egg-dropping-challenge is integrated in a project cycle which mirrors the phases of a project:

1. *Project initiation and definition*
   The task is explained and the materials available for building are announced. Students create a first sketch of their construction and draw up a material calculation.
2. *Project planning*
   Students create a work breakdown structure and a project schedule to plan phase 3.
3. *Project execution*
   Observers move between teams. The teams prepare their calculation, buy material and build their construction. The constructions are tested by throwing them out of the window.
4. *Project reflection*
   The cost-value ratios of the constructions are calculated and the winning team honoured. Supported by the observers the groups reflect their experience (cf. Kriz and Nöbauer 2003).
   My observations and students' reflection in their learning portfolio indicate that the method is a good way to help students gain a deeper understanding of PM in an enjoyable way. One student formulates this in her portfolio: "For me, the simulation game was the perfect deepening and application of theory. We had the opportunity to complete a project in class and were able to apply the learned tools. In addition, it was a lot of fun in the team and we have mastered the challenge in the end".

References

Kolb, D. A. (1984). *Experiential Learning: Experience as the Source of Learning and Development*. Englewood Cliffs, NJ: Prentice Hall.

Kriz, W. (2004). Planspielmethode. In G. Reinmann & H. Mandl (Hg.), *Psychologie des Wissensmanagements. Perspektiven, Theorien und Methoden* (S. 359–368). Göttingen: Hogrefe.

Kriz, W., & Nöbauer, B. (2003). *Den Lernerfolg mit Debriefing von Planspielen sichern*. Institut für Berufsbildung. Available at https://www.bibb.de/dokumente/pdf/1_08a.pdf. April 22, 2017.

16

Exploration: Public Engagement Activities for Chemistry Students

Dudley Shallcross and Tim Harrison

Introduction

Play and postgraduate research in Chemistry seem to be unlikely bedfellows. In the UK, Ph.D. study typically takes a minimum of 3 years and more likely 4 years to complete and revolves around the production of a thesis and defence of that thesis through a *viva voce* examination. The Ph.D. is viewed as a time for 'serious' study where one immerses oneself in a particular topic with the aim of becoming the expert in that particular part of that field (e.g. Powers and Swick 2012). The typical process will involve yearly reports and possibly yearly interviews with a thesis panel. The Ph.D. student (postgraduate) may be supervised by one person or several and may be part of one research group or more recently be part of a doctoral training centre (e.g. Govender and Dhunpath 2011). Whatever the mode, the interactions with the supervisory support can vary from daily to much longer

---

D. Shallcross (✉) · T. Harrison
Bristol ChemLabS, School of Chemistry, University of Bristol, Bristol, UK
e-mail: D.E.Shallcross@bristol.ac.uk

© The Author(s) 2019
A. James and C. Nerantzi (eds.), *The Power of Play in Higher Education*,
https://doi.org/10.1007/978-3-319-95780-7_16

timescales. Each postgraduate is different and each Ph.D. is different by definition, and so it is very hard to gauge how far along the road a student is at any one time. Since the Ph.D. is creating new knowledge, skills required are hard to define; whilst this can be an exhilarating experience, it can at the same time be terrifying when there seems to be no progress or no clear way to progress. Surely, the last thing that a postgraduate needs is a distraction, much less to spend time in play? In this exploration, we discuss how 'play' has enhanced the Ph.D. experience for Chemistry postgraduates engaged in outreach activities.

Setting the Scene: Postgraduate Study, Trials and Tribulations, Unspoken Issues

A postgraduate student faces many challenges such as the Ph.D. itself and the thought of not producing sufficient original material to warrant the award, mastering their particular subject area, connecting with their supervisor and research group and persevering when the inevitable problems arise during their study (e.g. Pearson et al. 2011). Ultimately, the student has responsibility for the production of the thesis, and if they are in a small research group and do not connect with others in the group, or are happy in their group but not making progress (in their eyes), it can be a tough road to travel. Are there ways that a postgraduate can be reinvigorated, have some fun, spend some time in play and in doing so move forward in their studies?

The Bristol ChemLabS Centre for Excellence in Teaching and Learning (Shallcross et al. 2013a, b) in the School of Chemistry at Bristol University started in 2005 and part of the CETL's programme involved Outreach to schools and the general public. Postgraduates were offered the chance to have training in a variety of outreach activities and to take part in the programme. The types of activity will be described in the next section, but one key aspect was that this programme was given total support by the senior management team in the department. All participants had to have the support of their Ph.D. supervisors and without it postgraduates were prevented from taking part. It is noteworthy that by the end of the first year, all supervisors were supportive of the programme, even those who were opposed at the start (see later). The programme was referred to as 'Play time for Ph.Ds' by the supervisors. This programme, as we shall discuss, does reinvigorate, support and challenge Ph.D. students through activities that were viewed as play. Although these excursions provided a much-needed opportunity to escape from the grind of intensive study, time and again these activities challenged the postgraduate and provided thinking space away from the laboratory.

Types of Play We Use

Bristol ChemLabS engages with between 25,000 and 30,000 school students, their teachers and the general public in several hundred face-to-face outreach activities per year and has done so for a decade. The wide portfolio of activities are predominantly organised through the department's School Teacher Fellow (Shallcross and Harrison 2007a, b; Shallcross et al. 2014) and Director of Outreach. Many of these involve suitably trained postgraduate chemists working with both primary and secondary school-aged students and their teachers. In outreach activities, postgraduates take on the role of teacher/educator and have a lot of fun doing so. Some of the types of outreach activity (play) are now described.

The Open Laboratories Programme (OLP)

Throughout the year, school students visit the undergraduate teaching laboratories at the university to engage in practical activities. Most of these students are aged 15–18 and are in groups of 20–80. The practical work that they engage in is not possible in most schools as they may lack appropriate equipment, space/time and expertise. Common practical workshops, lasting around three hours, include school students extracting caffeine from tea or synthesising an anaesthetic. Postgraduate chemists are allocated between 8 and 12 students to work through the exercise, demonstrating how to use the equipment and explaining what is going on. Occasionally, accompanying teachers also participate. An example of play that Ph.D. students have employed to be effective demonstrators is that of role-playing aspects of the chemical reaction the school students are studying. In Chemistry, not only is the shape of a molecule important but its stereochemistry, i.e. how the atoms that make the molecule are arranged. In some experiments, stereochemistry can be the reason why one product is preferred over another or why one reaction is faster than another. Using people to adopt different shapes (with hands usually), it can be demonstrated why this can make a difference to reactivity and product formation.

Primary Workshops

In teams of three, postgraduates visit a primary school within the geographical region and lead practical investigations in a two-hour workshop, and several Ph.D. students have reported that it is both fun and challenging guiding these students to carry out their own investigations without taking over (giving them insight into the Ph.D.—supervisor relationship) (Griffin et al. 2007; Harrison and Shallcross 2016; Shallcross et al. 2006; Shallcross and Harrison 2007b). Who wouldn't want to make their own slime or take the one minute challenge where they have to adjust the concentrations of the two chemicals provided so that the mixture turns from colourless to purple in as close to a minute as possible?

Residential Chemistry Camps

Residential chemistry camps, lasting between 2 and 5 days, allow school students to have an intensive university chemistry experience. During camps, school students spend each day in a combination of laboratory work, lecturettes (see next section) and tours. The camps take place throughout the year. Postgraduate chemists are involved in demonstrating in the laboratories as well as giving talks and occasionally participating in social events. The research talks force the postgraduates to really think through their research so that they can present it in a coherent way to the school students.

Postgraduate 'Lecturettes'

These are half-hour talks given by current postgraduate students, on a topic related to their research. They can also form part of school conferences, as evening lectures for school's science clubs and as part of teacher training events. Each talk, created in conversation with the School Teacher Fellow, includes the educational journey the postgraduate has had in reaching their current role, information on what it is like to be a postgraduate researcher and a suitable age-related treatment of their research area. There are always opportunities for questions from both teachers and students. Those postgraduates that have fed back have stated that it really did make them go back and cement their own understanding and in several cases that exercise alone prompted new ideas for their research. In addition, having mastered these type of talks, they were more confident in undertaking research talks at a variety of conferences associated with their Ph.D. Postgraduates have played with a variety of formats and modes of delivery including making animations, role playing how chemicals vibrate when exposed to infrared light, but the most memorable was the chocolate lecture where a postgraduate made chocolate for everyone whilst demonstrating aspects of colloidal chemistry.

Practical Competitions

Postgraduate chemists act as judges (and safety advisors) to visiting school teams participating in heats of national competitions. Here, postgraduates have to justify their decisions and argue their case, a valuable skill in the research arena, but they would not have an opportunity to do this under most Ph.D. training schemes. The competitions are themselves game based, e.g. there are a series of chemical tests that can be carried out on an unknown compound and based on the results of these chemical tests the students have to work out what the unknown compound must be.

Schools Lectures with Practical Demonstrations

Some postgraduates actively seek to be trained in the delivery of chemistry lectures with exciting practical demonstrations which are performed either at the School of Chemistry or in host schools. There is ample opportunity for this as the department gives 200–250 lecture demonstrations per year. Each postgraduate will impart their own personality into the delivery (Sunassee et al. 2012). Here, attention to health and safety is paramount (as it always is), timing of the talk and associated experiments and provides these young researchers with invaluable experience in delivering material at a variety of levels. However, using an exciting experiment such as the 'whoosh' bottle to demonstrate an aspect of Chemistry is extremely effective. Here, a whoosh bottle is a decommissioned 18 L water canister that has been emptied and dried to which a small amount of methanol is added. After vigorous shaking, the methanol evaporates and then a lighted wooden splint is placed at the entrance to the bottle and this ignites rapidly with a whoosh sound and blue flame.

Spectroscopy Tours

These are tours of the spectroscopic analytical equipment in the School of Chemistry for school-aged students (Harrison et al. 2010). Post-16 school students studying Chemistry in the UK will encounter spectroscopy but will not have access to these instruments at school. Each instrument/spectroscopy type (including a selection from nuclear magnetic resonance spectroscopy, infrared, mass spectrometry, scanning and transmission electron microscopy, gas chromatography and possibly x-ray crystallography) is presented to the school students with a short talk by an academic or postgraduate/postdoctoral researcher with a demonstration and possibly hands-on activity. The school students see the instruments in action, whilst learning about how they work and applications of the technique in support of their studies.

Postgraduates often use models of chemicals (ball and stick) as aides to demonstrate what happens when light interacts with these chemicals. Each postgraduate has developed a unique delivery and one even used a song from Saturday Night Fever to demonstrate the way that the molecules move when excited by light. The school students have an opportunity to talk with the postgraduates as they tour the department between workshops.

Science Writing

There are several publication outlets that are aimed at school students and their teachers, as well as the myriad social media platforms that now exist. Some postgraduates have taken the opportunity to work with the STF and others to produce work for publication to schools through these publication outlets. Writing in an unambiguous and scientifically rigorous way is vital to laying the foundations of a good thesis. Feedback from a wide range of people to these postgraduates has been extremely positive and has made cutting-edge research accessible to a wide audience. However, postgraduates have used great imagination to generate cartoons or diagrams that help to explain the science behind the article (Fig. 16.1).

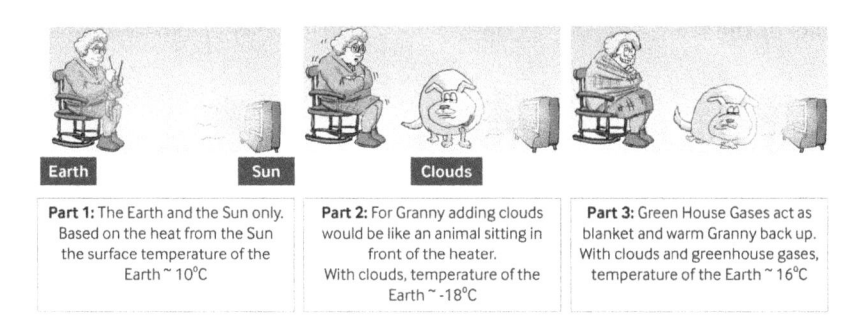

Earth	Sun	Clouds
Part 1: The Earth and the Sun only. Based on the heat from the Sun the surface temperature of the Earth ~ 10°C	**Part 2:** For Granny adding clouds would be like an animal sitting in front of the heater. With clouds, temperature of the Earth ~ -18°C	**Part 3:** Green House Gases act as blanket and warm Granny back up. With clouds and greenhouse gases, temperature of the Earth ~ 16°C

Fig. 16.1 The 'Granny' model of climate

Special Events

Participating in Bristol ChemLabS' organised events has empowered some postgraduate students to run outreach activities related to their own research groups' expertise. Examples include a 'School Protein Workshop', 'Antimicrobial resistance' and 'Discovery of Novel Antibiotics from Fungi Workshops' all of which involved talks, tours and hands-on practical work for senior local school students. A wide range of skills were developed by postgraduates and these too enhanced their research study. Helping students to build models of microbes and active sites in antibiotics and testing whether they can bind to each other is funny to watch but highly instructive. Polystyrene, blu tac, cocktail sticks and jelly babies have all been used, but regular chemistry kits are also used where available.

Postgraduates involved in the Outreach programme continue to have STEM Ambassador training through local STEM organisation. Here, the postgraduate acquire Disclosure Barring Service (DBS) clearance and are 'police checked' as suitable people to work with school students. The involvement of the external organisation also gives the postgraduates membership of a national programme and additional opportunities to engage in outreach activities outside of university events. Additional training occurs 'in-house' for those wishing to take part specific activities including for primary school workshops and the SIAS events. In the latter experienced, postgraduates cascade their training to newer members of the team.

Why This Play Is Effective

Effectiveness can be analysed from several points of view: from the school teachers involved, from the experiences of the students engaged and from the university from the postgraduates involved. The first two have been assessed by Bristol ChemLabS elsewhere (Shallcross and Harrison 2007c; Tuah et al. 2009; Harrison and Shallcross 2010). This section will concentrate on the impacts on the postgraduates. Powers and Swick (2012) outlined 10 top tips for successful survival of a Ph.D., and each aspect is supported through this programme. However, in particular; postgraduates find peers to engage with, they often find mentors (e.g. postdoctoral researchers), peers they can share their frustrations and issues with, their achievements no matter how 'seemingly' insignificant are celebrated, they hone their skills but in a different way to the regular Ph.D. and are required to use their knowledge in ways that demands a deep level of understanding. They also have an opportunity to disengage from their regular (intensive) Ph.D. but are still learning but through playful approaches.

What Do Ph.D. Students Gain from Engaging in Outreach?

When postgraduates are quizzed about what they gain from doing outreach, they usually state a rest from the pressures of their research or thesis writing, getting paid (though this is never the main driver) or to have some fun. Some simply see the passing on of their love for science as reward enough. On deeper reflection, they highlight a number of other positives.

- Postgraduate students have the opportunity to develop their communication skills, and here, a wide range of playful approaches are used, e.g. role play, video, making physical models.
  Communication skills, as part of a soft skills set, are highly desired by many employers whether in the chemical industry or elsewhere. Whilst many postgraduates have teaching duties with undergraduates as part of their workload, the ability to explain techniques or their research to much younger, less scientifically experienced students is far more challenging. Their experiences gained in outreach feeds back into their teaching of undergraduates and in their wider communication skills, being an advantage for the department. Several postgraduates have gone on to win prizes in competitions such as 'I'm a scientist-get me out of here' and in poster presentations.

For some overseas students, they cite an opportunity to practice English. Therefore, exposure to such audiences has led to confidence building and opportunities to explore through play different ways to communicate. In one memorable event, a student was working with visually impaired adults and got them to make a giant chemical structure which they quite naturally explored through touch. They made the structure using string and beads, and as they added their bit on to the rest of the structure, they were able to thread their bit on with a bead. They also repeated this using a more conventional chemistry molecule kit.

- An opportunity to experience school teaching as a career
  Regular postgraduate volunteers have ample opportunity to visit a variety of schools, to work with different age groups and to talk with teachers. This has helped them to decide on, or reject, teaching of specific age groups as a potential career. Some postgraduates have gone on to teach in institutions other than schools such as other universities or to become outreach directors at major research establishments. Feedback has shown that these playful excursions into teaching have been invaluable, first for those who are seriously thinking about a career in teaching, second for all to experience a wider range of teaching styles, establishments and student cohorts.
- The Social Aspects
  The School of Chemistry at the University of Bristol is one of the largest departments in the UK with around 230 Ph.D. students. The chance to meet other postgraduates is something that is often ignored, but for postgraduates to flourish, particularly those in small research groups, having a wider group of friends and colleagues is helpful. In some cases, peer-to-peer mentoring has arisen through these interactions and a positive impact on research is not uncommon. However, having fun using playful approaches has been very valuable for these postgraduates.
- Impacts on research
  Postgraduates engaged in outreach and studying seemingly disparate areas have, through informal conversation at outreach events found common ground that has aided both projects. Listening to the research talks of other postgraduates pitched at an appropriate level

has been invaluable to many postgraduates (they have found them easy to follow). Also, needing to explain a topic to school students or teachers such as infrared spectroscopy or interactions with people outside their normal research arena has helped their research. Ph.D. students have found that they have developed a deeper understanding of some area allied to their research because they have had to explain it in much simpler terms to someone else. In several cases, this has directly benefitted their research project.

What Are the Less Positive Aspects of Doing Outreach Activities?

In the early days of Bristol ChemLabS outreach, comments regarding commitments and attitudes of supervisors were present with some supervisors not recognising the value of outreach or seeing it as a drain on research time. However, having seen the positive effects on their research students in myriad ways, we have observed that supervisors are less reluctant to prevent their students from engaging in outreach.

Where Do We Go from Here?

These kinds of ideas can be ported into science-, engineering- and medical-related studies and the principles transferable into other subjects. These are primarily for Ph.D. students to be able to engage with peers and with a wide audience about their subject. For the School of Chemistry, health and safety restrict some areas of development but we are finding that postgraduates refine and sometimes develop new aspects to this programme. One particular programme, when working with disabled adults, was so impactful that every academic involved reviewed their mode of teaching, and most postgraduate students reported some impact either on the research focus or their future career direction. Exploring outside the Ph.D. incubator and playing has proved to have myriad benefits.

Conclusions

Facilitating 'play' in the Outreach programme has allowed postgraduates to reconnect with their love of the subject which can be lost due to the pressures of research and the time constraints hanging over that research. They could see others excited by Chemistry and met people who were genuinely interested in their research and wanted to understand more. Through the honing of their communication skills and not wanting to be floored by a question, many students took time to really understand the background to the research area they had undertaken and as a result their research flourished. Meeting other postgraduates from different groups helped socially but also scientifically as ideas were discussed and advice given. However, most of all, taking part in something where the audience is excited and appreciative makes a huge difference to one's psyche. These students all have personal stories to tell about how they engaged with child X or adult Y and had the most amazing conversation, how they made a connection that helped them in some way with their Ph.D., but most of all, how they had fun and enjoyed being part of this programme. The programme has taken these postgraduates out of their research bubble and given them the opportunity to play in the purest sense of the word, i.e. have fun with something they enjoy doing, as it turns out these forms of play feedback into their Ph.D. and postgraduate skill development in tangible and sometimes unexpected ways. Interacting with stakeholders outside their immediate research area has proved invaluable to these postgraduates.

References

Govender, K., & Dhunpath, R. (2011). Student Experiences of the PhD Cohort Model: Working Within or Outside Communities of Practice? *Perspectives in Education, 29,* 88–99.

Griffin, A., Harrison, T. G., & Shallcross, D. E. (2007). Primary Circuses of Experiments. *Science in School, 7,* 28–32.

Harrison, T. G., & Shallcross, D. E. (2010). What Should be Expected of Successful Engagement Between Schools, Colleges and Universities? *School Science Review, 91,* 97–102.

Harrison, T. G., & Shallcross, D. E. (2016). Chemistry Provision for Primary Pupils: The Experiences of 10 Years of Bristol ChemLabS Outreach. *Universal Journal of Educational Research, 4,* 1173–1179.

Harrison, T. G., Shaw, A. J., Shallcross, K. L., Williams, S. J., & Shallcross, D. E. (2010). School-University Partnerships: Lessons Learned from 10 Years of Spectroscopy for Teachers and Post 16 Students. *New Directions in Physical Science, 6,* 72–76.

Pearson, M., Cumming, J., Evans, T., Macauley, P., & Ryland, K. (2011). How Shall We Know Them? Capturing the Diversity of Difference in Australian Doctoral Candidates and Their Experiences. *Studies in Higher Education, 36,* 527–542.

Powers, J. D., & Swick, D. C. (2012). Straight Talk from Recent Grads: Tips for Successfully Surviving Your Doctoral Program. *Journal of Social Work Education, 48,* 389–394.

Shallcross, D. E., & Harrison, T. G. (2007a). A Secondary School Teacher Fellow Within a University Chemistry Department: The Answer to Problems of Recruitment and Transition from Secondary School to University and Subsequent Retention? *Chemistry Education Research and Practice, 8,* 101–104.

Shallcross, D. E., & Harrison, T. G. (2007b). The Impact of School Teacher Fellows on Teaching and Assessment at Tertiary Level. *New Directions in Physical Science, 3,* 77–78.

Shallcross, D. E., & Harrison, T. G. (2007c). Why Bother Taking University Led Chemistry Outreach into Primary Schools? Bristol ChemLabS Experience. *New Directions in Physical Science, 3,* 41–44.

Shallcross, D. E., Harrison, T. G., Wallington, S., & Nicholson, H. (2006). University and Primary School Links, the Bristol ChemLabS Experience. *Primary Science Review, 94,* 19–22.

Shallcross, D. E., Harrison, T. G., Obey, T. M., Croker, S. J., & Norman, N. C. (2013a). Outreach Within the Bristol ChemLabS CETL (Centre for Excellence in Teaching and Learning). *Higher Education Studies, 3,* 39–49.

Shallcross, D. E., Harrison, T. G., Norman, N. C., & Croker, S. J. (2013b). Lessons in Effective Practical Chemistry at Tertiary Level: Case Studies from the Bristol ChemLabS Outreach Program. *Higher Education Studies, 3,* 1–11.

Shallcross, D. E., Harrison, T. G., Read, D. R., & Barker, N. (2014). Lessons Learned from the Excellence Fellowship Scheme, the School Teacher Fellow Concept. *Higher Education Studies, 4,* 7–18.

Sunassee, S. N., Young, R. M., Sewry, J. D., Harrison, T. G., & Shallcross, D. E. (2012). Creating Climate Change Awareness in South African Schools Through Practical Chemistry Demonstrations. *Acta Didactica Napocensia, 5,* 31–48.

Tuah, J., Harrison, T. G., & Shallcross, D. E. (2009). The Advantages Perceived by Schoolteachers in Engaging Their Students in University-Based Chemistry Outreach Activities. *Acta Didactica Napocensia, 2,* 31–44.

17

Sketch: Playful Maths

Chris Budd

Maths and play in my opinion go very well together. This may sound odd to many readers, as maths is often perceived as being a dull, boring and very serious subject. However, nothing could be further from the truth! I argue that maths is a highly (if not the most) creative subject and that the best way to discover new maths is to play. What's this about new maths I hear you ask, surely all maths is known and what can be more predictable than the statement $1 + 1 = 2$. Again wrong! Maths as a subject is growing incredibly fast, with many new discoveries being made all the time. As well as being amazing intellectual achievements in their own right, these new mathematical discoveries are transforming the way that we live. For example, the Internet, Google, mobile phones and credit cards are founded on new mathematical discoveries.

So, back to my original theme of why maths is playful and creative. Firstly, maths as a subject takes you well past your imagination. Who could conceive of objects in 22-dimensional space, but such are

---

C. Budd (✉)
University of Bath, Bath, UK
e-mail: c.j.budd@bath.ac.uk

not only studied by mathematicians but have important applications in physics and engineering. Secondly, maths is the subject of many puzzles and games. Sudoku (both ordinary and killer), the Game of Life, logic puzzles, Griddler, magic tricks (as we shall see), jigsaws and mind reading, all rely on maths to work and in some cases (such as Sudoku) were actually invented by mathematicians. Thirdly, to make discoveries in physics you need an expensive and well-equipped laboratory. However to make discoveries in maths, all you need is a pencil and paper, and a bit of time (e.g. waiting for train in Reading station). The reason that maths is so playful is that it is all about finding and learning about patterns, and to find patterns you need to play. In fact, the process of doing maths could best be described as playing to find patterns, generalising and abstracting these patterns and then proving that they are always true. Mathematicians call the best of these patterns *Theorems* and perhaps best of all is Euler's fabulous result $e^{i\pi} = -1$. This is perhaps the most important formula in the whole of maths, and it also lies at the heart of much of modern physics and engineering. You are making use of this formula every time you use a mobile phone, watch TV or flick on a light switch.

Sadly, mathematics is often taught in school as a non-creative subject that comes pre-formed out of a text book. I argue that we should *always* emphasise the creative and discovery aspects of it in all of our teaching. Part of this involves explaining where the mathematical discovery came from (e.g. Euler's formula above). We should also always show the awe and wonder in maths and make clear that it is a subject full of surprises and mystery. My own personal favourite mathematical result is the fabulously useful and beautiful *Gregory's formula* which relates π (which comes from geometry) to the odd numbers and takes the form

$$\frac{\pi}{4} = 1 - \frac{1}{3} + \frac{1}{5} - \frac{1}{7} + \frac{1}{9} - \frac{1}{11} \cdots$$

What could be more mysterious and/or surprising than that? (Try playing with it to learn even more). It is so mysterious because it links two quite different things, namely geometry and the odd numbers, which seem to have no relation to each other at all. This is rather like finding that you are directly related to the Queen. Gregory's formula is (to a mathematician) sublimely beautiful because of its elegance and simplicity. It is also extremely useful as it gives us a way to calculate π to any desired precision. And without an accurate value of π, much or modern engineering (such as your mobile phone) would simply not be possible. Thirdly, find the links between maths and other 'creative' subjects. For example, maths is hugely important in music, dancing, art, magic and real life. Above all, show that maths is fun and that good maths is always useful. I personally take this approach in all of my teaching, whether it is to undergraduates, school children or the general public, and I believe strongly that it works. I was once asked what the term was for someone that could not enjoy or understand maths, and my reply was 'a figment of the imagination'.

Let's briefly see how this works by looking at a simple bit of mathematical magic. Brandishing a pack of cards you boldly approach a (friendly looking) person on the street. 'Give me a number between 10 and 19', you say. They reply, for example, 16. You count out that number of cards and then pick them up. You then ask them to add up the digits of their number. In this case, it is 5. You count out that number from the pack in your hand. Finally, you ask them if they like telling jokes. Usually, they say *yes*. Finally, you turn over the next card. It is the *Joker*. This trick is fun, mysterious and relies on a mathematical pattern. If you take *any* number add up its digits and subtract it from the original, then you *always* end up with a multiple of 9. (Remember that someone discovered this by playing around with patterns.) If the number lies between 10 and 19, then the number you get when you subtract off the sum of the digits is always 9. So you simply put the Joker in as the 9th card, and the trick works itself. Bravo and cheers all round. Go maths!

18

Sketch: Connecting People and Places Using Worms and Waste

Sharon Boyd and Andrea Roe

The veterinary professional has a role to play in sustainability, conservation and communication; something we are keen to address in the curriculum. We designed an activity where staff and students constructed personal wormeries using recycled plastic salad bowls, paper cups and food waste from the canteen, and soil and leaves from the campus. Each participant was given worms to look after for two weeks, and, in some cases, the worms were given names.

The wormeries were taken home and participants returned after a two-week period to release their worms in the vegetable garden compost bin. At this second meeting, experts in the field of soil ecology and entomology gave an open-air talk about microorganisms and the diversity of soil life. After the worms were released, we all returned indoors to

---

S. Boyd (✉)
Edinburgh College of Art, University of Edinburgh, Edinburgh, Scotland, UK
e-mail: sharon.boyd@ed.ac.uk

A. Roe
Royal (Dick) School of Veterinary Studies, Edinburgh, Scotland, UK

© The Author(s) 2019
A. James and C. Nerantzi (eds.), *The Power of Play in Higher Education*,
https://doi.org/10.1007/978-3-319-95780-7_18

reflect on the activity and to speak about our feelings of responsibility after caring for the worms.

The wormery creation was a stimulus activity (see Cotton and Winter 2010) to encourage discussion on recycling, and empathy within the role of the veterinary professional. The follow-up talk emphasised the importance of taking a holistic view of patient and client support and communication. Students and staff reported that they enjoyed the events, particularly the sense of care engendered by being responsible for their worms. Meetings involved students and staff sharing experiences; this was significant as the first event was scheduled during student welcome week. New students reported how important it was for them to be able to connect with teaching staff and senior students in a relaxed atmosphere. Participants were also connecting to the campus itself, by considering how to minimise waste, visiting the garden, making compost, walking the land. Through this, they could begin to develop a personal awareness of their relationship with the campus through our "landfull" teaching approach (Baker 2005).

In designing this task, we drew on our experience of previous opportunities for play such as interdisciplinary projects with the art college. Andrea's presence as Leverhulme Trust artist in residence was key, with her experience of running creative workshops with staff and students at Easter Bush. We recommend investigating similar collaborations as opportunities for creating exploratory and playful activities.

The strength of play is that it is flexible, allowing us to plan engaging activities with a clear veterinary application to incorporate sustainability concepts into a full curriculum, as successfully achieved here. We have founded a student- and staff-led well-being group to integrate play and learning. The next project is to "knit a zoo" incorporating veterinary medical knowledge, e.g. knitted pathology specimens and skeletons.

References

Baker, M. (2005). Landfullness in Adventure-Based Programming: Promoting Reconnection to the Land. *Journal of Experiential Education, 27*(3), 267–276.

Cotton, D., & Winter, J. (2010). It's Not Just Bits of Paper and Light Bulbs: A Review of Sustainability Pedagogies and Their Potential for Use in Higher Education. In P. Jones, D. Selby, & S. Sterling (Eds.), *Sustainability Education: Perspectives and Practice Across Higher Education* (pp. 39–54). New York, NY: Taylor & Francis.

19

Sketch: Maths, Meccano® and Motivation

Judith McCullouch

There is a sad propensity amongst many members of society, including primary school teachers, to harbour negative feelings about mathematics and thus perpetuate their angst through next generations. Learning about teaching through play that puts the learner at the centre makes a major contribution to readjustment of attitude, even to the point of evangelistic positivity! We want children to thrive within mathematics, not be outside whilst mathematics teaching is 'done to them'. Social constructivism holds that knowledge is not passively received but is actively built through participation and modelling this principle with teachers through playing with Lego® or Meccano® works. As the makers state: 'Model realisation using Meccano® is limited mainly by the imagination and ingenuity of the builder'.

Q: How can teachers learn to teach in this way? A: By experiencing it themselves!

Consider three groups of teachers. Group 1 has sets with the exact parts and instructions to build a bridge. With a little concentration,

J. McCullouch (✉)
University of Winchester, Winchester, UK
e-mail: judith.mccullouch@winchester.ac.uk

some reading and fine motor skills, the bridge can be built to a high standard, matching the illustration on the box. Group 2 has a box of parts (pieces missing—haha) with monochrome instructions. They have the security of instructions but are more challenged to build the exact model. The 3rd group have just a box of parts without instructions leaving no choice but to construct whatever bridge they can.

Some key messages, related to teaching mathematics:

Group 1: The instructions told them what to do—no need to know about bridges; they just carried out a series of steps. Despite a strong sense of accomplishment and satisfaction, in mathematics this has only

Fig. 19.1 LEGO® lifting bridge—full instructions

the short-term benefit of getting it right; the lack of active engagement means little is learned (Fig. 19.1).

Group 2: Although irritated by the unclear instructions and missing pieces, they shared thoughts and had to communicate to decide what to do. For learning mathematics, this challenge simulates engagement and creates opportunities for active learning through application.

Group 3: They had to consider what the parts did and how they worked together, working to improve on initial ideas. There was lots of animation (out of their seats), talking, listening and thinking. The immense pleasure at achieving the goal outweighed the frustrations encountered. For the mathematics learner, this approach needs well-judged teacher support to avoid counterproductive disheartening or giving up but the learning is powerful and long term (Fig.19.2).

One way does not suit all and all approaches provide success. The three models illustrate a range of teaching approaches for mathematics from procedural to discovery. Meeting a challenge is a bumpier road to learning than following instructions, but the outcome is satisfying and learning embedded. Working as part of a team in a social context helps construct knowledge and promote progress, enhanced by being at the centre of it; learning through doing and experiencing.

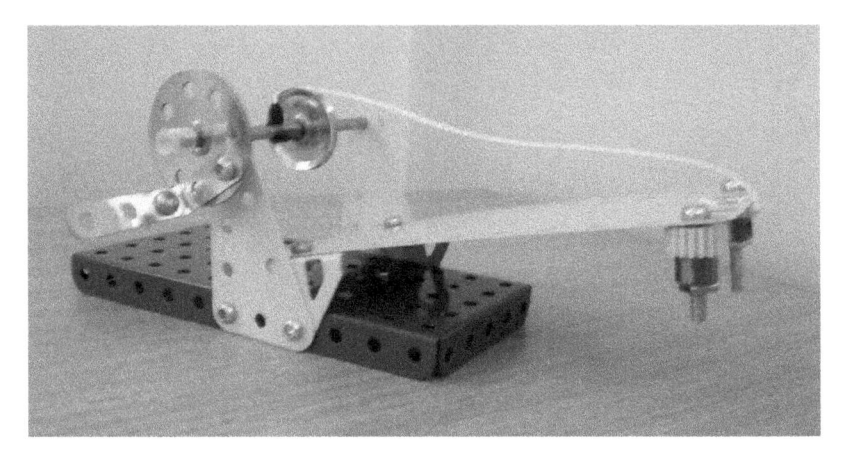

Fig. 19.2 LEGO® lifting bridge—no instructions

20

Exploration: Playful Urban Learning Space—An Indisciplinary Collaboration

Clive Holtham and Tine Bech

Introduction

This exploration reports on an unusual playful collaboration between a business school (Cass Business School; City, University of London) and a fine art practitioner (Dr. Tine Bech, Tine Bech Studio), supported by a Creative Entrepreneur in Residence funding scheme of Creativeworks, London. Here, the two are largely referred to impersonally as "the business school" and "the artist". The project involved four phases:

1. Context and partnership formation
2. The evolution and delivery of the installation "Spaces 2050"

C. Holtham (✉)
Cass Business School, London, UK
e-mail: C.W.Holtham@city.ac.uk

T. Bech
Tine Bech Studio, London, UK
e-mail: mail@tinebech.com

3. Reflection and direct follow up
4. Conclusion

Phase 1: Context and Partnership Formation

Both the school and the artist had strong interests in play (Bech 2014; Brady et al. 2005), and the Creativeworks funding scheme made it possible for the artist to explore the intersection between the two domains. Figure 20.1 summarises the overall aim of the collaboration. The collaboration created the conditions through which the artist could design and implement an installation. She summarised her initial proposals as follows:

> The Creative Entrepreneur residency will investigate how art, technology and play can create new systems of communication across the city and new ways of connecting with each other in public spaces. I will explore play and rule breaking, examining its role in the creation of public dissidence. I am interested in how these forms of play in public spaces can be link to disobedience and how this potentially can shape the future and enable change. In a wider context it is also important to explore how play and risk has implications for society. In particular, how the fear of risks suppresses play – an important aspect in social bonding.

What Is Meant by Play

Both partners had broadly similar generic concepts of play (Huizinga 1955; Papert 1980; Winnicott 1971), even though they were derived from art practice and a related Ph.D. on the one hand, and over a decade of research and experimentation into play-based methods specifically for business education on the other. Both had drawn on similar key influences in the literatures of play. Both partners had research and development experience in drawing on public spaces as spaces for informal learning and imaginative stimulation. There was not a narrowly

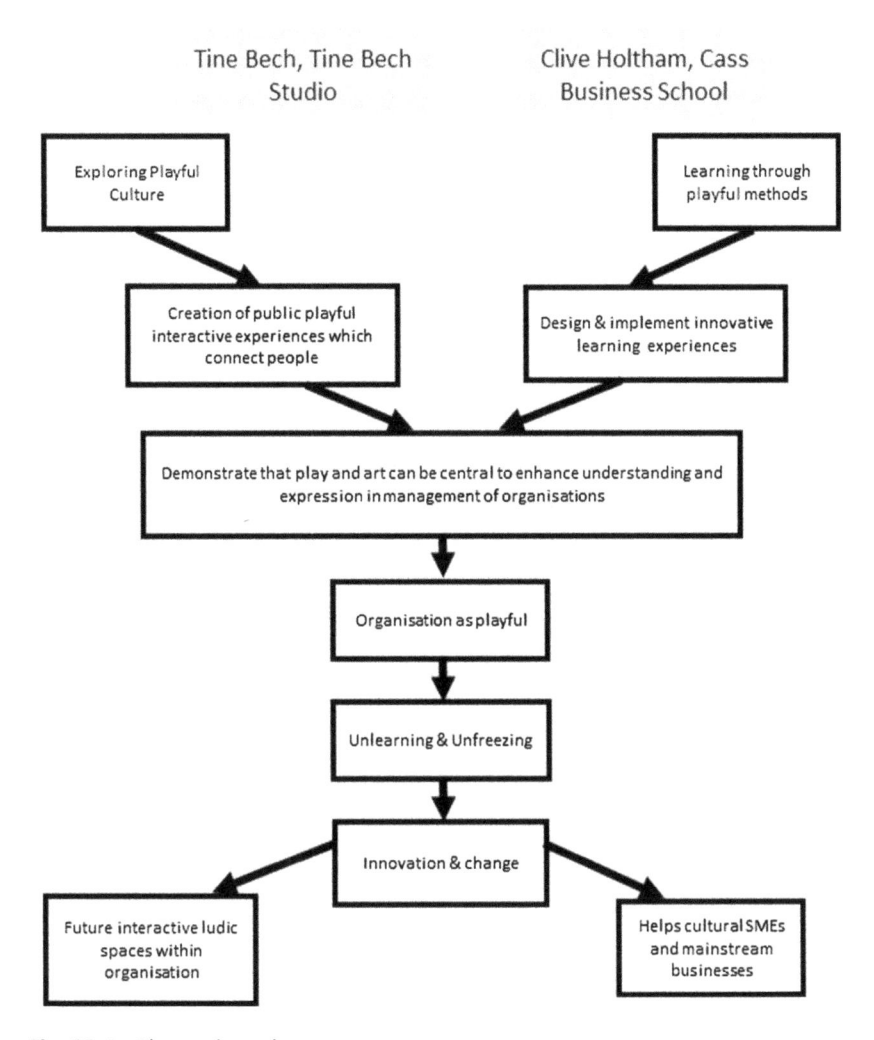

Fig. 20.1 The project plan

drawn boundary around the context of play, e.g. simulations, formal games or use of building bricks.

Being in a state of non-seriousness lies at the heart of encouraging playfulness. If serious means being driven by primarily rational ways of thinking and performing, this may be appropriate for much everyday conduct and decision making in organisations, precisely the type that may be increasingly delegated to machines in future. But there remain vital areas of management which cannot be reduced to rational models and thinking, and for these an intuitive approach is needed in addition.

Pedagogic Rationale

There was a strong interest in the business school in drawing on the residency to extend its existing arts-based management education and in turn, helping to improve the practices of business.

Importance of Play in Specified Context

Historically, play has been an important dimension in management education, not least at the strategic level where role-playing simulations, most particularly in the form of military war games, have centuries of tradition (von Hilgers 2012). The Cass partner business school in Paris, ESCP Europe (formerly the Ecole Superieure de Commerce Paris), was the location of a very rare, very early (1800s) and sadly doomed attempt to design business education around experiential simulations (Touzet and Corbeil 2015). During the twentieth century, the formalisation and accreditation of management education, shifted the centre of gravity from embodied activities to cognitive ones, with heavy emphasis on analytical methods that served the post-war world of relative stability well, but were unable to prevent the crashes and leadership failures of the twenty-first century. The shortcomings of this approach were exposed as the result of the crashes and crises in 2001 and 2007, leading to a reawakening of interest in non-analytical pedagogic approaches, including play-based learning methods. Much publicity has attached to the use of building bricks in management learning, but there is in fact a very wide spectrum of playful learning approaches, much of which stems from the sub-discipline of the Art of Management and Organisation.

In this case reported here, there was not only an interest in play for education, but it was also seen as an alternative route to the production of new knowledge, particularly in the area of ideation in the context of planning for unpredictable futures.

Phase 2: The Evolution and Delivery of the Spaces 2050 Installation

With adults, some specific professions (storytelling, the arts) positively encourage and promote imaginative thinking, but for many, conforming to standardised ways of thinking and doing is the norm. With the Creative Entrepreneur Residency, it was important to address a future-facing problem that positively demanded imaginative thinking, and which could find a way of unlocking the type of imaginative thinking that is discouraged, ignored or even suppressed in conventional meeting rooms and post-it note laden workshops. At least for the duration of the event, participants needed to be given permission to be playful.

During the residency, the artist explored how playful interactive spaces can help organisations innovate. She spent time in the business school both physically, and in engagement with faculty and students. As a result, she decided to build the theme of her event around space and knowledge, a crucial issue for the school in the light of its strategy looking for significant improvements in its physical estate.

The subject matter really was identified by the then new Dean of the Business School, Professor Marianne Lewis, when she announced that the school was looking to improve its estate, and encouraging ideas and views on that. From the viewpoint of the artist, her concentrated period of residency led to a decision to focus the installation on the design of a new business school building, under the heading of "playful urban learning space". The term indisciplinary was also used to highlight that this was not bounded by conventional silos such as art or social science.

The residency culminated with an event in January 2016 titled "SPACE 2050: Seeing and Seers". Participants were invited to be the masters of illumination—the future learners and researchers, whose mission it was to re-imagine future learning and research spaces. Wearing unique wearable lighting (by Tine Bech Studio) participants had to complete a quest—finding seven reflection colour zones and solving a challenge at each site with their power of radiance. Figure 20.2 gives a perspective on how this was achieved in practice.

Fig. 20.2 A group making reflections in the mylar wall covering and reflecting on the question posted beneath it

Using social media, players send illuminating messages back in time, reflecting what the future education spaces look like, to help year 2016 envision their twenty-first-century education space. The players' messages of images and text were gathered online—becoming a glowing legacy. In SPACES 2050, players were not simply passive observers, but actively participating and engaging, creating new artefacts which were shared with others digitally, both locally and globally.

How Play Has Changed Your Practice

For both partners, play was already a core aspect of their professional practice, albeit in the diverse domains of installation art and business education, respectively. The project was therefore aimed to widen and ideally deepen or reshape each partner's practice in play. For the business school, experimenting with different approaches to play, both up to and after the watershed of an innovative 2005 MBA elective on the "art of management" (Lampel et al. 2006), had been a vital part of the pedagogic innovation process. It had also become an integral part of the business school's approach to research-based and participative design of physical space for knowledge work.

Practical and Theoretical Aspects

In this case reported, there was not only an interest in play for learning, it was also seen as an alternative route to the production of new knowledge, particularly in the area of ideation in the context of planning for unpredictable futures. The Harvard University Press website (http://www.hup.harvard.edu/catalog.php?isbn=9780674005815) states of *The Ambiguity of Play* (Sutton-Smith 1997) that:

> This work reveals more distinctions and disjunctions than affinities, with one striking exception: however different their descriptions and interpretations of play, each rhetoric reveals a quirkiness, redundancy, and flexibility. In light of this, Sutton-Smith suggests that play might provide a model of the variability that allows for natural selection. As a form of mental feedback, play might nullify the rigidity that sets in after successful adaption, thus reinforcing animal and human variability.

The final sentence has very profound implications because play is one of relatively few methods that readily provides the key "slack" individuals and societies need to adapt and indeed survive.

Business schools are typically not heavily involved in processes to maintain the status quo. In fact, we are often called on to help challenge the status quo. We can draw on the art and science of managing the present, and our beacons of the future, to support effective change processes. A vital part of change management is "unfreezing" an organisation which has, like ice, solidified (Cummings et al. 2016). Since individuals and organisations do over time almost develop immunities to traditional forms of unfreezing, there is a continuing need to develop innovative forms of unfreezing, and we are at a point where arts-based approaches to unfreezing are becoming increasingly common and increasingly accepted.

Phase 3: Reflection and Direct Follow Up

In the formal evaluation of the residency, Clive Holtham concluded as follows:

> The Business School has not previously had a creative entrepreneur residency, though we do have a large and successful range of interactions both with generic entrepreneurs and also with artists who engage with management and organisations.
>
> In my view as sponsor, because Tine Bech has both an academic and an art practice background, she was able to create connections and relationships extraordinarily quickly, and developed an understanding of our community much faster than might normally have been expected. This enabled her to begin to participate in meetings, not as an external fly on the wall, but as an informed collaborator. She found this useful, but we in turn also were able to see ourselves in a different light, both strengths as well as weaknesses.
>
> Of the three phases of preparation, engagement and event, the event was an amazing success, beyond anything we could have envisaged at the start. The physical presence of an experienced artist valuably opened up the possibility of critical and constructive external and informed challenges to our discipline-based conventions.

Direct Outputs/Publications

One of the superb photographs of the event commissioned from then Maths Ph.D. student Lleonard Rubio y Degrassi was selected as the Business School's entry to the City University 2016 "Images of Research" competition and put on display in the main university.

Though the project funding finished three days after the installation took place, the partners had planned to seek out opportunities to disseminate the findings and we can identify a series of direct spin-off events. The most significant was the Creativeworks event at Kings London, where there was modest funding to enable a small form of the installation to be recreated, which was accessible over a full day. This again generated considerable interest from participants.

The installation inspired an undergraduate student to produce his own "mirror" installation at a first year BSc Management student exhibition of work in April 2016, imaginatively and economically using mirror card issued to visitors who then wrote their reflections on index cards.

The playful format, but without the lights and mirrors, was drawn on for several national conferences, most particularly the Playful Learning Conference at Manchester Metropolitan University in July 2016 (Holtham and Bech 2016), again using a campus location but with a very lo-fi form of lighting, namely tiny torches.

The Spaces 2050 event has also directly inspired walks at:

Association of Business Schools conference, Aston April 2016

Develop@City conference, City, University of London, July 2017.

Phase 4: Conclusion

Obstacles

The most serious obstacle at every stage of the project was time, although what modest time which was available was very efficiently used. For both partners, even though this was a relatively modest project, it was also perceived as high profile and hence high risk.

The word "play" potentially has risks in the environment of professional development, specifically here in the context of business education. It cannot be assumed that because many younger students welcome are familiar with play and games in their non-academic lives, that they will automatically realise that these are potentially valuable in their own business education. Although we noticed an undercurrent of anxiety about play-based learning methods after the first financial crisis of the twenty-first century (2001), this anxiety seemed to markedly increase after the second crisis of 2007–2008.

For the business school, the residency has led to augmented capacity in both teaching (learning by walking about) and designing of physical spaces for knowledge work. For the artist, she has broadened and deepened her understanding of similarities and differences between artistic and business practices, and also built linkages across other disciplines in city, University of London, particularly in the engineering discipline.

References

Bech, T. (2014). *Playful Interactions: A Critical Inquiry into Interactive Art and Play* (Unpublished Ph.D. thesis). Faculty of Arts, Creative Industries and Education University of the West of England, Bristol.

Brady, C., Holtham, C., & Melville, R. (2005). *21st Century Professional Management Education: Learning, Simulation, Emulation and Games*. Atlanta: International Simulation and Gaming Association.

Cummings, S., Bridgman, T., & Brown, K. G. (2016). Unfreezing Change as Three Steps: Rethinking Kurt Lewin's Legacy for Change Management. *Human Relations, 69*(1), 33–60.

Holtham, C., & Bech, T. (2016). *Playful Urban Learning Space*. Playful Learning Conference, Manchester.

Huizinga, J. (1955). *Homo Ludens: A Study of the Play Element in Culture*. Boston, MA: Beacon Press.

Lampel, J., Sims, D., & Holtham, C. (2006). *Can Artful Inquiry Help Investigate the Mystery of Management?* 3rd Art of Management and Organization Conference on September 5–9, Krakow, Poland.

Papert, S. (1980). *Mindstorms*. New York, NY: Basic Books.

Sutton-Smith, B. (1997). *The Ambiguity of Play*. Cambridge, MA: Harvard University Press.

Touzet, L., & Corbeil, P. (2015). Vital Roux, Forgotten Forerunner of Modern Business Games. *Simulation and Gaming, 46*(1), 19–39.

von Hilgers, P. (2012). *War Games: A History of War on Paper*. Cambridge: MIT Press.

Winnicott, D. W. (1971). *Playing and Reality*. London and New York: Tavistock Publications/Routledge.

21

Sketch: Novelty Shakes Things Up in the History Classroom

Carey Fleiner

Proactivity in the classroom seems like a no-brainer: to engage the students with lecture and seminar materials, to initiate curiosity, to retain the material. But sometimes the material is difficult to disseminate, and passive reading, hand-outs and lectures only lead to the dreaded fifty minutes of silence. Fortunately, desperation is a fruitful muse, especially when accompanied by careful planning and preparation.

So, how to light the blue touch paper? Initially, for me, traditional seminar groups where I assign a short reading to a group to prepare and discuss (as opposed to more creative activities) have worked well since my Teaching Assistant days. Since then, I've mixed it up with students debating (should the Romans adopt Hellenistic culture? Was Octavian a rebel or a reformer?), running political campaigns (complete with speeches, bribery and corruption), 'copying' medieval manuscripts, and marketing merchandise to 'sell' the Roman empire by designing museum gift shop tat.

One memorable activity occured when my students on my Carolingian module acted out the civil wars of Louis the Pious, a conflict with confusing contemporary accounts and a complex modern historiography. My own postgrad lecture notes on the subject included a desperate 'WTF' scrawled in the margin. Ha! I told colleagues, this is so damned complicated, and I should just assign the students parts and turn it all into a game of Twister …hmmm….

We dressed up the classroom as ninth-century Francia, tacking big sheets of A3 to the walls to represent territories and kingdoms. Students showed up for class with props and costumes (the Pope brought a palace made out of empty toilet rolls, and a strapping, bearded six-footer played Queen Judith). Everyone had coloured pencils, Sharpie markers and stickers. We put together a chronology, I called out instructions, and each character then moved to the designated area and tagged it—one 'king' annexed a territory by tearing a strip off the A3 and blue tacking it to his homeland. Lots of laughs, sure, but at the end, we could physically see how the tagged regions demonstrated why the sources are such a mess, but yet… clarified how things actually looked on the ground. Discussion then considered advantages and disadvantages of the wars, gaps in the sources, long- and short-term repercussions. Retention of the material remained high as evidenced on the exam several weeks later.

Novelty shakes things up—it can help to inspire analysis and allow students to engage memorably with the material. Balance is crucial—too much silliness grates; students appreciate a mix of activities. No matter how an activity seems to be borne of panic, no truly successful activity is. Planning (and experience) is essential. All of my weekly lecture/seminars come with 'kits'—a seminar guide with the readings, a suggested bibliography, prompt questions; complementary materials are supplied in class. I always have a backup plan of an in-class reading to unpack on the spot, should all else fail. As one of my students once remarked, 'She's not only a plan B and C, she's got the entire alphabet!'

Part IV

Wordsmiths and Communicators

22

Exploration: Don't Write on Walls! Playing with Cityscapes in a Foreign Language Course

Mélanie Péron

> I put a picture up on a wall. Then I forget there is a wall. (Perec 1999: 39)

Teaching a foreign language and its concomitant everyday culture is evidently easier in a homestay study abroad context than it is on campus. Language, in all its forms and registers, is everywhere outside of the classroom. The city represents a ubiquitous classroom where the locals act as avatars of the teacher. The actual difficulty is the desire of most students to stop being (seen as) tourists. Tourists could be defined as a peripheral and transient audience, passive observers who pass through while remaining marginal to the local scene. They might be noticed by the locals but are seldom listened to. In contrast, locals could be seen as consciously rooted in their environment and trying to make connections with it. Not only are they aware of the role played by the place in the construction of their own identity, but the place is also aware of the role locals play in the construction of its identity. So how to help

M. Péron (✉)
Department of French and Francophone Studies,
University of Pennsylvania, Philadelphia, PA, USA

© The Author(s) 2019
A. James and C. Nerantzi (eds.), *The Power of Play in Higher Education*,
https://doi.org/10.1007/978-3-319-95780-7_22

students develop a sense of belonging? How to help them become active participants in their new environment and be heard by the locals?

Another difficulty is connected to the highly competitive culture the participants experience on campus. It often leads them to feel overwhelmed and to forget the pleasure of learning. Therefore, how can a SA programme take advantage of its out-of-the-ordinary nature to turn the students into the curious children they once were?

To address these questions, the author developed the task-based project *Don't write on walls!* for an advanced French course taught during 6 weeks in the town of Tours, France.

Course Description

The course is listed as a writing course. Yet, on the first day of class, it is presented as a whimsical game aiming at rekindling a childlike wonder in all of us. It invites students to step into a world where familiar activities on campus—wandering the Internet, clicking, snapchat, posting—take on new meanings. This is how the web turns into the host city, the click of the mouse into the sound of heels on the pavement, the highlighted words on the screen into street names. Instead of sending impressions programmed to disappear, one is urged to capture fleeting moments and post them so they do not vanish. Students are asked to keep all their senses wide open, in a childlike way, to see the texts offered by the city and listen to the whispers of the walls. While life on campus is all about doing things quickly, this project requires them to slow down and forget about the destination. They morph into modern *flâneurs*. A *flâneur* is commonly defined as one who strolls aimlessly but enjoyably, observing life and his surroundings. When using *flânerie* as the framework of a course, one must be willing to accept the role serendipity will play on the everyday organisation. Even though the course has a planned weekly thematic syllabus, it may shift because of the apparition, overnight, of an image of a bird tagged all over town, for instance. One should be ready to allow the city hand out the script of the day and let one's imagination tackle the impromptu challenge. "Imagination is often playful and elusive. It revels in serendipity, in unexpected connections, chance meetings, and seeing the everyday and familiar in new ways" (James and Brookfield 2014: 3). This constant unpredictability helps breaking free from routine and monotony. It turns lesson planning into an exciting adventure.

Description of *Don't Write on Walls!*

Playing with Words

Students create a blog. Their first post is a video sharing their expectations for the programme. Throughout the following six weeks, they post a total of fifteen texts about the city. I give the titles one by one, a couple of days before the due date. This strategy aims at keeping a playful element of mystery and prevents students from falling back into their on-campus habit of rushing to cross assignments off of their to-do lists. Each entry must be the result of a paced peripatetic experience during which the student-observers took their time to decipher the signs offered by the city. One noted:

> Coming from a campus whose fast-paced and high-pressure culture promotes insularity and isolation, it stands as a refreshing reminder that in even the most ordinary of places on the most ordinary of days, there is much surrounding us yet to be experienced, uncovered and discovered. (student observer)

1. Seuil | Rives (Threshold | River bank)	4. Mur (Wall)	7. Nom (Name)	10. Pierre (*stone; Pierre*)	13. Carte (*map; card*)
2. Porte (Door)	5. Rue (Street)	8. Tu | Vous (You)	11. Tramway (Tram)	14. Mémoire (*memory; memoirs*)
3. Fenêtre (Window)	6. Paysage (Landscape)	9. Bribes (Bits of sentences)	12. Traces	15. Re-Tours | Dé-Tours (Return; Detour; re-Tours; de-Tours)

Once they have the new trigger word, students look in the city for an embodiment of what the word means conventionally, to them and/or metaphorically before writing a text about it. This is how *window* took the shape of stained glasses in a cathedral, the sunglasses of a customer at a café, the eyes of a statue on the façade of the theatre, among others. What appear at first to be banal words follow an architectonic progression deliberately leading the students from the frontiers (e.g. banks) to the centre (e.g. tram), from observation to participation and consequently from the unfamiliar to the familiar, from being marginal to being part of the local life. They are markers on the students' itineraries that will lead them to the feeling of localness. For each text, students are required to refer to their five senses. They include an illustration (e.g. picture taken at the scene, artwork the scene reminds them of) and a soundtrack (e.g. recording they made at the scene, a song they associate with their text). The city becomes the book the students read as well as the palimpsest they contribute to with the narratives they write. The students therefore take on the double identity of readers and authors.

Coming full circle, the last entry, playing on the name of Tours, is followed by a video where students talk about who they are *now*. At the end of the journey, they (re-)discover themselves recalling T. S. Eliot's lines in *Little Gidding*:

> We shall not cease from exploration
> And the end of all our exploring
> Will be to arrive where we started
> And know the place for the first time.

Playing with Space

Class meets three times a week for a total of six hours. On Mondays, we meet in a classroom at the university without confining ourselves to the four walls of the space. We take advantage of the geography of the building to enhance our exploration of the surrounding culture. The noticeboard covered with ads and pamphlets, the graffiti covering the desks and the bathroom walls become priceless textbooks.

On Wednesdays, we meet in the same small neighbourhood café frequented mostly by locals. Café scenes are linguistically chaotic. Overlapping conversations are muffled by the screaming steamer and the deafening horns coming from morning traffic. Yet it is authentic.

Fig. 22.1 Atypical classroom: a circus warehouse

In this setting, students learn how to act as locals: negotiating meaning with meta-language, raising their voice, speaking in public. Thanks to the frequency and expectedness of our presence, the class forges a rapport with their fellow patrons. Some of the latter eavesdrop on our readings and participate in our discussions. A woman joyfully greeted us each time with her "So what are *we* reading today?" When students are asked to read aloud, many customers kindly smile at them as a sign of support. The café is the stage where players and audience keep reversing roles and support each other.

On Fridays, the classroom is always shifting. It can be a tramway car, a medieval scriptorium, a circus warehouse (Fig. 22.1).

This manipulation of the notion of classroom aims at helping students step out of their comfort zone as tourists and passive language learners. It forces them to be active players in the life of the city. Most importantly, the excitement of discovery keeps the students fully engaged.

Class time is divided between reading literary texts to prepare the students lexically and conceptually for their assignment and prompts for short exercises using their surroundings: *Trace a graffiti found in the cathedral and incorporate it into a text.*

Behind what could be seen as superficial play stand strong linguistic and cognitive principles. In fact:

> the important point about using imagination is that we are using it to engage students with the most challenging, difficult, and substantial learning that we judge they need to undertake. (…) There is nothing inherently superficial or unchallenging about engagement; in fact it's the opposite of superficiality. (James and Brookfield 2014: 5–6)

Playing with Walls

Every week, the students are invited to turn one of their digital posts into posters (Fig. 22.2).

They tape them across the city after negotiating the mural space with locals. Thus, their work gains a wider audience. The city turns into an open gallery, the students into artists and the locals into visitors. The student-written impressions offer the city inhabitants new sets of eyes. They

El Cafecito | le 5 juin à 14:51 | nuageux, bruine

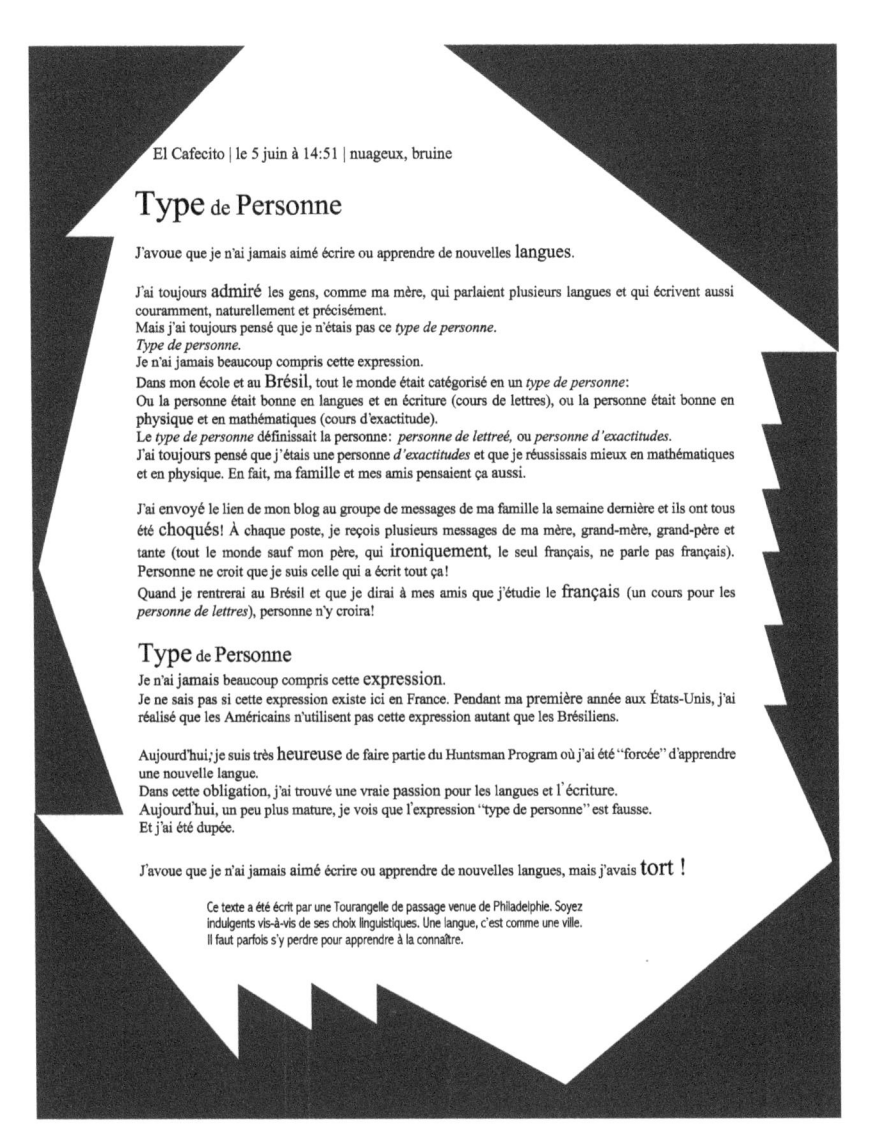

Type de Personne

J'avoue que je n'ai jamais aimé écrire ou apprendre de nouvelles langues.

J'ai toujours admiré les gens, comme ma mère, qui parlaient plusieurs langues et qui écrivent aussi couramment, naturellement et précisément.
Mais j'ai toujours pensé que je n'étais pas ce *type de personne*.
Type de personne.
Je n'ai jamais beaucoup compris cette expression.
Dans mon école et au Brésil, tout le monde était catégorisé en un *type de personne*:
Ou la personne était bonne en langues et en écriture (cours de lettres), ou la personne était bonne en physique et en mathématiques (cours d'exactitude).
Le *type de personne* définissait la personne: *personne de lettreé*, ou *personne d'exactitudes*.
J'ai toujours pensé que j'étais une personne *d'exactitudes* et que je réussissais mieux en mathématiques et en physique. En fait, ma famille et mes amis pensaient ça aussi.

J'ai envoyé le lien de mon blog au groupe de messages de ma famille la semaine dernière et ils ont tous été choqués! À chaque poste, je reçois plusieurs messages de ma mère, grand-mère, grand-père et tante (tout le monde sauf mon père, qui ironiquement, le seul français, ne parle pas français). Personne ne croit que je suis celle qui a écrit tout ça!
Quand je rentrerai au Brésil et que je dirai à mes amis que j'étudie le français (un cours pour les *personne de lettres*), personne n'y croira!

Type de Personne

Je n'ai jamais beaucoup compris cette expression.
Je ne sais pas si cette expression existe ici en France. Pendant ma première année aux États-Unis, j'ai réalisé que les Américains n'utilisent pas cette expression autant que les Brésiliens.

Aujourd'hui, je suis très heureuse de faire partie du Huntsman Program où j'ai été "forcée" d'apprendre une nouvelle langue.
Dans cette obligation, j'ai trouvé une vraie passion pour les langues et l'écriture.
Aujourd'hui, un peu plus mature, je vois que l'expression "type de personne" est fausse.
Et j'ai été dupée.

J'avoue que je n'ai jamais aimé écrire ou apprendre de nouvelles langues, mais j'avais tort !

> Ce texte a été écrit par une Tourangelle de passage venue de Philadelphie. Soyez indulgents vis-à-vis de ses choix linguistiques. Une langue, c'est comme une ville.
> Il faut parfois s'y perdre pour apprendre à la connaître.

Fig. 22.2 Blog post turned into poster

(re-)discover their city through the senses and the words of foreigners. On our class Twitter account, students post a picture of their work in its new environment with hashtags inviting the city to guess where the picture was taken and discover something new in a place they are familiar with. The double identity of the texts—digital and paper—is paramount. Blogging may help students develop their linguistic skills and intercultural reflection, yet it remains restricted to a closed conversation between them and the class. The old tradition of taping paper on a brick and mortar wall endows the project with its full anthropological and dialogical nature.

Public [Dis]Play

The project culminates with two public collective exhibits of the posters. One is hosted in the public library for several weeks. There, the students are able to interact with the visitors and answer their questions. They are asked by locals to tell them *their* city. The possessive pronoun here expresses mutual possession. Contrary to ethnographic student-led interviews where the student is clearly in the position of the one who knows less, the dialogues triggered by the posters posit both interlocutors on the same level of belonging and local knowledge. Each poster includes a QR code linking to a voice recording of the texts made by their respective author. In this manner, the students offer the city a sample of all the creative melodies its language can take on.

The other public event is a pop-up exhibit in a city garden. Posters are hung with clothespins on a rope running poetically from tree to tree. They become the pages of an open book read by local *flâneurs*.

Conclusion

This project teaches our students to slow down and look for the essential in life while still striving to reach their full potential. This academic interstice can provide them with the skills necessary to balance life and school once they return:

> [The course] has played a pivotal role in my life. The interactive writing workshop pushed me out of my comfort zone, opened my eyes to my creative capacity, and significantly changed the way in which I carry myself

throughout life. I learned about the importance of "allowing yourself to get lost," whether that physically meant getting lost in the town, losing my train of thought while writing, or letting go of agendas and perfectly planned *rendez-vous*. While bothersome at first, I slowly began to acknowledge the importance of the unknown (…). Several traces still find themselves in my daily routine: Admiring and taking note of the mundane, embracing the unknown, walking aimlessly, and relying on my five senses to savor memories.

The various forms of play revive the inquisitive child in the students and set them on the path to becoming responsible empathetic citizens. As James and Brookfield (2014: 16) explain, "[b]y working with visual, auditory, kinesthetic, discursive, and written modalities of teaching and learning, (…) learners can broaden and deepen their understanding of knowledge and open their minds to other ways of construing the world and their futures". One student talked about "the opportunity to be able to learn so organically, as [the course] really restored some of [her] faith in the purpose of higher education." She "carr[ies] those memories with [her] for when [she] feel[s] sad or stressed about [school]."

Another student explained:

> [the project] left me some words of wisdom that I hold near and dear to me today. [It] said that in order to truly immerse oneself into the culture of another society, one must become a local. Becoming a local is walking along the streets, alone, discovering. Becoming a local is talking to other locals and learning their stories. Becoming a local is having no boundaries - being absolutely open to the sights and sounds that occur around you. Before going on this experiential trip, I always had a "map" - I always had a direction and a plan to go from point A to B. The course, however, taught me the value of having no direction. It taught me the value of questioning myself and my surroundings. I am ever thankful for the opportunity to be able to grow as a human being in this way.

Moreover, the project enables the students to realise that one does not need to be born somewhere to be a local. Being a local is being emotionally connected to a place. It is to belong to a place where one has made memories for oneself and for others.

Finally, the students leave a trace in the city's history as much as the city is imprinted in their memory. The project relies on the principles of mutual discovery and exchange. While the students can eventually say that they are from their hometown *and* from a town in the Loire Valley, they were the catalysts of a magical moment for their hosts who, thanks to them, discovered the unsuspected amidst their ordinary. In what could be compared to the turn of a magic trick, the locals experienced *dépaysement*, which J. C. Bailly describes as the feeling of being situated in unfamiliar surroundings in your own environment "either because you effectively find yourself elsewhere, transported far away from what you know, or else because what you know or thought you knew has itself been transported to an elsewhere indiscernible yet present. What, then (you ask yourself), what is this elsewhere that is here?" (Bailly 2011: 409).

Introducing play and imagination in HE curricula helps knock down walls, whether linguistic, cultural or psychological. It encourages students to reconceive of learning as play as opposed to learning as work. This reframing of learning sets young adults on the enchanting path of edifying wonder and amazement.

References

Bailly, J. (2011). *Le dépaysement*. Paris: Le Seuil (my translation).
James, A., & Brookfield, S. (2014). *Engaging Imagination*. San Francisco: Jossey-Bass.
Perec, G. (1999). *Species of Spaces and Other Pieces*. London: Penguin Books.

23

Sketch: Poetry as Play—Using Riskless Poetry Writing to Support Instruction

Ann Marie Klein

Virtual reality cultivates self-imaging, scanning, and minute-messaging. Consequently, many students fear engaging with others in person. Ironically, I have found that riskless wordplay helps students return to the real world. They learn to contemplate as they articulate perceptions; they pause to ponder as they exchange observations on each other's anonymous verse.

In a literature course on the beatitudes, I assign weekly verse-writing. For instance, I ask students to email me a quatrain on meekness for two points regardless of quality. I collect their quatrains onto a handout without names. In small groups, students discuss three and present one to the class.

Upon hearing peers' insights into their poetry, students become passionate about verse that was neither graded nor identified. Composing for pleasure, they enhance not their GPA but their personal well-being. Penning a quatrain led one student to shift her view of the homeless:

A. M. Klein (✉)
University of St. Thomas, Saint Paul, MN, USA
e-mail: amklein@stthomas.edu

> Broken. Begging. As looked at from those 'above,'
> Souls with a richness they don't comprehend.
> What worldly things hold more power than love? --
> Soon the world shall beg *their* wisdom to lend. (Delexi Riley, 2.10.16)

It led another to value "losing time" by dismissing the drive for tangible results:

> Pluck a rose not to put it in a sack
> But to see it beautiful from two steps back.
> In that detachment love for God will bloom
> And teach you of the roses' sweet perfume. (Letizia Mariani, 26.2.16)

Composing a couplet drew one to recognize virtue in simple gestures:

> With breathing gaze and eyes that sing,
> Two hearts grasp hands and soon take wing. (Olivia Steeves, 18.9.16)

Wordplay endorsed unhurried delight in sensory knowledge, a stark contrast to the gratification of multitasking.

Longer verse afforded opportunities to process experiences. One sestet did so through imagination, like the play of galloping children. A freshman's quandary about transition found resolve through a seaman's navigation of the unpredictable "in-between":

> Called to sail the seas of life, a sailor sets out
> On a journey towards that land no man has seen;
> The wind billows his sails while waves churn about
> He knows not his course through this life in-between.
> Yet free as gulls that fly, not bound by earth or stone
> The Captain of his soul will surely lead him home. (Hannah Rose Smith, 9.3.17)

Another sestet became space for mulling over Shakespeare:
When you see this play, you notice the ruler:

> A strong and fearless king, who loves his daughters.
> How much can we, the watchers understand him?
> And for a few scenes, we find the mindful fool:
> Loves his king, knows more than jests and laughter.
> Don't we, the learners, love more this ironic random? (Patrick Lechner, 9.3.17)

The sonnet form was even found apt for releasing long-held grief.

By intriguing the powers of observation, memory, and imagination, riskless poetry writing offers even CEO- and MD-aspiring students room for play. It entices them to engage directly with the world around them—but not to measure and record it for their CV. Rather, to marvel at it.

24

Sketch: On Word Play in Support of Academic Development

Daphne Loads

Semantic Levity

As an academic developer, I encourage university lecturers in all disciplines to play with words. Together we read poems, policy statements, academic papers and song lyrics, paying attention to unexpected associations, ambiguities and contradictions. We read both literary and non-literary texts slowly and carefully, exploring words, sharing understandings, discovering new meanings and making connections with what we do and who we are as teachers. For example, we read Keats's poem and discuss what "gold" might mean:

> MUCH have I travell'd in the realms of gold….
> Keats (1988: 43)

One lecturer said,

> "gold" here reminds me of the excitement of teaching: of the treasure I bring from other lands.

Another commented that for him, "the realms of gold" evoked the world of business and profit and his weariness of that world.

Words do not straightforwardly contain or exclude meanings. They come to us with connections to previous times and different contexts. These associations may be idiosyncratic (my grandad's gold tooth), common to a particular community (Spandau Ballet's Gold album) or more widely shared (rarity and value). Each time we choose or respond to a word, we reactivate some connections and deactivate others. It's possible that any or all of these meanings of "gold" may have no relevance whatsoever to our teaching practice or teacher identity. However, openness to the possibility that they *might* be relevant is a valuable quality for university teachers.

I facilitate these activities as a way of using Maton's (2013) "semantic waves". Maton shows how effective teachers help students to move up and down in semantic waves, between simple and contextualised meanings, for example the everyday use of the word "gold"; and condensed and abstract meanings, for example the way chemists use the word "gold", where it is packed with meaning and plugged into a structured system of knowledge.

The waves help students to integrate different areas of skills and knowledge, the everyday and the academic, so that they can learn more systematically. This focus on well-organised learning is valuable, but I believe it neglects learners' and teachers' additional needs for open-ended exploration and playfulness. Wordplay enables us to go beyond "semantic waves" of contextualised and abstract, condensed and simple communications (Maton 2013) and to develop what I call "semantic levity": the capacity to move playfully between different contexts and meanings.

But it's not all plain sailing. Some colleagues hate my approach, feeling patronised and infantilised, or frustrated with what they see as a lack of rigour or of gravitas. Many more colleagues tell me that they find it liberating, restorative and fun.

Semantic levity is that disposition seen in both teachers and students who are able to keep in play a wide range of contexts and meanings when encountering and explaining new ideas and experiences. I intend to continue nurturing that precious quality in my colleagues.

References

Keats, J. (1988). *Complete Poems* (3rd ed.). London: Penguin.
Maton, K. (2013). Making Semantic Waves: A Key to Cumulative Knowledge-Building. *Linguistics and Education, 24*(1), 8–22.

25

Sketch: The Communications Factory

Suzanne Rankin-Dia and Rob Lakin

The International Preparation for Fashion (IPF) (Certificate of HE) course at the London College of Fashion (LCF) prepares international students for undergraduate study in fashion. Our diverse cohort of 250 students from approximately 35 different countries comes not only with cross-cultural misunderstanding, but also comedy. With a view to embracing the comedic nature of cross-cultural communication, we use play as a tool.

The 'Factory' model, developed in the Fashion Business School offers rapid-fire, interactive and playful workshops throughout the course of the one-day event. The Communications Factory is based on this model as well as Kuh and Zhao's (2004) findings, which suggest that the establishment of playful, co-curricular learning communities are

---

S. Rankin-Dia (✉)
London College of Fashion, University of the Arts London, London, UK
e-mail: s.rankin@fashion.arts.ac.uk

R. Lakin
Fashion Business School, London College of Fashion, London, UK

© The Author(s) 2019
A. James and C. Nerantzi (eds.), *The Power of Play in Higher Education*,
https://doi.org/10.1007/978-3-319-95780-7_25

positively linked to attainment and a sense of belonging. We use playful approaches to intercultural communication that value and at times laugh at our differences with a view to building an enhanced sense of belonging within a learning community. The day focuses on task-based learning encouraging transferrable academic skills such as creative thinking, project management, intercultural communication, critical discussion and teamwork.

The aim is to recognise and acknowledge that international students often experience culture shock, language shock and academic shock (Caroll and Ryan 2005). Sovic (2008) refines these observations to: integration with other students, English language and academic socialisation, respectively. Our own observations suggest that the main causes of concern are around food and getting lost and so, among other activities, we play tea parties, treasure hunt and, since we are fashion students, dressing up.

The *Global Dressing Up* workshop allows students access to a selection of cultural fabrics. In small multicultural groups, they select 5 pieces and create a look, which they then present to their peers. What was interesting was challenging pre-established cultural meanings and seeing them from different perspectives but also empowering students to use their own cultural capital to talk about fabrics from their own culture.

In *Global Treasure* hunt, one member of the group is blindfolded and relies on instructions from their group members to find random cultural objects around the building and peg them onto a washing line. Students then see these objects juxtaposed against each other and often see them as a metaphor for themselves. Informal discussion around the meaning of the objects follows and encourages the use of prior learning and experience.

At the *Global Tea Party*, students design a menu based on dishes from their own culture. They then make the pretend food out of whatever materials are at hand. Being an art school, the results are often of a high quality. They then serve their 'guests'—each other and dressmakers dummies. Again, there is informal discussion over 'dinner' and a lot of laughter.

Feedback has been largely positive. Once the students remember how to play, it can be a real leveller, removing any power dynamics.

In addition, *The Communications Factory* enables students to practise and develop academic skills, which they can draw on for range of tasks and assignments throughout the year. It also allows us all to have fun.

References

Caroll, J., & Ryan, J. (Eds.). (2005). *Teaching International Students: Improving Learning for All*. London and New York: Routledge.

Sovic, S. (2008). *Lost in Transition? The International Students' Experience Project*. London: CLIP CETL.

Zhao, C., & Kuh, G. (2004). Adding Value: Learning Communities and Student Engagement. *Research in Higher Education, 45*(2), 115–138.

26

Sketch: Playful Writing with Writing PAD

Julia Reeve and Kaye Towlson

The East Midlands Writing PAD Centre (EMWPC) has its roots in the meeting of Julia and Kaye as DMU Teacher Fellows in 2011. They discovered a shared passion for new, creative ways to overcome barriers experienced by students when approaching academic writing. Julia's background was Contextual Studies and Kaye's Information Literacy.

Inspired by the wider Writing PAD community, particularly the work of Francis (2009) and Gröppel-Wegener (2013), their work seeks to challenge established approaches to the thinking process for academic writing and research.

We started to collaborate, developing visual, embodied workshops for undergraduate students and Art & Design staff; subsequently we found our work appealed to all faculties, levels and directorates.

J. Reeve (✉) · K. Towlson
De Montfort University, Leicester, UK
e-mail: jreeve@dmu.ac.uk

K. Towlson
e-mail: kbt@dmu.ac.uk

Our guest-edited JWCP issue (Reeve and Towlson 2014) gave us the official seal of approval to base a Writing PAD Centre at DMU. We continue to promote our vision, launching our blog in 2015, developing techniques, publishing, events, curriculum and resources.

Our Manifesto defines our aims, and our blog documents our activities. Imaginative workshops with a playful approach epitomise the EMWPC ethos, using visual, tactile activities to engage students and staff with creative and reflective thinking. In a playful spirit, we offer our core activities below as a tasting menu, using a culinary metaphor.

A few dishes from our 'Playful writing menu':

Reframing Research
Recipe: A stage by stage exploration of an image or topic using concentric frames drawn on paper.
Tasting notes: A personal, playful way into academic writing.

Image-Enriched Mind Map
Recipe: Free-flow collage used to explore a topic.
Tasting notes: A vehicle for self-reflection and future planning.

Swollage
Recipe: Use of free-association, annotated collage for a personal SWOT analysis.
Tasting notes: Offers new insights for self-reflection.

Dress-up Doll (adapted from Groppel-Wegener 2013)
Recipe: Populating a paper doll outline with key words or images to inform research, reflection and writing.
Tasting notes: A playful route for self-reflection and research planning.

Research plait (inspired by Francis 2009)
Recipe: Weaving paper strips containing research elements together.
Tasting notes: A hands-on method for engaging with the interwoven concept of 'research'.

Action Handprint
Recipe: Drawing round own hand, then embellishing and annotating.
Tasting notes: An embodied approach to summing up one's key strengths or project planning.

These recipes are used to enrich approaches to academic research and writing, both in our institution and beyond. We 'Engage students with theory assignments through creative and playful learning experiences' (Reeve and Towlson 2015): overcoming barriers and enhancing engagement, reflection and joy.

References

Francis, P. (2009). *Inspiring Writing in Art and Design: Taking a Line for a Write*. Bristol: Intellect Books.
Gröppel-Wegener, A. (2013). *Tactile Academia*. Available at https://tactileacademia.com/. Accessed June 30, 2017.
Reeve, J., & Towlson, K. (2014). Welcome to Our Visual Learning Journey: Editorial. *Journal of Writing in Creative Practice, 7*(2), 229–232.
Reeve, J., & Towlson, K. (2015). *East Midlands Writing PAD Manifesto*. Available at http://writingpad.our.dmu.ac.uk/manifesto/. Accessed June 30, 2017.

Part V

Builders and Simulators

27

Exploration: Wigs, Brown Sauce and Theatrical Dames—Clinical Simulation as Play

Caroline Pelletier and Roger Kneebone

Walking into the store cupboard, just off the A&E ward, I see a pile of arms in a box. Two luxuriant scalps lay across a closed hospital laptop. Flaccid faces peak out of a drawer. Some brown liquid with a couple of blood-red specks is splattered across the base of a stainless-steel kidney dish.

That store cupboard is where a London hospital's simulation centre keeps its theatrical apparel (Fig. 27.1). This is brought out whenever there is a simulation-based medical education course, together with the toiletry bags of make-up and sacks of costumes. The doctors and nurses who work in the simulation centre dress up the mannequin to appear as a young man who has just had a motorbike accident; or an elderly lady unsteady on her feet; or a young woman with acute pain

---

C. Pelletier (✉)
UCL Institute of Education, London, UK
e-mail: c.pelletier@ucl.ac.uk

R. Kneebone
Centre for Engagement and Simulation Science,
Imperial College London, London, UK

© The Author(s) 2019
A. James and C. Nerantzi (eds.), *The Power of Play in Higher Education*,
https://doi.org/10.1007/978-3-319-95780-7_27

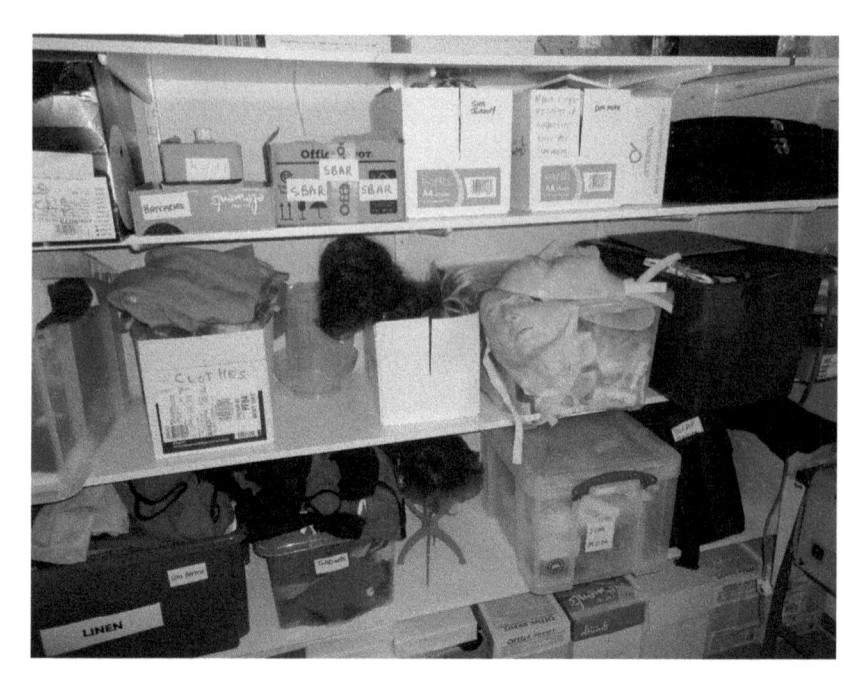

Fig. 27.1 Theatrical props for medical education

in her belly—the appearance of each character, as in countless episodes of *ER* or *Holby City*, provoking the summary telling of a backstory, the unfolding of a storyline structured around bodily trauma, and narrative crisis resolved in the saving of a life. The doctors and nurses also wear costumes, to enact the parts of the anxious relative, the elated drunk, or the cocksure orthopaedic surgeon.

The enactment of critical clinical situations has become integral to medical education. The argument for this is that healthcare workers can learn to practise safely away from real patients. In much of the clinical literature, simulation-based education is evoked in terms of skills training and is the very opposite of play. Issenberg et al. (2005: 23), for example, conclude their systematic review of medical simulation by defining it as an 'opportunity for learners to engage in focused, repetitive practice where the intent is skill improvement, *not idle play*' [our italics].

One doesn't need to be a Freudian to interpret this negation as pointing to a denied presence: there is indeed play going on in simulation centres. Take a look at Fig. 27.2. It shows a manikin dressed up for a scenario based around the simulation of an ectopic pregnancy. Note how the signifier for 'female body' consists of a large, colourful bra. The theatricality of the big, bright breasts ensures that junior doctors immediately ascertain the sex of their simulated patient, a crucial step in their differential diagnosis. The bra operates like a theatrical prop: it sets a scene; it provides a clue to the essential meaning of events. In our experience, it tells participants on a professional development course about emergency medicine that the mannequin is a patient whose condition pertains to gynecological intervention.

There is nothing idle about this play—contra Issenberg et al. It is precisely what makes simulation possible. Participating in a simulation-based course requires cooperative pretending, recognition of the

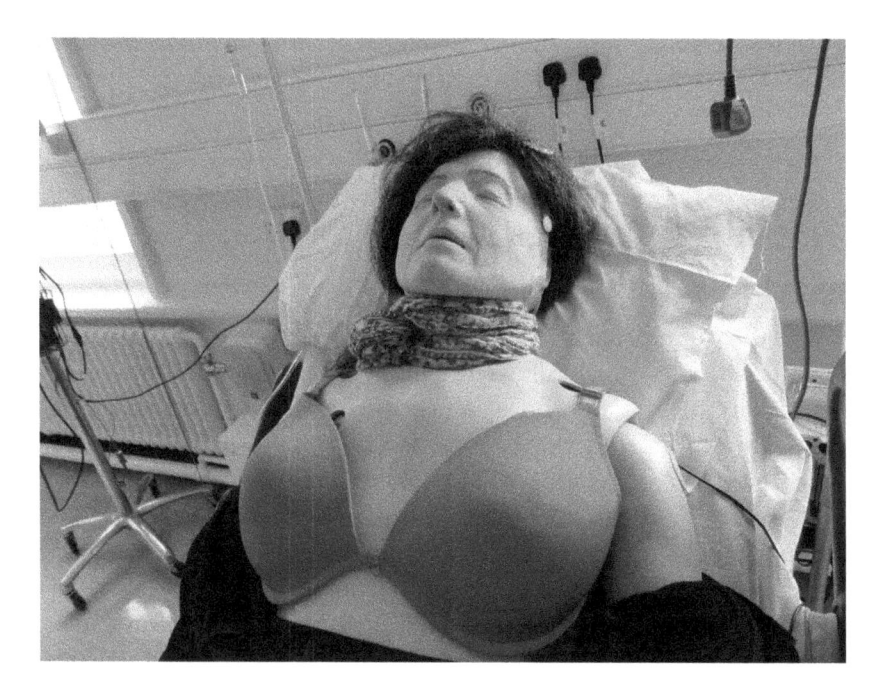

Fig. 27.2 Manikin with pink bra

narrative conventions by which scenarios unfold, and the display of traits and emotions appropriate to a fictional scene, but not necessarily outwith this. This is active, creative, and also ideological work which goes far beyond the passive 'suspension of disbelief' called for in clinical accounts of simulation-based teaching (e.g. Gaba et al. 2001).

Such work can be made sense of on the basis of literature that takes play seriously. The anthropologist of play, Brian Sutton-Smith (1997), describes different rhetorics by which play is understood in academic research. One of these—the rhetoric of the imaginary, summarised below—is particularly helpful for making sense of what happens in hospital simulation centres:

> We are eternally making over the world in our minds, and much of it is fantasy. The difference is that while children have toys, adults usually have images, words, music and daydreams, which perform the same function as toys. *Our fantasies are the microworlds of inner life that all of us manipulate in our own way to come to terms with feelings, conflicts, realities, and aspirations as they enter into our lives.* Children and adults may not really be so different in their use of fantasy play… (1997: 156)
>
> *Play is not based primarily on a representation of everyday real events - as many prior investigators have supposed - so much as it is based on a fantasy of emotional events.* (p. 158—our italics)

Within this rhetoric, play is understood to be motivated by feelings, rather than unmediated images of reality. It appears as an emotionally vivid experience, which allows the limits imposed by normal or non-play reality to be transcended; mocked as much as mimicked. Rather than representing the world, play deconstructs it, taking it apart in order to suit players' emotional responses to events.

If we draw on this rhetoric to examine field data generated in an ethnographic study of London-based simulation centres (Pelletier and Kneebone 2015, 2016a, b), we see phenomena that are rarely commented upon in the literature on medical simulation. These include the relish with which parts were played and the pleasure taken in acting 'out of character' at work. For instance:

> In the control room, John answers the phone, playing the role of a consultant. In a strong Scottish accent, he says: 'Hamish McTaggart by name…' The other educators in the control room laugh loudly. John then enters the simulated theatre. Lindsey, the trainee, says to him 'Hi John'. He responds in a heavy Australian accent: 'I'm Shane'. [Field notes]

The parody of accents and professional traits was mirrored in the exaggeration of symptoms. Educators explained this in terms of the importance of teaching trainees how to manage clinical situations: it was imperative, then, that trainees recognise a situation as pertinent to clinical knowledge. A scenario was deemed a failure if a trainee did not identify the clinical condition, or if the scenario did not make it sufficiently visible. For example, the following field note was made during one scenario in which a trainee had failed to identify symptoms manifested by the manikin:

> John asks the technician to increase the settings on the manikin, so that the heart rate falls even more quickly. He then turns to me and says: 'well, you have got to make it obvious what is going on, otherwise they just don't know'. [Field notes]

Symptoms and conditions therefore appeared heightened and exaggerated. The urgency, excitement and anxiety this generated contrast with how trainees represented their everyday work in discussions:

> During the coffee break, Susan, a trainee, says to another trainee standing next to her: 'In my hospital, there isn't a cannula on the whole ward. None of the equipment works. The seniors aren't at all interested in your situation. But I guess there would be no point in simulating this, as *what we want* to learn is the clinical stuff'. [Field notes]

The italics here highlight the expression of desire—'what we want to learn is the clinical stuff'—which illustrates Sutton-Smith's point that play is performed 'to come to terms with feelings, conflicts, realities, and aspirations as they enter into our lives' (1997: 156). The purpose of a course, and the principle according to which aspects of reality were treated as 'simulatable', was—in Susan's words here—the expression of a wish: of learning 'clinical stuff'; of doing meaningful, satisfying, effective and exciting work. It follows that what was not simulated were the dissatisfying, intractable, limiting aspects of life in hospital. This is one way of understanding why paperwork, administration and record-keeping—which take up significant amounts of a junior doctor's time, in 'real life'—were absent from simulation-based practice.

When clinical simulation is treated as a form of play, which is meaningful *because* of its emotional vividness, its educational rationale is affected. It needs no longer be accountable solely in terms of developing skills, and apologetic about its simplification of medical work. Rather, there is scope then to explore how it can sustain the deconstruction and analysis of medicine as an emotional practice. These contrasting rationales are not mutually exclusive. However, treating simulation as an imaginative exercise is one response to 'simulation deniers' (Turkle 2009) who state that it can never be like real life; that it is trapped within its own magic circle, inherently separated from the real world (Caillois 1967; Juul 2005). This stance on medical simulation characterises the clinical literature, including the arguments of those who advocate its use: Gaba (2004), for example, justifies simulation in medical education in terms of one day achieving something akin to Star Trek's holodeck, a claim which celebrates the achievements of current technologies while simultaneously deferring their full benefits to some point in the future. Others argue that simulation cannot replace work-based learning, but only supplement it (e.g. Issenberg et al. 2005; Ziv et al. 2003). Both of these qualifications treat simulation as a form of illusion: a fake/unreal/inauthentic version of reality.

It is this distinction—*'skill improvement, not idle play'*—that upholds a view of play as trivial. But if we follow Sutton-Smith in defining play as the exercise of imagination, it becomes possible to see how the boundaries between reality and non-reality are anything but firm, but rather negotiated and shifting. Simulating professional practice is then not simply a question of learning skills for subsequent transfer to 'real life'. It is also an exploration of, and an experimentation with, what makes those skills meaningful; worth exercising. Rather than simulation acting only as an anteroom to the workplace, it can then be imagined as a space in which the emotional experience of work is manipulable, and thus transformable in ways that go beyond the transfer of skills, to touch on the meaning of those skills for the experience and quality of work. Simulation becomes then a resource with which to explore and manipulate the pains and pleasures of work, its failures and frustrations; and an occasion on which to work through them to develop better responses to its tribulations.

One incident during fieldwork illustrates our point. It happened as part of a course intended to address a high rate of 'failure to rescue' incidents on one ward. ('Failure to rescue' is a category in the health service's taxonomy of errors, and refers to a failure to identify a rapidly deteriorating patient, who then goes on to die.) The course involved all staff on that ward. On the day Caroline—one of the authors of this chapter—observed, several of the ward's nurses interrupted the introductory lecture on communication skills to interject that 'failure to rescue' incidents were not caused by a dearth of such skills, but rather by management's irresponsible cost-cutting exercises:

> So what are you going to do if you come round to my ward and I have seven patients to look after, two post-ops, and no Healthcare Assistant (HCA). What are you going to say or do? [Field notes]

The presence of 'management', in the form of the deputy director of nursing, meant that this version of reality was counter posed by another: that the hospital's funding was being cut, with little prospect of future increases. The debate that followed set versions of the reality of work against each other. Nurses pointed to the fictional status of work systems designed to identify deteriorating patients; 'management' disclaimed the power to resolve this. The exchanges shaped what was treated as the object of the simulation: a scenario was not seen as indicative of an individual's capacity to respond to an emergency, but rather of working conditions; and, most importantly, of the different ways in which these were being made sense of in the hospital.

The discussion was heated, which was indicative of what was at stake: how the hospital's failure to rescue patients should be interpreted. The skill exercised by the educators however ensured it did not degenerate into a shouting match: by repeatedly asking both nurses and 'management' to respond to each other's accounts, to acknowledge their lived and felt reality, the educators enabled the course to become an occasion on which to rethink how clinical work was done, and how the division of labour could be altered to achieve different outcomes. Agreement was not reached on the day Caroline visited the hospital. However, a principle of ongoing collective review appeared to have gained support among both staff and 'management'.

The course illustrates Sutton-Smith's account of the benefits of imaginary play: it sustained explorations of versions of reality. This suggests how training-oriented simulations can give rise to aesthetic reconfigurations that make the world appear alterable; and in this sense, make it playful, in the most profoundly serious and non-trivial sense of the word. This has implications for imagining the ethics of professional simulation: simulation may be ethical not because it is safe, but precisely because it is dangerous. It puts versions of reality at stake. It opens up reality to critical transformation. It is on this basis that it might be understood as a central pedagogic resource in professional and higher education.

References

Caillois, R. (1967). *Les jeux et les hommes*. Paris: Gallimard.
Gaba, D. M. (2004). The Future Vision of Simulation in Health Care. *Quality and Safety in Health Care, 13,* i2–i10.
Gaba, D. M., Howard, S. K., Fish, K. J., Smith, B. E., & Sowb, Y. A. (2001). Simulation-Based Training in Anesthesia Crisis Resource Management (ACRM): A Decade of Experience. *Simulation & Gaming, 32*(2), 175–193.
Issenberg, S. B., McGaghie, W. C., Petrusa, E. R., Gordon, D. L., & Scalese, R. J. (2005). Features and Uses of High-Fidelity Medical Simulations That Lead to Effective Learning: A BEME Systematic Review. *Medical Teacher, 27,* 10–28.
Juul, J. (2005). *Half-Real: Video Games Between Real Rules and Fictional Worlds*. Cambridge: MIT Press.

Pelletier, C., & Kneebone, R. (2015). Learning Safely from Error? Reconsidering the Ethics of Simulation-Based Medical Education Through Ethnography. *Education and Ethnography, 11*(3), 267–282.

Pelletier, C., & Kneebone, R. (2016a). Fantasies of Medical Reality: An Observational Study of Simulation-Based Medical Education. *Psychoanalysis, Culture and Society, 21*(2), 184–203.

Pelletier, C., & Kneebone, R. (2016b). Playful Simulations Rather Than Serious Games: Medical Simulation as a Cultural Practice. *Games and Culture, 11*(4), 365–389.

Sutton-Smith, B. (1997). *The Ambiguity of Play*. Cambridge, MA: Harvard University Press.

Turkle, S. (2009). *Simulation and Its Discontents*. Cambridge: MIT press.

Ziv, A., Wolpe, P. R., Small, S. D., & Glick, S. (2003). Simulation-Based Medical Education: An Ethical Imperative. *Academic Medicine, 78*(8), 783–788.

ated trust and enabled students to relate to clients as people, rather than as a list of symptoms or problems.

28

Sketch: Using Play to Bridge the Communication Divide

Jools Symons, Nancy Davies, Marc Walton and John Hudson

Bright Sparks Theatre Arts Company and the University of Leeds have utilised drama to improve the communication skills of medical students. As future doctors, our graduates will be expected to communicate challenging concepts and procedures to a huge variety of people with a wide range of communication issues. In the drama sessions, students collaborated with learning disabled adults from the Potternewton Fulfilling Lives and Aspire Centres and adults living with dementia from Inkwell Arts, all based in Leeds. Communicating with both sets of clients through drama presented unique challenges and opportunities for the students.

In non-formal settings, we encouraged the clients and students to voice opinions and interact in ways that challenged formal communication methods by allowing them to "play." The drama activities cultivated

---

J. Symons (✉) · N. Davies · M. Walton · J. Hudson
Institute of Medical Education, University of Leeds, Leeds, UK
e-mail: J.E.Symons@leeds.ac.uk

N. Davies
e-mail: n.e.davies@leeds.ac.uk

a creative, fun and playful environment, in which we promoted equal participation. In one exercise, participants are split into two groups, each must create a frozen moment in time and the other group must guess what scene is being portrayed. Many of the activities featured group devising work, in which the content of the drama was decided democratically. In order to achieve this, groups had to negotiate; and in order to negotiate, they had to communicate.

Running the workshops alongside the formal communication teaching allowed the students to use their learnt skills in different ways. Improvisation helped build confidence, and by practising new strategies and techniques, the students were able to develop a rapport with the clients. Students participating in the projects are left with a feeling of improved understanding of issues the clients often face. One element that we find particularly important is the way in which the realisation that "I've learnt something today" comes on reflection. The participants are caught up in the moment, as we move from one drama exercise to the next, and everyone is having too much fun to get overly focused on the actual reasons why we are doing what we are doing.

Although the focus of the activities often deals with fantasy scenarios, the personal experiences and stories of the participants inform the themes and situations explored through the drama. Through the workshops, we have become more conscious of the opportunities for the students to have fun whilst learning. Students were overwhelmingly positive about the workshops, particularly the contrast to their usual lessons.

Play through collaborative drama exercises enables the students to focus more on the clients' abilities rather than their disabilities as they work together for a shared outcome. The clients invariably have more theatre experience than the students, as a result the clients often lead in the activities reversing the usual power balance found in the doctor/patient relationship. Through non-didactic learning and cooperative negotiation, the clients experience an equality of voice and status they do not usually experience in healthcare settings.

As well as the students desire to have more fun learning, we noted that the clients came away with reduced anxiety about clinical environments and the health professionals with whom they come into contact in their real lives. It also helped cultivate a feeling of being valued and that their voices were being heard. We are currently seeking a way in which to embed this in the curriculum permanently so that all students can benefit including those who might shy away from more creative projects and who are arguably more in need of help with their communication skills.

29

Exploration: Building the Abstract—Metaphorical Play-Doh® Modelling in Health Sciences

Rachel Stead

This exploration discusses an ongoing research project established in 2014 with Health Science students at the University of Surrey, which engages nurses, midwives, paramedics and operating department practitioners in making metaphorical Play-Doh® models of abstract concepts from their studies. The author is a Learning Developer supporting students from our Faculty of Health and Medical Sciences. These students are expected to be highly reflective, forge links between theory and practice, and articulate the meanings of abstract concepts in critical discussions from their first year. However, they typically include a high percentage of under-represented students (i.e. mature learners) from non-traditional routes to HE, for whom discussion of the impersonal and abstract is extremely challenging. This exploration examines the rationale and key underpinning literature for the workshop, an outline of the activity and discussion of perceived benefits to student learning. To finish, the author outlines other recent work following similar approaches.

R. Stead (✉)
University of Surrey, Guildford, UK
e-mail: r.stead@surrey.ac.uk

© The Author(s) 2019
A. James and C. Nerantzi (eds.), *The Power of Play in Higher Education*,
https://doi.org/10.1007/978-3-319-95780-7_29

Background

My initial foray into playful practices four years ago was driven by a desire to inject more fun into my teaching which, according to James and Brookfield (2014), helps students take a more critical approach to their work and deepens understandings of difficult concepts. This desire was coupled with simultaneous frustration over student expectations of pre-packaged solutions and 'correct' ways of approaching academic tasks. Because much learning is what Morrison (2002, in Cohen et al. 2007) terms 'emergent or constructed', our role as developers of learning in HE is not to try to determine what is learnt, but rather to create appropriate conditions for learning to occur. The creativity and risk-taking inherent in play are two key conditions under which learning will most likely flourish (McIntosh and Warren 2013), yet little space is made for these within our 'testist' education culture, favouring prescription and measurement (see Barrington 2004).

Despite varying definitions, one consensus in the literature is that play or playfulness is as crucial for adults as it is for children (Brown 2009), for feeding the imagination, driving creativity and developing problem-solving skills (Ackermann 2004; Robinson 2006). Gray (2013) defines play as voluntary, process-driven, self-directed and imaginative. To him, play has no prescribed rules and players should be active but relaxed. This aligns well with our metaphorical modelling because the self-directed nature of play in the workshops and the intrinsic motivation borne of this is what makes it so educationally powerful (Gray 2013).

Underpinning Theory

A number of multidisciplinary theories underpin these workshops, and whilst space here does not permit in-depth examination, a brief summary below helps to explain their pedagogical significance.

The project is grounded in Papert's Constructionism, which explores the ways the makers of creative artefacts discuss what they make, leading to reflection, and self-directed construction of new knowledge

(Ackermann 2004). From a psychological perspective, creating a metaphorical model of an abstract concept draws on what Jung termed the 'creative unconscious' (in Gauntlett 2007), containing the often hard-to-express but nonetheless powerful, emotional and tacit knowledge gained through experience. It is argued that Western societies tend simultaneously to overestimate the power of conscious thinking whilst undervaluing tacit or embodied knowledge (Jung, n.d. in Gauntlett 2007; Sotto 2007; Ridley and Rogers 2010).

A central tenet of Constructionism is that concrete thinking is an alternative and complementary way of representing the world, which Sotto (2007) terms holistic thinking. Modelling concepts makes them tangible and concrete, aiding discussion, in an education system where privilege is awarded to knowledge that is 'abstract, impersonal, and detached from the knower' (Papert and Harel 1991) and other forms of knowledge are viewed as inferior. Attaching verbal meanings to models and their components, which are personal and subjective, and sharing them, promotes discussion of multiple individual perspectives (Sotto 2007) and subsequently reflection, the objective of which is learning and improvement.

A great deal of research has explored the relationship between the hands and cognitive and emotional processes, too extensive to explore here. However, one influential neuroscientist and author, Wilson (1999), argues that the hand figures critically in cognitive, emotional and physical development, with a fundamental role to play in art, design, music, language and communication, expressing emotions, construction and many other human endeavours. This can be explained from a scientific perspective by looking at the disproportionately large section of the primary cortex in the human brain dedicated to the hands, fingers and thumbs which means engaging the hands in manipulating materials, such as Play-Doh®, activates millions of neural pathways. In addition to the fine motor stimulus, if other stimuli are activated, for example auditory (via discussion) and visual (via the colours and visual impact of the models) and even olfactory (the smell of the Play-Doh® invoking experiential memories from childhood), the potential for deep learning is enriched (Carlson 1998).

The Workshops

We ran two workshops: one with 20 final-year dissertation students and one with 27 first years preparing their first essay. The workshops did not replace our usual learning and writing development workshops, were purely voluntary and were offered as an additional opportunity to discuss and reflect upon difficult concepts from within their essays or dissertations in order to deepen understanding.

The Preamble

Rather than simply a characteristic of language, metaphor is common place. It is central to understanding experiences, enabling discussion of intangible concepts such as life and death, love, knowledge and time (see Lakoff and Johnson 2003). So it was crucial at the start of the session to establish levels of understanding and then to encourage the students to use metaphor, however personal, in order to be able to participate fully in the activity.

The Main Activity

The individual Play-Doh® modelling exercise involved creating, in 15 minutes, a representation of one or more key concepts, e.g. advocacy, spirituality, ethics (from their professional codes of practice), with which they were struggling in their work. Participants were given very few guidelines and no specific rules to follow. In small groups of 4 or 5, the students then shared their models, explaining the significance of particular components and relating these to any personal meanings the build had brought to the fore. Articulating their thinking generated much discussion, questions from others and reflection on both their models and the building process. From my own and my observers' perspectives, the conversations throughout the building stage were as powerful and insightful as the reflections which followed (see Papert and Harel 1991). Participants were also actively encouraged to take

Fig. 29.1 Metaphorical models of barriers to trust, advocacy and death in Play-Doh®

photographs of their models in order to reinforce their memory and prompt later reflection. Below are examples of models from both workshops (Fig. 29.1).

Evaluation

Whilst ethical approval was deemed unnecessary by the University, students were asked to sign release forms for images and feedback collected during the workshop. Data was collected via individual reflective questionnaires, whole group debriefing, and observer comments. Overall, evaluations were extremely positive, with 72% (34 out of 47) reporting that they found the workshop beneficial in terms of positive development and only 6.5% (3 people) reporting no perceived benefits from participating. There were very few wholly negative responses, and even those who reported no perceived benefits evaluated the session as fun, relaxing and thought-provoking. The results, in fact, showed far more engagement and perceived benefits than initially predicted.

We didn't win everyone over but this is to be expected when individual attitudes, cultural preconceptions and learning preferences are taken into consideration. The most powerful negative comment, 'I can't do art and it's not necessary for science', is value-laden and contentious and deserves far more unpicking than this paper has scope for. Among the more considered negative responses, however, was that it simply did not suit a student's learning style, but these comments were in the minority. What is important to remember is that these are individuals' perceptions and, therefore, not empirical evidence that learning either has or has not occurred. Unsurprisingly, overarching themes of 'creativity' and 'learning styles' emerged in the data. However, others of greater pedagogical significance to the project aims are summarised below.

Themed Findings and Discussion

When asked what they liked about the workshop, the students responded largely in two ways: what they were 'allowed' to do and what they liked 'not having to do'. What they seemed to enjoy was being allowed to express themselves physically, use their hands and put their ideas into model form. And many students reported their appreciation of not having to write anything down and the freedom of not having to use language to express their ideas. The ability to avoid using language, or as one student put it, 'it's easier to express without words', resonates with Gauntlett's (2007) findings that language is not necessarily the best way to explain the coexistence and interrelatedness of separate concepts. The use of models instead allows ideas and relationships to be presented without the need to arrange them in a set order. Gauntlett (2007) argues that due to the challenge some students face in discussing complex abstract concepts, creative research methods provide a powerful alternative, and this is one of the driving forces behind this project. Alternative ways of seeing, helping the brain to work in new ways and permission to think outside the 'normal boxes', were also recurrent themes in the data as well as being dyslexic (4 students self-identified). These responses point to the possibility of projects like this contributing to a more inclusive learning and teaching environment in line with recent government-endorsed statements (see Department for Education 2017).

Another notable trend throughout the feedback relates to the memorable nature of this activity. Students felt that models served as useful mnemonics for revision and could help with learning human anatomy. This relates very well to James' (2013) findings that the three dimensional, sensory nature of the approach, in her case with LEGO® SERIOUS PLAY®, is what makes it memorable. This was not a surprise outcome, however, it was encouraging to see these ideas emerging unprompted from the students.

The workshops certainly proved meaningful and thought-provoking. Building models, it was reported, provoked deeper thinking about the topics and helped participants gain greater, or indeed new, perspective on their role as health care professionals. They also felt it allowed them to get in touch with how they felt about particular subjects. This last point resonates with both Gauntlett's (2007) and James' (2013) work, and is particularly significant for reflective assignments, but also for other types of academic writing where it is nonetheless important to separate personal emotions from objective academic statements. It was apparent that the activity gave participants a strong visual reference to distinguish between the descriptive and emotive in their concepts. One student reported, 'it reminds me that everything is attached to emotions - but you feel that you have to separate them at uni (sic)'.

The following comments are of particular value to this research reflecting one of the central constructionist themes: that participants do not tend to plan, nor indeed need to know what to build before they begin (Ackermann 2004). Students reported that, 'it made me create and then think about why' and 'my ideas developed while I was building'. This is reminiscent of writer's block: once an individual begins to manipulate and work with the materials, be they Play-Doh® or words for example in freewriting, ideas will start to build. In playful building activities, eventually the imagination takes over and inner unconscious thoughts and memories can surface (Papert and Harel 1991). Several responses about feeling more focused, 'when my hands were busy' closely mirror both Wilson's (1999) and Carlson's (1998) research regarding the activation of multiple neural pathways when the hands are engaged in building.

Keywords which surfaced repeatedly in the feedback were *informal, calm, relaxing, therapeutic* and *fun*. Whilst perhaps not directly educational, these factors are nonetheless significant at a time when the mental well-being of university students is reported by Universities UK to be at an all-time low (Coughlan 2015) leading to both an increase in demand for counselling services and rising dropout rates (Yeung et al. 2016; Marsh 2017). Students enjoyed the calm environment, found the activity itself to be stress-relieving, and this was recognised by some as beneficial to their learning styles, particularly for but not limited to those with dyslexia.

As previously stated though, not all feedback was positive. There was a recurrent fear of 'doing it wrong' and some initial scepticism due to the lack of explicit instructions and students being unaccustomed to learning this way. One particular student reported finding it 'scary to have no rules'. These feelings are not unusual. Peabody and Noyes (2017) report a similar situation of their students being expected to switch into a different mode of learning and being 'temporarily separated from what is known' in what Mezirow (1991) terms a 'disorienting dilemma' but one which is fundamental to transformative learning. On the plus side, most reported the discomfort to be short-lived and that the novelty of the activity made it fun, 'a different but enjoyable experiment'.

Challenges

Notwithstanding the usual issues of time, large cohorts and limited resources, the main difficulty was collecting useful feedback from students about their learning. Many struggle to evaluate a session objectively if their perception is that their immediate needs were not met, however clearly stated the objectives are from the outset. To give an example, the few students, who negatively appraised the workshop due to it not directly helping them to write their essay, not only missed the point of the workshop but may negatively have impacted upon their own openness to engage in activity which could in fact have had a positive effect on their current piece of work. When compared to other students who reported that they felt better prepared for their assignments, it serves to highlight the complexity of learning (Morrison 2002, in Cohen et al. 2007), and the differences in what students take away from the same activity. According to Marton and Saljo (1976: 10), 'A highly significant aspect of learning is…the diversity of ways in which the same phenomenon, concept or principle is apprehended by different students', which is clearly relevant to this project. What I have found particularly enabling though is the encouragement and freedom I have been afforded by my department and staff in faculty to try out new approaches.

How Has Play Changed My Practice?

This project, and others since, has had a profound effect on my teaching: it has made me less risk-averse and has taught me to seek innovative means by which to elicit ideas from students. The focus now is always on drawing out from them what they already know, even if they are unaware of this prior knowledge, and highlighting its significance as a starting point. Using playful making-to-learn approaches such as Play-Doh® and LSP has highlighted how much we may be missing in terms of accessing and harbouring the knowledge and the capacities of our students.

Related Work with Play-Doh® and LEGO® SERIOUS PLAY®

The playful learning agenda is gaining momentum at the University of Surrey, with continuing professional development (CPD) sessions now running for new teaching staff, using both Play-Doh® and LEGO® to explore approaches to teaching troublesome knowledge in their disciplines. My most recent research with Child Nursing (the subject of an upcoming paper) has been the application of LEGO® SERIOUS

PLAY® methodology to critical thinking and care planning, and collaborations are ongoing with BSc Acting courses using LSP for conceptual understanding. Play-Doh® has also been trialed extensively with great success in Veterinary Medicine for teaching and revising anatomy (the subject of another upcoming paper) and in Electrical Engineering for shrinking transistors. Despite the literal nature of the building in these Play-Doh® sessions, they nevertheless prove playful, engaging and memorable learning experiences.

References

Ackermann, E. K. (2004). Constructing Knowledge and Transforming the World. In M. Tokoro & L. Steels (Eds.), *A Learning Zone of One's Own: Sharing Representations and Flow in Collaborative Learning Environments*. Available at http://jotamac.typepad.com/jotamacs_weblog/files/Constructing_Knowledge_Ackermann2004.pdf. Accessed May 30, 2018.

Barrington, E. (2004). Teaching to Student Diversity in Higher Education: How Multiple Intelligence Theory Can Help. *Teaching in Higher Education, 9*(4), 421–434. Available at http://dx.doi.org/10.1080/1356251042000252363. Accessed May 30, 2018.

Brown, S. (2009). *Play Is More Than Just Fun*. TED Talk. Available at http://www.ted.com/talks/stuart_brown_says_play_is_more_than_fun_it_s_vital. Accessed June 16, 2017.

Carlson, N. R. (1998). *Physiology of Behaviour* (6th ed.). Boston: Allyn and Bacon.

Cohen, L., Manion, L., & Morrison, K. (2007). *Research Methods in Education* (6th ed.). London and New York: Routledge.

Coughlan, S. (2015). Rising Number of Stressed Students Seek Help. *BBC News*. Available at http://www.bbc.co.uk/news/education-34354405. Accessed May 30, 2018.

Department for Education. (2017). *Inclusive Teaching and Learning in Higher Education*. Available at https://www.gov.uk/government/publications/inclusive-teaching-and-learning-in-higher-education. Accessed June 21, 2017.

Gauntlett, D. (2007). *Creative Explorations: New Approaches to Identities and Audiences*. London: Routledge.

Gray, P. (2013). Play as Preparation for Learning and Life. *The American Journal of Play* (Spring). Available at http://www.journalofplay.org/sites/www.journalofplay.org/files/pdf-articles/5-3-interview-play-as-preparation.pdf. Accessed May 30, 2018.

James, A. (2013, November). Lego Serious Play: A Three-Dimensional Approach to Learning Development. *Journal of Learning Development in Higher Education* (6).

James, A., & Brookfield, S. D. (2014). *Engaging Imagination: Helping Students Become Creative and Reflective Learners.* San Francisco: Jossey-Bass.

Lakoff, G., & Johnson, M. (2003). *Metaphors We Live By.* Chicago and London: University of Chicago Press.

Marsh, S. (2017, May 23). Number of University Dropouts Due to Mental Health Problems Trebles. *The Guardian.* Available at https://www.theguardian.com/society/2017/may/23/number-university-dropouts-due-to-mental-health-problems-trebles. Accessed May 30, 2018.

Marton, F., & Saljo, R. (1976). On Qualitative Differences in Learning: I—Outcome and Process. *British Journal of Educational Psychology, 46,* 4–11.

McIntosh, P., & Warren, D. (Eds.). (2013). *Creativity in the Classroom: Case Studies in Using the Arts in Teaching and Learning in Higher Education.* Bristol, UK: Intellect (ebook).

Mezirow, J. (1991). *Transformative Dimensions of Adult Learning.* San Francisco, CA: Jossey-Bass.

Papert, S., & Harel, I. (1991). *Constructionism.* Available at http://www.papert.org/articles/SituatingConstructionism.html. Accessed February 16, 2014.

Peabody, M. A., & Noyes, S. (2017). *Reflective Boot Camp: Adapting LEGO® SERIOUS PLAY® in Higher Education.* Available at http://www.tandfonline.com/doi/pdf/10.1080/14623943.2016.1268117?needAccess=true. Accessed June 20, 2017.

Ready Set Design. Available at http://cdn.cooperhewitt.org/2011/09/02/Ready%20Set%20Design%20vX.pdf. Accessed June 21, 2017.

Ridley, P., & Rogers, A. (2010). *Drawing to Learn: Clinical Education, Health and Social Care.* Brighton: Visual Learning in Higher Education Series, University of Brighton, Learnhigher.

Robinson, K. (2006). How Schools Kill Creativity. [ONLINE] Available at http://www.ted.com/talks/ken_robinson_says_schools_kill_creativity.html. Accessed December 2017.

Sotto, E. (2007). *When Teaching Becomes Learning: A Theory and Practice of Teaching* (2nd ed.). London: Continuum International Publishing Group.

Wilson, F. (1999). *The Hand: How Its Use Shapes the Brain, Language and Human Culture.* New York: Vintage Books.

Yeung, P., Weale, S., & Perraudin, F. (2016, September 23). University Mental Health Services Face Strain as Demand Rises 50%. *The Guardian.* Available at https://www.theguardian.com/education/2016/sep/23/university-mental-health-services-face-strain-as-demand-rises-50. Accessed May 30, 2018.

30

Sketch: Our Learning Journey with LEGO®

Alison James and Chrissi Nerantzi

For nearly a decade, we have been using play in HE to create stimulating learning and development experiences that are immersive and explorative. We discuss these in detail elsewhere (e.g. James 2013, 2015, 2016; James and Brookfield 2014; Nerantzi 2015; Nerantzi and Despard, 2014; Nerantzi and McCusker 2014; Nerantzi et al. 2015), in particular our extensive use of the LEGO® SERIOUS PLAY® methodology in higher education. Here we summarise part of that activity to emphasise the extent to which playful methods can become embedded in the fabric of university learning.

We were part of an 'advance guard' of accredited practitioners applying these techniques in HE, at a time when play was still a taboo for

---

A. James (✉)
University of Winchester, Winchester, UK
e-mail: alison.james@winchester.ac.uk

C. Nerantzi
Centre for Excellence in Learning and Teaching,
Manchester Metropolitan University, Manchester, UK
e-mail: c.nerantzi@mmu.ac.uk

© The Author(s) 2019
A. James and C. Nerantzi (eds.), *The Power of Play in Higher Education*,
https://doi.org/10.1007/978-3-319-95780-7_30

many in universities. We were greatly influenced by the work of David Gauntlett, a pioneer of research in collaboration with the LEGO® Group. David also produced a community guide to the method which can be found online (2010) and Alison created a guide for the Higher Education Academy (James 2015).

We were accredited by the LEGO® SERIOUS PLAY® Master Trainers and this certainly contributed to the credibility of what we were doing for our institutions and beyond. We draw on its metaphorical and constructionist approach to create 3-D models of experiences, ideas and actions in HE contexts. The method involves posing a question, building a response, sharing that response and then reflecting on the discussion and the insights. Questions and topics are any to which there is no straightforward answer and have included aspects of academic development, personal learning and goals, stuckness, motivation, quality of teaching, evaluation, industrial collaboration, research supervision, Erasmus partnerships and school outreach activities. Constructions are created individually first but can also be collaboratively produced, resulting in intricate and colourful LEGO® landscapes. While these can have powerful meanings for participants, they can also look mystifying to anyone who has not been part of their physical construction. This is an important and symbolic illustration of the importance of being present and participating in play; it is not possible to miss these sessions and ask for the handouts you missed in compensation. Even when colleagues take away photographs and videos of their constructions these cannot fully recreate the feeling and depth of the exploration together.

From early on, we have adopted an evidence-based approach to our use of LEGO® and have carried out research in this area, informed by our work in universities and also beyond. In conjunction with this, we have both—especially Chrissi—used social and open media to disseminate LEGO® practices and inspire others to adopt these. We want participants in our workshops to learn to use the techniques just as they would other approaches or strategies, so they can grow and develop in their application of them. Outside the academic arena we have both used the methods for professional coaching, at conferences, even during open online courses, webinars and tweetchats. We have found the method to have a complexity and robustness that lends itself to any discipline and can transform academics' wariness of engaging with it into recognition of how it can inspire insights and learning. We hope our forthcoming separate publication on practices and proponents of LEGO® SERIOUS PLAY® in HE will become a useful guide for practitioners in multiple university settings.

References

Gauntlett, D. (2010). *Open-Source: Introduction to LEGO® SERIOUS PLAY®.* Available at http://davidgauntlett.com/wp-content/uploads/2013/04/LEGO_SERIOUS_PLAY_OpenSource_14mb.pdf. Accessed May 30, 2018.

James, A. (2013). Lego Serious Play: A Three Dimensional Approach to Learning Development. *Journal for Learning Development in Higher Education, 6.* ISSN:1759-667X.

James, A. (2015). *Innovative Pedagogical Practices: Innovating in the Creative Arts with LEGO.* Commissioned by the Higher Education Academy. Available at https://www.heacademy.ac.uk/innovating-creative-arts-lego.

James, A. (2016). Play and 3D Enquiry for Stimulating Creative Learning. In L. Watts & P. Blessinger (Eds.), *Creative Learning: International Perspectives and Approaches in Higher Education. Routledge.* New York: Routledge.

James, A., & Brookfield, S. (2014). *Engaging Imagination: Helping Students Become Creative and Reflective Thinkers.* San Francisco: Jossey-Bass.

Nerantzi, C. (2015, June). The Playground Model for Creative Professional Development. In C. Nerantzi & A. James (Eds.), *Exploring Play in Higher Education, Creative Academic Magazine* (Issue 2A, pp. 40–50). Available at http://www.creativeacademic.uk/.

Nerantzi, C., & Despard, C. (2014). Lego Models to Aid Reflection: Enhancing the Summative Assessment Experience in the Context of Professional Discussions Within Accredited Academic Development Provision. *Journal of Perspectives in Applied Academic Practice, 2*(2), 31–36. Edinburgh Napier University. Available at http://jpaap.napier.ac.uk/index.php/JPAAP/article/view/81. Accessed May 30, 2018.

Nerantzi, C., & McCusker, S. (2014). A Taster of the LEGO® Serious Play® Method for Higher Education. *OER14 Conference Proceedings.* Available at http://www.medev.ac.uk/oer14/19/view/.

Nerantzi, C., Moravej, H., & Johnson, F. (2015). Play Brings Openness or Using a Creative Approach to Evaluate an Undergraduate Unit and Move Forward Together. *Journal of Perspectives in Applied Academic Practice, 3*(2), 82–91. Available at http://jpaap.napier.ac.uk/index.php/JPAAP/article/view/141. Accessed May 30, 2018.

31

Sketch: Using LEGO® to Explore 'Professional Love' as an Element of Youth Work Practice—Opportunities and Obstacles

Martin E. Purcell

LEGO® was used with two cohorts of second year Youth Work students in sessions designed to encourage discussion about themselves and their practice, and about education as: dialogue, transformation, and an 'act of love' (Freire 1970). Specifically, the sessions sought to deepen students' understanding of the concept of 'professional love' (Page 2014; Purcell 2018), acknowledging the importance of 'love' in professional relationships between adult practitioners and young people in their care, both to strengthen the relationship and to enhance the young person's sense of self-worth and flourishing.

Activities where students used models to represent themselves as practitioners generated candid self-appraisals: "There's a flower on my head, coz I'm a bit of a plant pot"; "I'm a Princess, *with Jesus on my shoulders*". Such revelations opened spaces for conversations not previously pursued (e.g. convictions and aspirations), helping strengthen bonds of mutual support and understanding.

M. E. Purcell (✉)
University of Huddersfield, Huddersfield, UK
e-mail: m.purcell@hud.ac.uk

Students demonstrated enthusiasm, imagination and humour in their discussions. Dialogue stimulated by their freeform creations allowed participants to discuss themselves freely in their role as Youth Workers. They displayed a profound awareness of the purpose and challenges of their profession, the modelling opening up broader and deeper discourse within the groups, including discussions around 'professional love'—a concept that students often struggle to grasp. Although students became less fluid in their discussion about this concept ("Love made my ladder fall down"), they articulated benefits of bringing 'love' into professional relationships with young people: "I wanted to show I could empathise with the young person, to show that I kind of know where they're coming from, and help them cope".

Metaphors repeated throughout both sessions. Several students said ladders allow them to support young people's progress towards their own goals (one positioning herself with a young person at the bottom of the ladder, saying she encourages them to take "one step at a time; don't rush them; let them go at their own pace"). Other metaphors included 'toolkits' of artefacts or activities, with students ascribing specific functions or characteristics to some LEGO® pieces. Fencing featured in several representations of practice: sometimes representing professional boundaries (although one participant cautioned: "I don't want it too high, or we'll never make connections"); alternatively representing "protection", "safeguarding" and "promoting young people's wellbeing and safety".

While concentrating on the exercises, different neural networks seemed to open up in some participants' brains, occasionally revealing the darker side of their personality: "I love it when people fail" claimed the usually most caring member of one cohort; participants cheered her hubris soon after, as her own model collapsed. For other students, however, the process remained alien, with one asserting "I feel the session was great for others, but not for me. I don't feel I'm imaginative enough to work with LEGO®". The session left her feeling tearful and exposed, and prompted me to ensure other resources were available for the second session.

This kind of play has brought a new dynamic into my teaching, embedding dialogical learning at its heart, and profoundly enhancing students' understanding of their professional identity.

References

Freire, P. (1970). *Pedagogy of the Oppressed*. New York: Continuum.

Page, J. (2014). Developing 'Professional Love' in Early Childhood Settings. In L. Harrison & J. Sumsion (Eds.), *Lived Spaces of Infant-Toddler Education and Care—Exploring Diverse Perspectives on Theory, Research, Practice and Policy* (1st ed., pp. 119–130). London: Springer.

Purcell, M. E. (2018). Investigating the Transformational Potential of 'Professional Love' in Work with Young People. *Radical Community Work Journal, 3*(1), 14pp.

32

Sketch: Creating LEGO® Representations of Theory

Nicola Simmons

Sir Ken Robinson notes that 'the dominant forms of education actively stifle the conditions that are essential to creative development' (2001: 49). In resistance to these dominant forms, I use play-based activities with Masters of Education (M.Ed.) students to help them uncover implicit thinking and lateral connections.

Over the years I have found that integrating LEGO® play into my classroom has helped alleviate student stress and, more importantly, supports students conceptualising and synthesising their ideas. Innovative thinking in play may require stepping from linear paths and bringing a more creative flow to cognitive processes (Gauntlett 2007). With adult students, play helps students set aside preconceptions of the 'right' answer or approach, allows them to laugh at themselves a bit, and engages a more holistic perspective on the task at hand.

M.Ed. students often struggle learning to synthesise theories towards new models. I invite them to play with LEGO® to make their thoughts

N. Simmons (✉)
Brock University, St. Catharines, ON, Canada
e-mail: nsimmons@brocku.ca

© The Author(s) 2019
A. James and C. Nerantzi (eds.), *The Power of Play in Higher Education*,
https://doi.org/10.1007/978-3-319-95780-7_32

about theory concrete. I purposely provide few if any instructions, simply providing an assortment of LEGO® and asking them to start building, and as they put together the blocks, to think about how their constructions are like the theory about which they are writing. The play allows them to move their thinking forward; often they create lateral connections of which they were not consciously aware. Students say this unlocks their thinking by allowing them to think about theory applications in concrete terms:

> It is a great way for me to see connections and themes that may not have occurred to me.
> Her creative assignments allowed for more learning than I have gained in any other course this semester.

Much of my teaching is about identity development. Building on Gauntlett's (2007) work in which clients construct their identities with LEGO®, my graduate students play their way into understanding. Playing with LEGO® allows childlike inquiry, with a focus on thinking processes instead of pursuing the 'right answer.'

In addition, students have commented on how LEGO® breaks their writer's block:

> My greatest challenge of the entire program is writing ... I can explain the entire paper but to put it on paper it then becomes a struggle. This assisted me in finding words to put to writing.

In summary, LEGO®: (1) provides a platform for creative play that may lead to innovation, (2) helps students make their implicit ideas concrete, and (3) supports students conceptualising their ideas, allowing them to literally construct relationships amongst topics as they play. In one student's words:

> It surprised me how much it contributed since on the surface it seemed to be a very playful activity. But maybe because of this freedom of mind, it actually allowed you to do some free associations and make connections with the work. This activity helped me to reflect on what I considered were the key concepts of this course.

References

Gauntlett, D. (2007). *Creative Explorations: New Approaches to Identities and Audiences*. Abingdon, Oxon: Routledge.

Robinson, K. (2001). *Out of Our Minds: Learning to be Creative*. Westford, MA: Capstone.

Part VI

Gamers and Puzzlers

33

Exploration: A Dancer and a Writer Walk into a Classroom

Seth Hudson and Boris Willis

Introduction

Incorporating play-centric learning into higher education may seem like a stretch in some disciplines, and though it may seem an obvious fit in the emerging field of computer game design, the conventions of higher education still present challenges. For us, play is exploration. All games provide an opportunity space that allows players to express themselves through interacting with the world of the game (Salen and Zimmerman 2004) and our classes are no different. Keeping game design principles in mind through course and exercise development allows us to engage students as we might players, challenging them to excel rather than demanding they follow rigid instructions.

S. Hudson (✉) · B. Willis
George Mason University, Fairfax, VA, USA
e-mail: shudson3@gmu.edu

B. Willis
e-mail: bwillis3@gmu.edu

Backgrounds in dance and writing mean years of experience teaching from different professional perspectives, but years teaching game design have allowed us to harness our prior knowledge, and experiences, of play. Through personal narratives and reflection on classroom experience, what follows is an exploration of two game design professors embracing play in the college classroom.

Journeys Back to Play

The Dancer, Boris: There were several impactful moments in my life as a designer of games and dances. After seeing Mikhail Baryshnikov on the children's television show *Captain Kangaroo* as I kid, I wanted nothing more than to dance. The episode found Baryshnikov arguing with one of the show's main characters Mr. Moose, a moose puppet, that male dancers were not sissies. My desire to entertain made me somewhat of a class clown; I looked to make everyone laugh. I did just that until my mother's calls to discipline myself finally, and perhaps unfortunately, succeeded. She pushed me to grow up fast and contain my enthusiasm. My ability to learn as my authentic class-clown self was stifled in order to meet traditional expectations of a model student.

The Writer, Seth: As a youngster, school provided more social interaction than it did intellectual or creative stimulation. As a faculty member reflecting back on that period in my development, I realize that playfulness learned outside of the classroom really drives my practice. This playfulness was manifested through a game called *Spontaneous*.

Spontaneous was a component of the Odyssey of the Mind program, a competitive months-long problem-solving competition for teams of youngsters from around the globe. Sitting around a table with a deck of cards, ace through five: "Name containers and things they contain." "Explain what's happening in the Rembrandt's *The Night Watch*." In turns dictated by the flip of a card, our team would produce as many answers to the same question in the allotted time—not one narrative for *The Night Watch*, but as many as we could concoct in a few minutes. The five of us sat in a quiet room with the judges looking on, competing with teams we could neither see nor hear. Frustration, laughter, and a range of competitive emotions were all at play.

Both

Spontaneous showed Seth the potential to amplify creativity in competitive, collaborative setting. Reflecting back, he sees it as one of the most vital contributors to his higher-order thinking skills. Boris's reflection on struggling with the constraints of traditional student expectations still serve as a constant reminder that students learn best through exploration while being true to their authentic selves.

Playing in the Classroom

Even after decades of living, learning, and teaching, those play experiences are still a part our practice. Our students tend to be avid game players with ample experience playing and discussing the medium they are so passionate about. Some even begin making games before they step foot on campus. They, like many others, assume that work in computer game design will happen in front of a monitor, spending hours coding, animating, and creating audio for an interactive experience. As such, our playful approaches to teaching can throw them a bit off guard at first. The following classroom narratives offer a look.

The Dancer: When students walk into my game design studio class the first day, I introduce myself and then ask them to leave. The first assignment is to go out into the world, off campus, and take photos of a sculpture. They must go on a journey, examine art, experience nature, observe lighting, and listen to sound as the first step in creating a game experience.

Curious looks from students reveal their assumptions. Students prepared to ask questions like "What software will we be using?" or "Do I have to know C++?" instead of leave on a sculpture hunt. Upon returning students are directed to recreate the scene captured in their photos using a game engine, the creation software where digital games are ultimately built.

Setting the tone of the course with this playful act is challenging and fun, but fun isn't the goal. From day one, students learn that our focus is creating experiences rather than merely learning software.

The Writer: "This class is where fun comes to die." I repeat this statement multiple times throughout my game design courses. While it tends to get a laugh, it also serves to remind students that the playful work we do in the classroom is ultimately designed to provide rigorous preparation in the field of games. In my writing course, after a brief introduction, the first day looks like this:

Write me a 100-word story.

Mouse clicks and keystrokes are heard as some students begin; I interrupt the students.

You may not use any word more than once.

Near silence. Some students smile as their eyes widen at the challenge; others draw their hands away from the keyboard with looks of confusion or timidity. After asking students to wait while I field questions, they are invited to begin. But…

You have ten minutes. Bon courage.

Students take a few precious moments to consider strategy, basic story, and characters, but soon find that tactics are more vital than creative invention in approaching this task. The game at hand has the simple goal of finishing rather than crafting a masterpiece.

It is exercises of this kind, driven by competition and play, that make class meetings most valuable to students. The rationale of this activity is explained to students upon completion, highlighting the importance of creative flexibility in the field and the role of such exercises in our course. As one student recalled, "You do kill fun in this class, but then we build it back up again."

A Dancer and a Writer Walk into a Classroom

We have some major theoretical differences in our approach to teaching and creation, due in large part to our disparate disciplinary backgrounds. Play is the central factor that unites our pedagogies.

The Dancer: I understand the importance of play in any artistic process. Every work begins with an idea that transforms into something more practical or coherent. The evolution of the initial idea depends on the creator's ability to work within the constraints of the project; play gives time and space for those explorations.

The Writer: Over the years I have developed a firm, at least for now, belief that although artistic expression and creativity are fundamental to the process. A pragmatic, craft-based approach is the key to creative writing development. The rhetorical situation can be understood as the rules of the game; the writing is how you play it.

As experienced faculty in higher education, we now realize that our former, playful selves are at the core of our teaching identities. Boris' experience with dance opened his eyes as a student, feeling empowered with the freedom of creativity valued by that discipline; Seth's hours of playful practice with his Odyssey of the Mind teammates showed him how the constraints of competition can breed creativity.

Learning the Rules of the Game

Students must play. We must provide a learning experience that, much like a game world, rewards exploration. Boris' students gain XP, game speak for experience points, for completing and iterating work—a technique outlined in Lee Sheldon's *The Multiplayer Classroom: Designing Coursework as a Game* (2012). Rather than a linear progression of assignment and execution, followed by summative assessment, students have freedom to approach assignments at different times. The course is designed so that students must revise and resubmit work until it fulfills the associated learning outcome just as they would replay levels in a game.

Failure must be followed by reflection. Harnessing the power of play and encouraging students to explore requires failure, the freedom to iterate. Seth's students learn to make use of failure through reflection. Exercises like the 100-word story mentioned above are thankless tasks. Once students realize that it is nearly impossible to create something polished within the constraints given, they can free themselves of anxiety and just write. To help students learn they reflect on the experience: "What were their first impressions when given the prompt?" "Why was it difficult to complete?" Incorporating reflection with playful acts reveals their importance to students, they begin to understand the value of play. These honest self-assessments allow greater insight into student growth.

Playful professors must be prepared for challenges. The two preceding examples share challenges in assessment. While our years of experience have solidified its value in instruction, play still faces scrutiny in higher education for not being properly academic. Students, along with their parents and institution administrators, are steeped in the conventions of our American education system structured around letter grades A through F that are often accompanied with percentage-based scoring. Unfortunately, play may seem extraneous to the goals of students solely focused on getting a good grade rather than growing creatively and intellectually.

The Potential of Play

Playful approaches actually benefit from preconceived notions that play is casual and childlike, centered on fun. Rather than assessing students on a scale that places them at some increment below a perfect, 100% A+, these approaches encourage students to explore and try new things. While all game design starts on paper, creating the space and rules for players' interaction, those initial design ideas must be tested through play. Implementing a design is akin to cooking in this way; following a recipe to the letter and using the finest ingredients doesn't ensure the quality of the final product, it is the taste of the food that matters (Despain and Acosta 2013). To assess the quality of their work, our students must play. Realizing the following affordances of play have helped us demonstrate the value of this approach.

Professional Development

Providing students with an education that prepares them for the relatively young, ill-defined field of game design—few practices are standard across the games industry (Newman 2013)—requires finding novel approaches to instruction. With no definitive list of what students need to know or be able to do, instruction that focuses on creativity, collaboration, and communication is called for: playful approaches are most conducive to meeting these goals. Pedagogy that gives primacy to process, rather than product, is the key.

The Writer: Writing courses that focus on what we want students to do, more than what we want them to know, best prepare them for life post-graduation (Russell 2001). Learning to write through these games requires great effort: one high-performing student used to top marks complained, "My brain hurts." This "effortful" learning results in strengthened mental representations associated with retrieval and making connections (Brown et al. 2014), but it also aids in students' professional development by requiring them to work collaboratively in order to solve problems.

Given rising tuition costs and mounting student debt, the value of a university degree is under continual scrutiny (Selingo 2013). Students expect an education that prepares them for the professional world post-graduation, but there is no set path to the games industry. A pedagogical approach that values collaborative process prepares students for far more than filling an entry-level position at a company. Playful approaches to instruction demand flexibility and creativity of students, perhaps preparing students for jobs that may not yet exist.

Empowerment

The potential of play beyond enhanced teaching and learning is empowerment, offering students motivation beyond marks, and fear of failure. Creating a learning environment that complicates prevailing structures of education opens new paths for student development

The Dancer: When I took my first dance class, my world changed. I felt smart, capable, and empowered to make a contribution. Dancers create moments of play in the improvisation of movement that ultimately becomes choreography. In some of my classes, students create movement-focused games for the XBox Kinect.

Rather than have them focus on conceptualizing an experience for the player, they start with the movement itself—using their bodies to get a visceral sense of what they as players would enjoy experiencing. This challenges their notions of what it means to design, and instead focus on the human experience in a very real way.

Rather than students acting as obedient pupils, they are active participants in the creation of knowledge through experience. Everyone expresses themselves through play and explores identity in the process. Demonstrating to students the value of challenging conventions can go beyond the classroom, helping students avoid the replication of hierarchical structures in society.

Conclusion: A Return to Play

Extending the "games are cooking" metaphor above, following traditional models of education and assessment would be akin to presenting students with recipes, discussing them, then asking them to recall all the ingredients and instructions through some sort of assessment. This won't work for aspiring game designers who seek to provide engagement and enjoyment for others. While knowing the ingredients and where to find them is important, taking time to savor the dish and relish that experience is the key to educating in our field.

Play is the free will to explore, without having to be right, without having to solve anything or come to any new conclusions. Play puts students on an equal footing, regardless of prior knowledge or learning style. One of the most basic tenets of game design, attributed to Nolan Bushnell (1996), is that good games should be easy to learn but difficult to master. Structuring pedagogy in that light, creating experiences that challenge students while inviting them to experiment, has enhanced our practice and fulfills us as educators.

Reflecting on the power of play in the classroom has revealed an unexpected resource, our experiences of play. Decades of training and preparation for our current roles enhance our ability to harness those past experiences. Educators who go on the journey to harness this power in the classroom undoubtedly have the same rich resource to draw from.

References

Brown, P., Roediger, H. L., III, & McDaniel, M. A. (2014). *Make It Stick: The Science of Successful Learning*. Cambridge, MA: Harvard University Press.

Bushnell, N. (1996). Relationships Between Fun and the Computer Business. *Communications of the ACM, 39*(8), 31–37. https://doi.org/10.1145/232014.232025.

Despain, W., & Acosta, K. (2013). *100 Principles of Game Design*. Indianapolis, IN: New Riders.

Newman, J. (2013). *Videogames* (2nd ed.). New York, NY: Routledge.

Odyssey of the Mind. (n.d.) Available at https://www.odysseyofthemind.com/. Accessed May 30, 2018.

Russell, D. R. (2001). Where Do the Naturalistic Studies of WAC/WID Point to? In S. H. McLeod, E. Miraglia, M. Soven, & C. Thaiss (Eds.), *WAC for the New Millennium: Strategies for Continuing Writing-Across-the Curriculum Programs* (pp. 259–298). Urbana, IL: NCTE.

Salen, K., & Zimmerman, E. (2004). *Rules of Play: Game Design Fundamentals*. Cambridge: The MIT Press.

Selingo, J. (2013). *College (Un)bound: The Future of Higher Education and What It Means for Students*. Boston, MA: Houghton Mifflin Harcourt.

Sheldon, L. (2012). *The Multiplayer Classroom: Designing Coursework as a Game*. Boston, MA: Course Technology.

34

Exploration: From the Players Point of View

Maxwell Hartt and Hadi Hosseini

Introduction

Despite advances in active and other participatory learning methodologies, instructors know all-too-well how difficult it can still be to intrinsically motivate students. As a result, pedagogical research continues to explore innovative approaches to further engage and motivate student learning. New methods emerging from the coalescence of games and pedagogy encourage intrinsic motivation for learning by tapping into students' sense of play and competition (Hollander and Thomas 2009; Hosseini and Hartt 2016). Deterding et al. (2011: 10) define a subset of the methods, gamification, as "the use of game design elements in a non-game setting."

M. Hartt (✉)
School of Geography and Planning, Cardiff University, Cardiff, Wales, UK
e-mail: harttm1@cardiff.ac.uk

H. Hosseini
Department of Computer Science, Rochester Institute of Technology, Rochester, NY, USA
e-mail: hhvcs@rit.edu

Gamification, or game-based learning, uses gameful interaction and design to motivate students to engage with the course material. By introducing elements of play into the classroom, games and game-based activities entice internal learning motivation. Several empirical examinations have shown gamification to increase students' intrinsic learning motivation, emotional involvement and enjoyment (Gee 2003). In addition to incentivizing learners to engage in the classroom (Lee and Hammer 2011; Richter et al. 2015), games and game dynamics also activate positive psychological arousal—increasing the player's focus and memory. Enjoyable group activities that stimulate a level of competency indirectly influence the analytical cognition to capture the principal concepts involved as positive emotions and experiences cause cognitive activation and psychological arousal. Positive emotions, caused by excitement, such as hope and group synergy, increase learners' attention and motivation and, as a result, help students develop competencies (D'Mello and Graesser 2012; Linnenbrink 2007; Pekrun et al. 2002).

The majority of gamification techniques, and the associated academic literature, concentrate on technology-based games; game-based learning that relies upon the use of computers, handheld devices and online applications. Furthermore, the gamification literature lacks descriptive accounts of game-based learning deployment in the classroom (Deterding et al. 2011; Zichermann and Cunningham 2011). In our research, we concentrate on gameplay in its most fundamental way by examining games played without the use of technology. More specifically, our study focused on undergraduate student perceptions (the players' point of view) of game-based teaching techniques. Conducted at a medium-sized Canadian university in the autumn term of 2015, our study was an interdisciplinary project between the School of Computer Science and the School of Planning. The primary objective of the study was to examine the importance of interactivity, communication and social belonging through the deployment of game-based teaching techniques. In this exploration, we provide a summary of our research findings and reflect on our own experiences (as well as the academic literature) to highlight the opportunities and challenges of designing and executing game-based teaching techniques.

Designing Games and Engaging Players

Gamification is the use of game elements, game thinking and game mechanics in non-game contexts to engage users in an activity (Tu et al. 2014). Games enable the integration of both intrinsic and extrinsic motivational components to cultivate an environment where players feel more motivated to engage in the target activities. There are many ways to design effective game-based lesson plans to blend learning and fun in higher education. Based on our experience and the current literature on designing games, we classify all game-based activities into two major categories: Immersive Game Design (IG) and Modular Game Design (MG).

In IG activities the entire session (or even the entire semester) is designed as a game; students may choose a character (e.g. an avatar), collect points or badges and develop their avatar throughout the semester. In contrast, MG focuses on gamifying a single activity by designing game modules that are independent of one another. Students get engaged in various game modules and move to another activity or section of the session after the game. The instructors can include one or several independent activities in a single session and there is no need for continuity.

The choice of game design depends on the subject matter, class time, number of students and the discretion of instructors. MG activities are easier to implement and often more practical because tasks or activities are not required to contribute to the same theme. On the other hand, IG activities can create a sense of community and social connection through continuity and cohesiveness. One may use a hybrid approach where some learners' activities are designed towards an immersive experience and other activities are independent of the immersive theme.

The overarching game design, rules, rewards and all other game components are all tailored to motivate student engagement with each other and the course material. Reflecting on our experiences and the psychology of motivation, we offer four key recommendations for designing and executing game-based techniques:

1. Know your audience. Design reward systems and game dynamics that are appropriate for your audience in terms of their age, skill sets, major and personality.
2. Provide some degree of autonomy in the design of the game. For instance, a game in which there is only one way to win provides less autonomy for players compared to a game where the players can employ various strategies to win the game.
3. Include features/components that involve social interaction. A game in which the players interact (e.g. help, compete, trade, etc.) with each other is more motivating.
4. Provide feedback at the end of each task in the game. Feedback is what motivates players to go forward in the game. Any type of feedback such as visual feedback (e.g. an explosion), a verbal feedback (e.g. recognition by an instructor) or reward feedback (e.g. gaining points) is vital in keeping the players motivated in moving forward in the game.

Of course, the use of game-play as a novel tool for encouraging learning and classroom participation is not without its challenges. In order to overcome any potential student scepticism towards a new learning technique, we recommend game-based activities be introduced slowly along with full step-by-step instructions to eliminate any confusion about the rules and mechanics as well as the objectives of activities. This subtle introduction of activities together with the interactions between students will contribute to longer activity times. Therefore, managing class time becomes even more crucial. As a result, instructors must carefully choose topics that are most suitable for game-based activities.

Gamification and Student Perceptions of Effectiveness

Gamification can be applied to any discipline, however, planning and computer science education are particularly well suited for game-based learning. Traditionally, computer science education involves a variety of technical, and often dry, concepts that make it inaccessible for a large group of students. As a result, many students drop out of computer science programs. Combined with the clear parallel to video game culture, computer science education in universities is a prime candidate for game-based learning to enhance the quality of learning and in-class experience.

Planning also has many natural ties to gamification. According to Myers and Banerjee (2005), planning education should focus on the skills distinct to planning, including the facilitation of civic engagement, stakeholder collaboration, negotiation and communicative action. Game-based learning provides a vehicle to build these necessary skills. Much like projects, workshops, or studios (which are all familiar pedagogical tools in planning), gamification promotes deep learning and helps develop interpersonal and problem-solving skills. Learning techniques that incorporate autonomy require students to take responsibility, and team-based work reflects modern-day planning and necessitates leadership (Frank 2007). Malone (1981) demonstrates that including an element of randomness in games forces students to be creative and adapt (much like planning practice). Hollander and Thomas (2009: 109) note that gameplay can help "facilitate self-discovery about the complexity of urban systems."

In order to explore the effectiveness of game-based techniques in improving students' perception of learning, engagement and teamwork, we analyzed student feedback to a pair of lectures in both the School of Computer Science and the School of Planning. In both disciplines, we identified two topics within an undergraduate course with similar pedagogical outcomes and student perception by reviewing previous offerings of the course and student performance. The first topic was delivered using traditional teaching techniques heavily reliant on lecturing and the second topic incorporated newly designed gamified tasks and activities. Student feedback was gathered through an online questionnaire and semi-structured interviews. In the computer science course, *Data Types and Data Structures*, the lectures were delivered to 80 students, mostly in second year or third year. The planning lectures were delivered as part of a first-year undergraduate course, *Introduction of Planning Analysis*, which had 60 students.

The traditional lecture in computer science introduced students to the concept of searching over unsorted and sorted sequences. The games-based lecture that followed focused on the topic of sorting algorithms. The intended learning outcomes for the game-based lecture were for students to learn various efficient algorithms for sorting sequences of elements and to analyze the running time of each of these algorithms. Students were asked to sort a set of playing cards in groups of 2, 3 or 4, and develop a set of steps that could be generalized to any sequence of cards or ordered elements. The goal was to design algorithms that are (1) correct (applicable to any set of ordered elements) and (2) fast (in terms of number of steps required), under some mild assumptions. A few groups were randomly chosen to send their representatives to the board and explain their algorithms. The teams with the best algorithms received candy as prizes. Throughout the gamified sessions, we observed more active participation from students who were often silent and tend to participate in fewer activities in previous sessions. In fact, one of the most passive students got very excited and started to volunteer himself to share his solutions. We observed a similar trend about female students that became more engaged in the gameplay and group activities. These observations suggest that perhaps game-based activities are capable of involving a more diverse set of students with variety of learning types and behavioural traits.

The first (traditional) lecture in planning, an introduction to regression-based population forecasts, was followed by an introduction to cohort-based population forecasts. In the latter, students actively demonstrated the different demographic processes that impact population change by participating in a board game ("The Game of a Lifetime") designed specifically for the lecture. The students were organized into groups and at each turn were exposed to one of four random life events: survival, death, birth or migration (in which they would move to another group). The goal of the game was to live as long as possible and birth as many children as possible. In the gamified lecture, we observed that every single student was actively participating and engaged in the material. Although there was significant engagement (questions, comments, etc.) in the traditional lecture, it was primarily from the same small subset of students.

From the online questionnaire and semi-structured interviews that followed the lectures, we found that student enjoyment, peer interaction and ability to share ideas were more pronounced in the gamified lecture. As one planning student noted, "[in the traditional lecture], I took notes, I asked questions. I didn't talk to my peers, because when you are in a lecture, you are usually listening. [In the gamified lecture], I got to help out. I found myself really wanting to talk to my peers about the material and I was excited." Both the computer science and planning students felt the gamified lecture was more effective for thinking about how to solve problems but less effective for working on a specific skill or technical procedure. Responses also showed that 97% of the computer science students and all of the planning students found the gamified lectures to be well organized, and clearly recognized the relevance of the material being taught. This result challenges the myth that game-based activities produce misunderstanding and chaos in the learning process. Moreover, students' perceptions of teamwork and working together were significantly higher in the game-based lecture (with statistical significance and p-value of 0.003). With regard to problem-solving skills, students also felt that game-based learning was slightly more effective, however, we could not draw any conclusion due to the insignificance of the difference.

Conclusion

Overall, we, and our students, found game-based learning to be effective, exciting and fun. For us, the design and implementation of gamified teaching techniques was as educational as the results themselves. As with other teaching techniques, the explanation and execution of game-based activities becomes smoother over time as both student and instructor familiarity with the technique grows. Our own comfort and proficiency has increased significantly since first starting this project. One future direction we are interested in exploring is to combine game-based learning with flipped classrooms. Encouraging students to acquire basic knowledge and comprehension prior to class time, and designing in-class game-based activities to further students' learning towards higher levels of analysis and thinking. Ideally this would allow more in-class time to be spent engaging with each other and the material. More time to play and more time to have fun.

References

Deterding, S., Dixon, D., Khaled, R., & Nacke, L. (2011). From Game Design Elements to Gamefulness: Defining "Gamification." In *Proceedings of the 15th International Academic MindTrek Conference: Envisioning Future Media Environments* (pp. 9–15). ACM Press.

D'Mello, S., & Graesser, A. (2012). Dynamics of Affective States During Complex Learning. *Learning and Instruction, 22*, 145–147.

Frank, A. I. (2007). Entrepreneurship and Enterprise Skills: A Missing Element of Planning Education? *Planning Practice and Research, 22*(4), 635–648.

Gee, J. P. (2003). *What Video Games Have to Teach Us About Learning and Literacy*. New York: Palgrave Macmillan.

Hollander, J. B., & Thomas, D. (2009). Virtual Planning: Second Life and the Online Studio. *Journal of Planning Education and Research, 29*, 108–113.

Hosseini, H., & Hartt, M. D. (2016). Game-Based Learning in the University Classroom. *Teaching Innovation Projects, 6*(1), 4.

Lee, J. J., & Hammer, J. (2011). Gamification in Education: What, How and Why Bother? *Academic Exchange Quarterly, 15*(2), 146.

Linnenbrink, E. A. (2007). The Role of Affect in Student Learning: A Multi-Dimensional Approach to Considering the Interaction of Affect, Motivation, and Engagement. In P. A. Schutz & R. Pekrun (Eds.), *Emotion in Education* (pp. 107–124). Burlington: Elsevier.

Malone, T. W. (1981). Toward a Theory of Intrinsically Motivating Instruction. *Cognitive Science, 5*(4), 333–369.

Myers, D., & Banerjee, T. (2005). Toward Greater Heights for Planning: Reconciling the Differences Between Profession, Practice, and Academic Field. *Journal of the American Planning Association, 71*, 121–129.

Pekrun, R., Goetz, T., Titz, W., Perry, R. P., & Pekrun, R. (2002). Academic Emotions in Students' Self-Regulated Learning and Achievement: A Program of Qualitative and Quantitative Research. *Educational Psychologist, 37*(2), 91–105.

Richter, G., Raban, D. R., & Rafaeli, S. (2015). Studying Gamification: The Effect of Rewards and Incentives on Motivation. In T. Reiners & L. C. Wood (Eds.), *Gamification in Education and Business* (pp. 21–46). Cham: Springer.

Tu, C.-H., Sujo-Montes, L. E., & Yen, C.-J. (2014). Gamification for Learning. In R. Papa (Ed.), *Media Rich Instruction* (pp. 203–217). Cham: Springer.

Zichermann, G., & Cunningham, C. (2011). *Gamification by Design*. Beijing: O'Reilly Media.

35

Exploration: Wardopoly—Game-Based Experiential Learning in Nurse Leadership Education

Bernadette Henderson, Andrew Clements, Melanie Webb and Alexander Kofinas

Introduction

Developing leadership qualities in undergraduate nurse programmes is firmly embedded within the NMC Standards and Code for Pre-registration Nursing (NMC 2010, 2015). The Francis report (2013) on patient mortality at the Mid-Staffordshire NHS Foundation Trust called for strong leadership at all levels of the nursing profession and therefore the need to develop leadership skills within pre-qualification

---

B. Henderson (✉) · A. Clements · M. Webb · A. Kofinas
University of Bedfordshire, Luton, UK
e-mail: bernadette.henderson@beds.ac.uk

A. Clements
e-mail: andrew.clements@beds.ac.uk

M. Webb
e-mail: melanie.webb@beds.ac.uk

A. Kofinas
e-mail: alexander.kofinas@beds.ac.uk

© The Author(s) 2019
A. James and C. Nerantzi (eds.), *The Power of Play in Higher Education*,
https://doi.org/10.1007/978-3-319-95780-7_35

nursing education set out by the NHS Leadership Framework (NILD 2016). Embracing the leadership initiative, this exploration outlines the development, implementation, student evaluation and facilitator observations following introduction of a playful approach to learning in the shape of Wardopoly. Wardopoly is a practice-based board-game informed by the Monopoly genre and aiming to increase the engagement and understanding of health-care leadership required in preparation for interdisciplinary professional clinical practice (NMC 2017), in a pre-registration BSC (Hons) Nurse programme.

The Game

Wardopoly is a clinical simulation board game which facilitates the use of explicit knowledge and critical reflection of factors affecting clinical leadership and hospital patient flow. Wardopoly is preceded by a survey which students complete revealing personal leadership styles, and concludes with the creation of a personal action plan (Fig. 35.1).

Based on experiential, constructivist and reflective learning philosophies associated with adult learning (Knowles 1970), Wardopoly promotes an informal, collective problem solving yet competitive interactional context of play evidenced in both early learning philosophies and adult pedagogies (Berland and Lee 2012; Whitebread et al. 2012; Tanis 2012).

Rooted in clinical practice, the game narrative focuses on managing patient flow through designated territories (patient bed spaces), while dealing with events which may promote or threaten patient safety and effective team-working. Simulating clinical conditions, players form teams and select a specific area of the ward they will control in terms of patient flow, making decisions about admission of new, or discharge of existing patients. Play then involves turn-taking opportunities to lead, contribute, or challenge decisions brought about from the chance outcome of rolling a dice to move a counter around the board pathway in a clockwise direction (Fig. 35.2). Responding to the instruction on

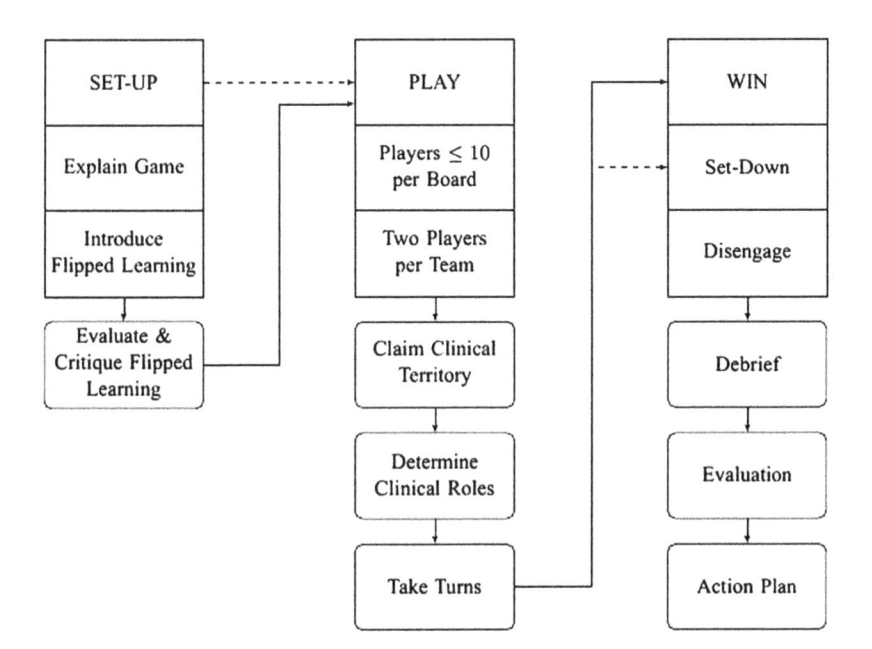

35 Exploration: Wardopoly—Game-Based Experiential Learning ...

Fig. 35.1 Wardopoly preparation, play and debriefing cycle

the board spaces, drama is added by the need to resolve variable conditions presented through either *Patient* or *Chance* cards depicting brief patient information and diagnosis, or contemporary examples of clinical management challenges, before the next player's turn. To reinforce opportunities to identify and analyse leadership styles, landing on a *Chance* space requires a second dice roll, this time determining 1 of 6 leadership approaches to be used to resolve the *Chance* situation. As the game progresses, teams acquire more patient cards, bed spaces fill up, complexity and negotiation increase to ensure bed space capacity is not exceeded, maintaining expected standards of quality care and patient safety.

Victory is based on luck of the dice by the team first landing directly on the 'Thumbs-Up' Friends and Family Quality Test Space (Fig. 35.3). As Wardopoly can be played independently by multiple groups of students, multiple boards may be in play at any one time. Once play stops

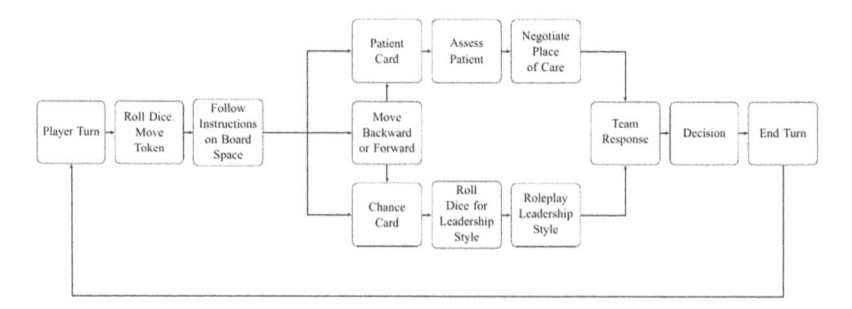

Fig. 35.2 Wardopoly player action and team response

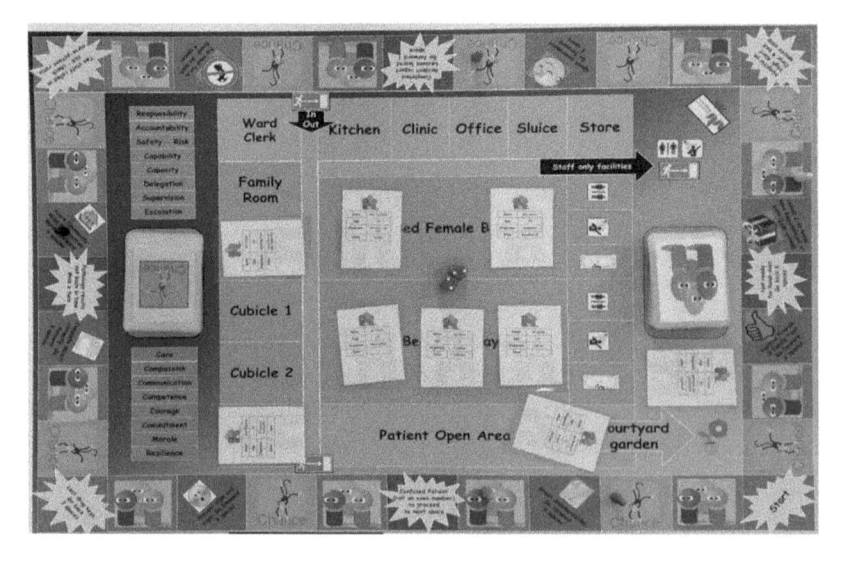

Fig. 35.3 Wardopoly

across all board teams, reflection on play begins using debriefing principles (Ng and Ruppel 2016). While the debriefing process provides insight to the play based approaches as a learning strategy, the main function helps players make meaning of their experience, encouraging further learning and application of learning to practice.

Outcomes

As facilitators, we observed how Wardopoly play and debriefing reduced previous student passivity and dependency on 'being taught'; replicated opportunities for spontaneity, collegiality and collaborative problem-solving (Proyer 2014; Mainemelis and Ronson 2006; Duncum 2009). Debriefing further revealed the depth of meaningful dialogue, exposing reflective critical thinking about the playful learning process and intentions to apply the principles to personal practice.

As game developers, we were conscious of the voluntary engagement and contribution condition for game play (Mainemelis and Ronson 2006), though in all sessions where Wardopoly was played, attendance was slightly higher than usual. Wardopoly also transformed a quiet learning space to a camaraderie based noisy buzz. While apparently chaotic, engagement in Wardopoly helped players contextualise leadership learning outcomes, underpinning the self-awareness, self-determination, self-regulation and positive regard through safe face-to-face challenge described as relevant leadership qualities by Barnett (2011) and Whitebread et al. (2012). Player behaviour and self-report identified how a playful mindset helped foster positive peer relationships noted by Yu et al. (2007) and Yue et al. (2016).

Discussion

In establishing a culture of play, we feel we facilitated students' independence and deeper appreciation of leadership directly and positively. Splitting a large class into 'player-teams' and instilling 'turn-taking' reversed expectations of individual engagement, creating more opportunities for educators to speak to individual students than previously achieved in a lecture. Game playing provided players opportunities to shape their own game and feel the dynamic interplay between leadership styles, teamwork and management of the *patient* or *chance* scenarios.

In turn, we felt players gained agency through advocacy where dependence on the facilitator shifted from information provider to that of coach.

We have used play and game-based learning techniques before, however, Wardopoly was our first experience as game developers, helping us to shape our appreciation of play and game dynamics and to give rise to six key insights:

1. **Preparation.** By applying expectancy theory (Smith and Lazarus 1990), we explained the flipped learning exercise and demonstrated the game in advance to increase understanding of meaningfulness and the anticipatory "willingness to engage based on perception of realism" (Rudolph et al. 2014: 342). However, even though students were given autonomy to decide team composition and size (i.e. they were seen as adults) it was soon apparent that support was required when it came to forming teams as some students were 'on their own'. The uncomfortable experience of 'not being picked' suggests sensitive pre-briefing is needed to explain the value of early inclusion, facilitating player team if necessary if congruence between learning objective, game narrative and mode of play is to be achieved.
2. **The state of winning.** Players felt we were less clear about the winning state than we could have been. While inclusion is imperative to progress (Hainey et al. 2013), we identified two types of player: those more concerned with fully exploring the game process; or pragmatic players who focused on winning, and in doing so, were willing to curtail discussion. Wardopoly was dedicated to the process of understanding of nurse leadership and social interaction reinforcing learning through enjoyment (Cessario 1987). However, we failed to appreciate was the importance some students placed on 'winning' and the disappointment when the game flow was interrupted by another team winning. While the game session is scheduled to last 90 minutes (including briefing and debriefing), having closure 'robbed' by a competing team left some groups expressing the desire to play longer, which we felt was evidence of the success of the play intervention.
3. **Facilitate choice—Avoid control.** While we created simple rules and were concise with *patient* and *chance* card information to create

'thinking challenges' and encourage curiosity to ask questions upon which decisions could be made (Pluck and Johnson 2011), some students wanted more information which we used coaching approaches to resolve. In facilitating freedom for teams to create their own game management rules, students were able to identify their own internal goals (the way they wanted to play). In doing so, creativity and experimentation gave rise to additional challenges and confusions, created new discovery cycles, supporting the process of increasing the responsibility and satisfaction of decision making by the teams as illustrated by Kangas (2010). For example, when bed spaces were full, rather than review priorities and discharge, *Patients* were placed in any other possible space, revealing the need to explore patient safety, clinical risk, discharge criteria and process. At times, we (the tutors), acted in 'agent provocateur' roles to prompt evidence-based ways of thinking about patient flow and leadership decision making.

4. **Be ready for change**. The extent of player immersion and submission to the role-play leadership condition surprised us. Players built on tacit knowledge of game play, took control of the game, ensured equity in opportunity and sought to balance bed space territory with patient advocacy. The size of the board (A1) and seating all use far more space than is usually accounted for in the classroom size calculation, leading player teams to move into adjacent areas, requiring more mobility on our behalf. However, where classroom space is limited, and learning spaces are shared, the experience brought home the importance of managing the impact noise may have on other learners.

5. **Relationship developmemt**. Wardopoly enhanced the relationship between ourselves and players which endured beyond the session (Spralls et al. 2010). We felt we got to know individuals students more holistically, contributing to co-creation activity through constructive contributions of specific clinical additions, more sophisticated game play ideas.

6. **Resource management**. Educational resources can be expensive, though as an in-house production, being in use since 2015, Wardopoly has shown itself to be cost-effective, durable and versatile pedagogic tool.

Conclusion

We have explored how game-based learning and the board game Wardopoly enabled student activity in the learning process and positive experiences in learning clinical leadership concepts. Co-creativity and positive feedback from game-strategy savvy students also pushed us towards evolving the complexity and mastery criteria for winning. In retrospect, we should also have anticipated the noise escalation brought about by engaged players, alongside our naïve game developer errors counting on students not to game the game, where we observed pragmatists who aimed to win the game rather than reflect on the process. However, the pragmatists learning experiences were equally relevant, shedding light on an important discussion dimension of how teams work to completing a goal. The design of Wardopoly is still evolving and will continue to evolve as we attempt on the one hand to counter the gaming behaviours that may hinder learning whilst enhancing the education benefits brought about through Wardopoly as a game-based intervention.

References

Barnett, L. A. (2011). How Do Playful People Play? Gendered and Racial Leisure Perspectives, Motives, and Preferences of College Students. *Leisure Sciences, 33*, 382–401. Available at https://experts.illinois.edu/en/publications/how-do-playful-people-play-gendered-and-racial-leisure-perspectiv. Accessed November 3, 2017.

Berland, M., & Lee, V. R. (2012). Collaborative Strategic Board Games as a Site for Distributed Computational Thinking. *International Journal of Game-Based Learning, 1*(2), 65–81. Available at https://www.researchgate.net/publication/254317022_How_Do_Playful_People_Play_Gendered_and_Racial_Leisure_Perspectives_Motives_and_Preferences_of_College_Students. Accessed November 3, 2017.

Cessario, L. (1987). Utilization of Board Gaming for Conceptual Models of Nursing. *Journal of Nursing Education, 26*, 167–169. Available at http://europepmc.org/abstract/med/3035132. Accessed November 3, 2017.

Duncum, P. (2009). Toward a Playful Pedagogy: Popular Culture and the Pleasures of Transgression. *Studies in Art Education, 50*, 232–244. Available at http://naeaworkspace.org/studies_single/Studies%2050(3)_Spring2009_individual/A2_Studies%2050(3)_Spring2009-3.pdf. Accessed November 3, 2017.

Francis, R. (2013). *Report of the Mid Staffordshire NHS Foundation Trust Public Inquiry*. London: The Stationery Office. Available at https://www.gov.uk/government/publications/report-of-the-mid-staffordshire-nhs-foundation-trust-public-inquiry. Accessed November 3, 2017.

Hainey, T., Westera, W., Connolly, T. M., Boyle, L., Baxter, G., Beeby, R. B., & Soflano, M. (2013). Students' Attitudes Toward Playing Games and Using Games in Education: Comparing Scotland and the Netherlands. *Computers & Education, 69*, 474–484. Available at http://dspace.ou.nl/bitstream/1820/5037/1/Students%20attitudes%20toward%20playing%20games%20and%20using%20games%20in%20education%20Comparing%20Scotland%20and%20the%20Netherlands.pdf. Accessed November 3, 2017.

Kangas, M. (2010). Creative and Playful Learning: Learning Through Game Co-creation and Games in a Playful Learning Environment. *Thinking Skills and Creativity, 5*, 1–15. Available at http://psycnet.apa.org/record/2009-24961-001. Accessed November 3, 2017.

Knowles, M. S. (1970). *The Modern Practice of Adult Education*. New York: New York Association Press.

Mainemelis, C., & Ronson, S. (2006). Ideas are Born in Fields of Play: Towards a Theory of Play and Creativity in Organizational Settings. *Research in Organizational Behavior, 27*, 81–131. Available at http://www.mainemelis.com/userfiles/articles/ROB2006_378019994.pdf. Accessed November 3, 2017.

Ng, G. M., & Ruppel, H. (2016). Nursing Simulation Fellowships: An Innovative Approach for Developing Simulation Leaders. *Clinical Simulation in Nursing, 12*, 62–68. Available at http://daneshyari.com/article/preview/2645953.pdf. Accessed November 3, 2017.

NILD. (2016). *Developing People—Improving Care: A National Framework for Action on Improvement and Leadership Development in NHS-Funded Services*. National Improvement and Leadership Development Board. Available at https://improvement.nhs.uk/uploads/documents/Developing_People-Improving_Care-010216.pdf. Accessed November 3, 2017.

NMC. (2010). *Standards for Pre-registration Nursing Education*. London: Nursing and Midwifery Council.

NMC. (2015). *The Code for Nurses and Midwives*. London: Nursing and Midwifery Council.

NMC. (2017). *Enabling Professionalism in Nursing and Midwifery Practice*. London: Nursing and Midwifery Council.

Pluck, G., & Johnson, H. (2011). Stimulating Curiosity to Enhance Learning. *GESJ: Education Sciences and Psychology*, *2*(19). Available at http://eprints.whiterose.ac.uk/74470/1/Pluck_and_Johnson_2011_Curiosity.pdf. Accessed November 3, 2017.

Proyer, R. T. (2014). To Love and Play: Testing the Association of Adult Playfulness with the Relationship Personality and Relationship Satisfaction. *Current Psychology*, *33*, 501. Available at https://www.zpid.de/psychologie/PSYNDEX.php?search=psychauthors&id=0288266. Accessed November 3, 2017.

Rudolph, J. W., Raemer, D. B., & Simon, R. (2014). Establishing a Safe Container for Learning in Simulation: The Role of the Presimulation Briefing. *Simulation in Healthcare*, *9*, 339–349. Available at https://www.ncbi.nlm.nih.gov/pubmed/25188485. Accessed November 3, 2017.

Smith, C. A., & Lazarus, R. S. (1990). Emotion and Adaptation. *Handbook of Personality: Theory and Research* (pp. 609–637). Available at http://people.ict.usc.edu/~gratch/CSCI534/Readings/Smith&Lazarus90.pdf. Accessed November 3, 2017.

Spralls, S. A., Garver, M. S., Divine, R. L., & Trotz, H. (2010). Needs Assessment of University Leadership Programs. *Journal of Leadership Studies*, *4*, 20–35. Available at http://onlinelibrary.wiley.com/doi/10.1002/jls.20152/full. Accessed November 3, 2017.

Tanis, D. J. (2012). *Exploring Play/Playfulness and Learning in the Adult and Higher Education Classroom.* State College: The Pennsylvania State University. Available at https://etda.libraries.psu.edu/files/final_submissions/8092. Accessed November 3, 2017.

Whitebread, D. B., Marisol, K. M., & Verma, M. (2012). *The Importance of Play: A Report on the Value of Children's Play with a Series of Policy Recommendations.* Brussels, Belgium: Toy Industries of Europe (TIE). Available at https://www.toyindustries.eu/wp-content/uploads/2012/11/Dr-David-Whitebread-The-importance-of-play-final.pdf. Accessed November 3, 2017.

Yu, P., Wu, J.-J., Chen, I.-H., & Lin, Y.-T. (2007). Is Playfulness a Benefit to Work? Empirical Evidence of Professionals in Taiwan. *International Journal of Technology Management*, *39*, 412–429. Available at https://www.deepdyve.com/lp/inderscience-publishers/is-playfulness-a-benefit-to-work-empirical-evidence-of-professionals-ExvldFn4xf. Accessed November 3, 2017.

Yue, X. D., Leung, C.-L., & Hiranandani, N. A. (2016). Adult Playfulness, Humor Styles, and Subjective Happiness. *Psychological Report*, *119*, 630–640. Available at http://journals.sagepub.com/doi/abs/10.1177/0033294116662842?journalCode=prxa. Accessed November 3, 2017.

36

Exploration: Using Play to Design Play—Gamification and Student Involvement in the Production of Games-Based Learning Resources for Research Methods Teaching

Natalia Gerodetti and Darren Nixon

Background Literature

Although the benefits of using serious games (games with informational and/or educational components) in HE are increasingly recognized in the emerging literature, much of it focuses on technologically sophisticated games rather than on what has come to be called 'new traditional games for learning' (Moseley and Whitton 2012). Within this body of literature, attention is mostly focused on the benefits of *playing* games for students. However, in this exploration, we focus on the benefits of student involvement in the *design* and *creation* of games-based learning (GBL) resources and explore how this creative process can itself be gamified. Importantly, there is a difference to be drawn between GBL

N. Gerodetti (✉) · D. Nixon
Leeds Beckett University, Leeds, UK
e-mail: n.gerodetti@leedsbeckett.ac.uk

D. Nixon
e-mail: D.Nixon@leedsbeckett.ac.uk

© The Author(s) 2019
A. James and C. Nerantzi (eds.), *The Power of Play in Higher Education*,
https://doi.org/10.1007/978-3-319-95780-7_36

and gamification. GBL refers to the integration of games into learning experiences to increase engagement and motivation. Whereas gamification refers to the use of game mechanics and dynamics (point systems, leaderboards, badges, etc.) as a pedagogical system to improve motivation and learning (Whitton 2015; HEA 2017). To some extent, there is little that is new about the link between learning and playing and the twentieth-century theorists such as Piaget (1951) or Vygotsky (1978) have argued for the crucial role of play in the cognitive development from birth and through adulthood.

Games may be presented as merely another option within a diversified teaching and learning strategy but their characteristics, such as clear, achievable goals and rules which challenge students, can make them a good tool to be used in teaching, particularly when they draw on Problem Based Learning (PBL) which can then be turned into Problem Based Gaming (PBG) (see Kiili 2007). Games, particularly traditional games (board and card games), are interactive (collaborative and/or competitive) and can be played in safe environments which provide the opportunity to make and learn from mistakes (Whitton and Moseley 2012). The interaction and feedback resulting from this process is, therefore, a key part of the games-based learning environment. Curiosity, permission to fail and engagement with others can provide students with contextual challenges in which they have opportunities to gain a sense of control and power to make judgments and decisions (Knapp 2012). Collaborative and problem-solving skills are thus often emphasized in the skills development that is part of the learning outcomes within games-based learning activities.

Whitton (2015) and Hand (2016) underline important warnings about the lack of reflective and purposive use of gamification within HE. We suggest that gamification and games-based learning can be combined to provide students with the opportunities to engage in failure or shortcomings, something that normally is penalized and discouraged in HE and its assessment structure but something that is both integral to the gaming experience and to reflective learning. Thus we agree with Whitton (2015: 23) that playful learning is not a simple solution and is 'more than a pedagogic technique, it is a philosophy of learning'. In acknowledging a more fundamental shift, moreover, we would like to suggest that it is important to involve students in the design of games for the purposes of learning.

Students as (Games) Producers

The concept of 'students as producers' has emerged over the last decade as a critical response to the dominant contemporary construction of 'students as consumers' (Neary 2012).

Several key insights from this model have informed the design and development of the project reported here. Firstly, this discourse asks us to rethink or reconsider how we teach in Higher Education. Through the traditional lecture and seminar model, students are often cast as passive recipients of academic knowledge transmitted by a lecturer. In its place, 'students as producers' seeks to recast students as active producers of socially useful academic knowledge. Yet, embedding such an approach to learning in the undergraduate curriculum suggests not only a reconstruction of our image of the student but also a reconstruction of the relationship between students and academics. Here the academic is cast not as the transmitter of knowledge, but as a facilitator of student learning who enables students to take responsibility for directing their own enquiries, and as a collaborator (alongside students) in the co-production of academic knowledge.

In developing this student-staff collaborative project, it was our contention that the teaching of research methods and ethics in the social sciences is particularly ill-suited to the 'transmission model' of teaching and learning. This made research methods teaching ripe for potential gamification. However, it was not our intention to redesign the curriculum based on our reflections of our teaching practices. Rather, we asked our students: What are your experiences of teaching and learning research methods and ethics? How can we make teaching more productive? Can we develop a game that might improve teaching for future cohorts of students? Central to our approach was a very careful consideration of how we designed the project in order to facilitate the development of games *for* the students *by* the students.

Using Gamification to Create Games

In this exploration, we suggest that the students as 'partners' or 'producers' or 'communities of practice' framework can be fruitfully applied to the gamification of HE teaching practices. Little has been written on gamification in the social sciences, and even less on involving non-game design students in the conceptual development of games as well as their production, application and evaluation (Gerodetti and Nixon 2014). We attempt to demonstrate the benefits of working with students to design and produce games for use in sociology teaching. We show how a playful gamified approach that engages students can be mobilized to facilitate student game design and the production of game resources that have real pedagogic value and impact. We suggest that this approach generates a range of benefits for the students involved and the games produced. In particular, the project demonstrates that students:

- thrive working in a playful context to produce serious teaching materials
- develop a wide range of skills (such as leadership, collaboration and confidence)
- value working with other years, cohorts and academics
- develop a sense of engagement, belonging and ownership through mobilizing and embedding their knowledge and experience in practice.

The exploration is based on a curriculum innovation initiative funded by the HEA to 'gamify sociology teaching' several years ago. Set up as an extracurricular project, a series of workshops created an environment where—through play—students were charged with designing a games resource to be used in research methods teaching. Central to the project design was the adaptation of the format of the TV Gameshow *The Apprentice* for the games creation process (discussed below). The project led to the development of two research methods games which students co-presented at the HEA Annual Conference in 2013. One of the games was also presented and short-listed at ECGBL 2014 in Berlin. The games have been successfully used and evaluated at universities in the UK, Spain and Switzerland. Using play to design play has been a valuable, effective and joyful approach for us that we continue to use (the most recent project is developing a game that deals with the transition to university life).

Gamification—Workshops 1 and 2

Involvement in the project was entirely voluntary. Importantly, we invited both second- and third-year social science students to take part. The benefits that accrued from mixing different cohorts of social science students were greater than we expected and extolled by students in both cohorts. Second years were delighted to be able to talk to 3rd years about the experience of doing a dissertation, while the 3rd years seemed to revel in passing on their knowledge and experiences to other students.

The aim underpinning this project was to create a learning environment that fostered student collaboration but with a competitive edge that might provide extra motivational impetus. Thus, we decided that we would loosely base our initial workshop—which was focused on reflecting on students' experiences of research methods teaching, identifying what needed to be changed (in the students' words: make teaching and learning more fun) and designing a game to do that—on the format of the popular reality TV game show 'The Apprentice'. Attractive from that show was the idea of collective problem-based learning and the competitive edge generated by challenging groups to go up and against one another in the attempt to solve a problem or achieve a task. What emerged was that the students really liked the competitive component and some became very focused on 'winning'.

Upon arrival at the first extracurricular event students were allocated to a group, provided with an academic facilitator and given the following brief:

> **Aim:** For UG students to create a game-based learning approach to methodological and ethical dilemmas in planning and carrying out UG research/dissertations.
>
> 1. Think of a plethora of difficult areas to research/difficulties encountered in planning empirical research.
> 2. Think of ways of resolving these problems/dilemmas.
> 3. Perhaps consider some generic advice for another UG cohort? Good experiences, bad experiences?
> 4. Create a game/interactive approach for other UG students to use as a resource.

Students were told that by the end of the day, they would be expected to present their game concept to the whole group and that the whole group would adjudicate on the winning game. After the initial briefing, the structure of the day consisted of separate group workshops whereby the groups worked on their own specific ideas, interspersed with plenary sessions whereby the academic facilitators of each group fed back key or interesting issues generated within their own group. This idea of cross-fertilization between the groups, however, met with some resistance from the students who were less keen on revealing their ideas to their competitors than the group facilitators!

The first workshop day morning was spent by the two groups of students brainstorming around their acquired and shared experiences of methodological and ethical problems encountered when doing undergraduate research. As such, students were drawing on their 'authentic' experiences, a key principle highlighted in the gamification literature (Kiili 2007). In the afternoon, the two groups worked on thinking about how these problems could be incorporated into a game that could be used as a pedagogical tool in the future within methods modules.

The first workshop produced the winning game 'Curveball'. However, both tutors felt that a second concept ('RollWithIt') that got 'buried' held great promise so it was taken forward for development as well. A second workshop day two months later continued the content development. The incentive underpinning the second workshop was the opportunity to take any games that were sufficiently developed to the Higher Education Academy conference that year. This second workshop abandoned the competitive component and gave way to the collaborative effort of formulating learning outcomes—which the students found hard but interesting to do—and trialling the games on themselves, in order to revise and modify.

Conclusion

As we have suggested above, student game producers developed a range of skills and competencies through their involvement in this project. However, the benefits of our approach also extend to the nature and quality of the games produced and to future cohorts of our students. In our most recent project (based on the same workshop methodology but aimed at producing a game to address the first-year student transition), we have managed to develop a small 'community of practice' whereby some of the students who played the game during their own induction have now become student game designers as we evaluate and further develop the game. These students will then facilitate the game with new cohorts of students, potentially contributing to the establishment of a stronger peer-mentoring network across the different cohorts.

It is our contention that the gamification of the initial workshop event played a key role in the success of this project, particularly in terms of generating a competitive element that stimulated student motivation and engagement further. Nonetheless, we would also suggest that creatively involving students in curriculum development, particularly so that they are enabled to have increased 'ownership' of their learning and teaching experience, can create high levels of intrinsic motivation in the first place.

References

Gerodetti, N., & Nixon, D. (2014). Students as Producers: Designing Games to Teach Social Science Research Methods and Ethics. In *Proceedings of the 8th European Conference on Games Based Learning* (pp. 143–150).

Hand, B. (2016). *Designing Successful Gamification in Higher Education*. Available at http://www.gettingsmart.com/2014/02/gamification-successes-and-failures-higher-education/.

HEA. (2017). *HEA Starter Tools: Gamification and Games-Based Learning*. Available at https://www.heacademy.ac.uk/enhancement/starter-tools/gamification-and-games-based-learning. Accessed May 30, 2018.

Kiili, K. (2007). Foundation for Problem-Based Gaming. *British Journal of Educational Technology, 83*(3), 394–404.

Knapp, K. (2012). *The Gamification of Learning and Instruction: Game-Based Methods and Strategies for Training and Education*. San Francisco: Jossey-Bass.

Moseley, A., & Whitton, N. (Eds.). (2012). *New Traditional Games for Learning: A Case Book*. London: Routledge.

Neary, M. (2012). Teaching Politically: Policy, Pedagogy and the New European University. *Journal for Critical Education Policy Studies, 10*(2), 233–257. Available at http://studentasproducer.lincoln.ac.uk/files/2014/03/10-2-08.pdf. Accessed May 30, 2018.

Piaget, J. (1951). *Play, Dreams and Imitation in Childhood*. London: Routledge.

Vygotsky, L. S. (1978). *Mind in Society: The Development of Higher Mental Processes*. Cambridge: Harvard University Press.

Whitton, N. (2015). Beyond Gamification: Play in Higher Education. In N. Jackson, C. Nerantzi, & A. James (Eds.), *Exploring Play in Higher Education, Creative Academic Magazine* (Issue 2). www.creativeacademic.uk.

Whitton, N., & Moseley, A. (Eds.). (2012). *Using Games to Enhance Learning and Teaching*. Abingdon: Routledge.

37

Tabletop Gaming in Wildlife Conservation—'Park Life'

Louise Robinson and Ian Turner

Park Life is a 2–4 player board game developed to bring together the topics of wildlife crime and wildlife conservation delivered within a level 6 module on the BSc (Hons) Zoology programme at University of Derby. It is delivered towards the end of the module as a way to review taught concepts and demonstrate the interaction between conservation themes to overcome fragmented learning.

In the first year of development, Park Life was created using simple resources (e.g. Printed playing boards, cocktail sticks, and plastic counters) to play test the game with undergraduate students. After positive feedback, it was decided that Park Life would be developed by a bespoke board game company in order to produce a limited number of copies for teaching purposes. The professional production enhanced the overall

---

L. Robinson (✉) · I. Turner
University of Derby, Derby, UK
e-mail: L.Robinson@derby.ac.uk

I. Turner
e-mail: I.Turner@derby.ac.uk

© The Author(s) 2019
A. James and C. Nerantzi (eds.), *The Power of Play in Higher Education*,
https://doi.org/10.1007/978-3-319-95780-7_37

appearance and impact of the game whilst also improving its durability and re-usability. The finished product can be seen in Fig. 37.1.

The aim of the game is to develop a conservation park containing a breeding pair within each area of land, all of which are tracked, along with any offspring, through the completion of an adapted stud book. Players can also invest money within eco-tourism which provides an additional annual income to their park and must purchase fences to protect their land. Within the game, players may chance upon positive events which supply funds or increase breeding stock as well as negative events such as poaching and disease. Although players compete to win, they can also play co-operatively to transfer animals between parks to improve upon genetic stock and purchase resources from one another should they require funds. The player who declares themselves the winner is then questioned by the other players regarding the genetic history of a randomly selected animal from within their developed park. If full details can be obtained from the stud and all objectives are complete, they are declared the winner; if these details cannot be extracted that animal is lost and the player must re-enter the game.

Fig. 37.1 The current version of Park Life including the main board, player boards, breeding pair pieces, and resources used within the game (Photograph courtesy of David Bryson)

Park Life has been delivered for three years at the University of Derby, and each year, students are asked to evaluate the game via a short voluntary questionnaire. The majority of students report the game as both enjoyable and a useful memory aid for revision purposes. Additionally, respondents agree that the game has helped link and reinforce concepts within the module and aided their understanding of the importance of stud book completion.

Park Life has a much broader reach than undergraduate Wildlife Conservation students. Because the game does not require an in-depth understanding of the subject (as it was produced as a revision and not teaching tool) it provides an awareness of conservation topics to people with no previous knowledge of the subject or scientific background. The removal of the genetic component (stud book completion) also provides the opportunity to use Park Life to promote conservation to a younger audience.

38

Sketch: 'Frogger It, I'd Rather Be Playing Computer Games Than Referencing My Assignment'— A Harvard Referencing Game

Tracy Dix

This play initiative is a remix of the traditional referencing style guide into a retro arcade game. While style guides from universities such as Anglia Ruskin and Leeds are useful and relevant, they are also highly technical and complex in order to cover the breadth of modern research sources. So, this game aspires to help students remember how to cite common resources (such as monographs, journal articles and websites) in a compelling and interactive way.

Although citation games have been created before, they consist of simple ordering exercises, whereas Harvard Referencing incorporates the pixelated graphics, animation, repetitive music, scoreboard and simple gameplay of classic arcade games such as Pac-Man and Frogger (J. Sargeant Reynolds Community College Library 2017). Frogger involves navigating frogs past speeding vehicles and river hazards to their lily pad home. In a library context, each 'frog' is a book which the user takes from a shelf and adds to their reference list. The player moves

---

T. Dix (✉)
University of Leicester, Leicester, UK
e-mail: tracy.dix@leicester.ac.uk

© The Author(s) 2019
A. James and C. Nerantzi (eds.), *The Power of Play in Higher Education*,
https://doi.org/10.1007/978-3-319-95780-7_38

it using library carts and must avoid rushing students in the process. Books are each labelled 'title', 'year' and so forth to aid memory as the user's gaze follows it to its correct position in the citation, completing a full reference before moving onto other resource types.

Being a simple game, this took about three weeks to create, and was developed in Warwick Medical School Harvard style to cater to most academic departments at Warwick (2016). Graphics were easily drawn and animated using an open source application called Piskel, with coding in Javascript by the Library's IT specialist (Fig. 38.1).

The idea has enjoyed positive feedback at Warwick and elsewhere. However, due to limited resources, the labels on each book were omitted from the first working prototype. Evaluation by doctoral students at network events and undergraduates during embedded sessions suggested that the game was fun, but its effectiveness as a learning tool was adversely impacted without the labels. Academics also suggested that the use of worked examples would help to reinforce learning.

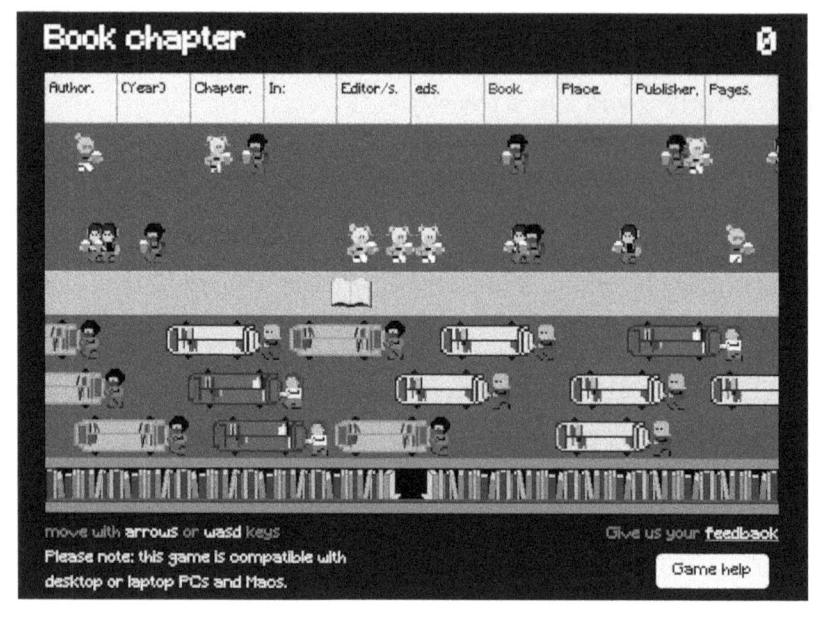

Fig. 38.1 Harvard Referencing Game

These issues have also been acknowledged by library professionals when it was entered into Lagadothon (part of the Librarians' Information Literacy Annual Conference 2017), with personal feedback from judges that it 'makes libraries look cool' and winning funding towards further development.

Following evaluation, the initial goal is to restore the book labels and introduce some worked examples so it is fit for purpose. Longer term, it would be ideal to redesign the game as a template, allowing departments to enter their own citation styles, so that bespoke versions for any institution can be generated without the need for coding.

References

J. Sargeant Reynolds Community College Library. (2017). *Citation Games—Citation Sources—Research Guides* [Online]. Available at http://libguides.reynolds.edu/cite. Accessed July 7, 2017.

University of Warwick Library. (2016). *Harvard Referencing Game.* Available at http://www2.warwick.ac.uk/services/library/students/referencing/referencing-styles/harvard-game. Accessed July 7, 2017.

University of Washington TRIO Training. (n.d.). *Citation Game Home Page: APA and MLA Citations.* Available at http://depts.washington.edu/trio/quest/citation/apa_mla_citation_game/index.htm. Accessed July 7, 2017.

39

Sketch: Using Play to Facilitate Faculty–Student Partnership—How Can You Co-design a Module?

Sarah Dyer and Tanya Lubicz-Nawrocka

We describe an experiment in creating playful spaces to facilitate partnership in learning and teaching by reframing the roles we inhabit in higher education. Student–faculty partnership, where all 'involved are actively engaged in and stand to gain from the process of working together to foster engaged student learning' (Higher Education Academy 2014: 2) is a valuable goal. However, the challenges entailed have led partnership to be characterised as a 'threshold concept', as troublesome as it is potentially transformative (Cook-Sather 2014).

Designing modules is often 'backstage' work, which is traditionally the responsibility of faculty, following on from academic expertise and freedom. Student–faculty partnership in module co-design involves surfacing students' valuable input and

S. Dyer (✉)
University of Exeter, Exeter, UK
e-mail: s.dyer@exeter.ac.uk

T. Lubicz-Nawrocka
Moray House School of Education, University of Edinburgh, Edinburgh, Scotland, UK

addressing differential access to bureaucratic frameworks and terminology used in curriculum development. One approach is training students, but this risks co-opting or silencing students' voices. Another approach is mediating contributions with a student representative, academic developer, or students' association staff member acting as a 'translator'. Reflecting on case studies of module co-design (Bovill et al. 2016; Cook-Sather et al. 2014), we wanted to try creating a parallel ludic space that would destabilise expert and bureaucratic power.

During the University of Edinburgh's Innovative Learning Week, we ran a workshop to challenge students, academics and support staff to co-design a board game together. We started with an exercise in 'appreciative partnership learning' (Dyer 2016) setting a tone of openness and respect. Then, from possible briefs designed to level the playing field of student and staff expertise, participants chose to design a game with the object of learning to fly. We encouraged participants to play with tactile materials including paper, pens, string, Playdoh, paper clips and wings whilst sharing ideas. The board game serves as a metaphor for a module, both with rules for engagement and success. We concluded by reflecting on examples of module proposal forms, their emphasis and omissions, from our perspective as co-designers (Fig. 39.1).

This was a standalone, experimental event and proof of concept to introduce co-design. We played with ideas to 'denaturalise' academic power so that module design decisions became more visible. The event posed questions about power, facilitating participants' reflections on implications, for the objectives of higher education. Using the principles of play and partnership helped academics explore the potential of students' contributions; furthermore, this workshop provided students with opportunities to explore previously hidden aspects of higher education.

Fig. 39.1 Co-design of a module as a board game

References

Bovill, C., Cook-Sather, A., Felten, P., Millard, L., & Moore-Cherry, N. (2016). Addressing Potential Challenges in Co-creating Learning and Teaching: Overcoming Resistance, Navigating Institutional Norms and Ensuring Inclusivity in Student–Staff Partnerships. *Higher Education, 71*(2), 195–208.

Cook-Sather, A. (2014). Student-Faculty Partnership in Explorations of Pedagogical Practice: A Threshold Concept in Academic Development. *International Journal for Academic Development, 19*(3), 186–198.

Cook-Sather, A., Bovill, C., & Felten, P. (2014). *Engaging Students as Partners in Learning and Teaching: A Guide for Faculty*. San Francisco, CA: Jossey-Bass.

Dyer, S. (2016). *Appreciate: Cards to Support Appreciative Partnership Learning—A Guide*. York: Higher Education Academy.

The Higher Education Academy. (2014). *Framework for Partnership in Learning and Teaching in Higher Education*. York: Higher Education Academy.

40

Sketch: Imagination Needs Moodling

Debra Josephson Abrams

> So you see, imagination needs moodling - long inefficient happy idling, dawdling and puttering.—Brenda Ueland

Buzzing, clamoring, muttering, arguing, whispering, laughing. Students are delightfully loud with learning.

As a student, I've had wild success creating projects that tapped many of my intelligences (beginning decades before Dr. Howard Gardner articulated them). As a teacher, I've therefore been mindful to fashion activities nurturing students' intelligences. In a pre-university high-intermediate English as a Second Language reading course in which popular sixth-grade novels were the core material, I had small student groups develop board games based on the novels.

Learners and I discussed game characteristics, games we enjoy, and games we have played and do play. I outlined the activity and the project they would create and said they could meet out of class should they

D. Josephson Abrams (✉)
Seoul National University of Science and Technology, Seoul, South Korea

wish. Classes met five days/week for 80 minutes, and I allotted 20-plus minutes per class for the project (about 3.5 hours total). I provided butcher paper, colored markers, colored paper, scissors, glue, and a stapler. Learners could bring additional materials, and they did.

I created a game assessment rubric and a rubric for groups' game presentations (Fig. 40.1).

Most groups and their projects were, pun intended, 'at the top of their game'. The results demonstrated learners internalized major themes and key vocabulary. Equally, students' aesthetic skills and talents were nurtured and highlighted. I was gobsmacked. The students who had done little all semester blossomed in this activity because they tapped their strengths: a bright but uninvolved, disinterested reader flourished when she applied her artistic talent to designing the game board. Students who read but contributed little to literature circles or class discussion were talkative, fascinated by the activity's kinestheticism. However, even with this inventive activity and my encouragement, not all were engaged. They squandered time as they had all

Final Project Presentation: Grading rubric

You must:

1. Introduce your game:
    - explain how you decided to create it;
    - explain what steps you took to create it;
    - share what mistakes you made in the creation process and how you solved them;
    - explain how you decided on the name and what the name means.

2. Explain the instructions and rules (how to play).
3. Speak loudly and clearly for everyone to hear and understand.
4. Look at everyone (make eye contact with everyone) when you speak.
5. Give everyone in your group a turn to speak for an equal amount of time (total group time=no more than 10 minutes).
6. Be prepared to answer questions from your instructor and your classmates about your game; all group members have a chance to answer.
7. Make sure that everyone in the room can see your game.
8. Give everyone a chance to play.

Fig. 40.1 Extract from a game rubric for English as a Second Language students (Created by the Author)

semester. Perhaps their behavior was because the program allowed students multiple course failures before passing or losing their visa status. It was no secret that some students used the system to extend their visas. Although these individuals were not active obstructionists to their classmates' creativity and learning, they were passive obstacles, distractions to the learning community.

Students crossed cultural boundaries, honed their English language and critical and creative thinking and analysis skills, and practiced their presentation skills. Moreover, they demonstrated their otherwise hidden talents.

When I present this activity again, we will examine what we do not like about games and why and discuss how to address the concerns. We will review Kapp's *Eight Game Elements to Make Learning More Intriguing* (2014), and I will revise the assessment accordingly. I will spend more time developing students' presentation skills, have students write reflectively about what they learned, and have them assess their engagement level. I will consider offering other activities from which students can choose; therefore, if creating a game is not appealing, they can choose another, comparable project.

Reference

Kapp, K. M. (2014). *Eight Game Elements to Make Learning More Intriguing*. Available at https://www.td.org/Publications/Blogs/Learning-Technologies-Blog/2014/03/Eight-Game-Elements-to-Make-Learning-More-Intriguing. Accessed June 21, 2017 (Online).

41

Exploration: It's a Serious Business Learning How to Reference—Playfully

Juliette Smeed

The Background

Academic referencing: now there's a phrase to strike fear into undergraduate breasts.

Surely nothing can be more pedantic or joyless. In a video by Alan Tsibulya, shared through the Student Problems Facebook page, he quips, 'Did you know Satan actually has a son? Yeah, his name's referencing' (2017).

For many years I have taught the academic skills of referencing and avoiding plagiarism to students new to Higher Education. It was my good luck to start with students who had well-defined ideas about teaching and learning: Early Childhood Educators (ECE) working towards a Bachelor of Teaching qualification. In the New Zealand early childhood curriculum, the value of play is widely known and appreciated. Taking cues from our students, my colleagues and I created

J. Smeed (✉)
University of Buckingham, Buckingham, UK
e-mail: juliette.smeed@buckingham.ac.uk

© The Author(s) 2019
A. James and C. Nerantzi (eds.), *The Power of Play in Higher Education*,
https://doi.org/10.1007/978-3-319-95780-7_41

teaching resources inspired by games and play activities commonly used to engage young children in learning.

During study skills classes, after a brief topic introduction, I would present students with cut up references and ask them to fit the puzzle pieces together using a combination of visual clues and informed guess work. The reference pieces were made oversize, and slightly mixed up, to encourage conversations and physical engagement. When they had finished, groups of students ranged the room using guide sheets to identify the different types of references pieced together, with this part of the class run as a low-stakes competition to improve focus and add an element of fun. Similarly active mix-and-match and spot-the-difference games helped students identify different types of plagiarism or learn citation conventions. Because all these games were staples of the ECE classroom, referencing became instantly less mysterious and more do-able.

By the time I began teaching the same range of academic skills to undergraduate and postgraduate students in business-related disciplines (now in the UK), my playful puzzle-based approach to teaching referencing and avoiding plagiarism had become routine. Except—business students weren't having it. While their initial reactions to the prospect of learning academic referencing were comparable to early childhood educators—expressions of anxiety or boredom were common—business students responded to puzzles and guessing games differently. Some students were baffled, unable to link such apparently puerile activities to the serious, if boring, task of learning how to reference. Still others made it clear—either through time spent on task or more directly—that they thought the exercises trivial. Only occasionally would a group of business students have a playful response comparable to those I observed in groups of ECE educators. More commonly they expressed concern that I'd asked them to do something they hadn't been properly taught yet.

Throughout this exploration I stress 'playfulness' rather that 'play' because it is not straightforward to fit what happens in HE classrooms into commonly used definitions of play. For example Peter Gray notes that a defining characteristic of play is its 'self-chosen' nature, which includes 'the freedom to quit' (2013). When students engage in or disengage from planned classroom tasks their behaviour is not the same as that of intrinsically motivated players negotiating participation in a self-chosen activity. However, the responses of ECE students to my referencing games fit well into Bateson and Martin's definition of 'playful play' as play 'accompanied by a particular positive mood state in which the individual is more inclined to behave (and … think) in a spontaneous and flexible way' (2013). Therefore, I will use the terms 'play-based' (activities/tasks) and 'playful' (behaviours) to describe activities in HE classrooms.

The Challenge of Teaching Academic Referencing Playfully—Some Contexts

Strange as it seems now, it did not occur to me at the time that ECE teachers responded well to my referencing lessons because of their professional understanding of play-based learning. I somehow thought we'd discovered a universal solution to the problem of getting students to focus sufficiently on their academic skills. My oversight is particularly notable because Education in a discipline steeped in sociocultural understandings of how people learn. According to sociocultural theory, learning occurs as a result of social interactions that use socially produced artefacts within culturally specific settings (both symbolic, e.g. language, and physical, e.g. a puzzle) (Ratner 1998).

Within their cultural setting, ECE teachers have endless opportunities to see how play activities support learning in young children, opportunities that are then reinforced and legitimised by their formal disciplinary learning. However, for business students the playful lessons of childhood must seem a long way away. For many their most recent learning experiences are in A-level classrooms that are 'generally didactic' and 'teacher centred'; learning environments where '[t]eachers typically provide all of the information that their students will require to pass their examinations so that nothing is left to chance' (Jeffery 2012: 3).

Ken Robinson, among others, has written and spoken extensively about how schools educate children out of their creativity by stifling 'the processes and conditions that are most likely to bring it about' (2011). Students who are used to responding to classroom tasks as if they were the antithesis of play—dictated (not actively negotiated) and compelled (not self-chosen)—cannot be expected to automatically embrace a return to learning playfully after years of mental hard labour. These students are likely to be frustrated by the meandering lines of enquiry that characterise creative problem solving and unwilling to engage in helping to create the learning outcomes of a lesson. It is not that creativity or play have no part in their lives. Rather, play happens somewhere else in their lives: online, on sports fields, in pubs, or anywhere that isn't a classroom with a teacher in it.

In Defence of Playful Learning Approaches with Business Students

In addition to the challenges noted above, my difficulty is compounded by the fact that learning a 'study skill' such as referencing is peripheral to the interests of most business students, who are understandably more motivated to engage with their chosen subject. To make my provision more accessible to business students, for some time I switched to instruction-based lessons and sidelined playful learning by turning puzzles and games into sober quizzes. Students appeared more comfortable, but they did not learn better, nor did their engagement improve. Eventually, I returned to using playful puzzles and games for the reasons stated below.

First, academic referencing does not suit didactic teaching, or even particularly suit the demonstration and test method of teaching. A fundamental difficulty of learning to reference is that it is technical and fiddly. It requires attention to detail, but hardly ever inspires focused engagement and the right level of attention. A puzzle-based teaching approach encourages students to be curious while it incentivises them to grapple with difficulty. Players do not ration or rationalise effort because they are motivated by an intrinsic creative impulse which exceeds the task (Gray 2013). Playful behaviour, therefore, contrasts directly with the behaviour of surface learners, or even of strategic learners, who tend to focus on the outcome or products of study (Entwistle 2001) rather than engaging with the learning process.

Any lesson that successfully invokes students' capacity for play benefits from the excess effort they bring to the tasks. Once I have buy-in with the lesson, it becomes much easier to convey to students just how important academic referencing is to their lecturers, their discipline, and the wider academic endeavour. And there is a further benefit to this playful approach to teaching. When students engage playfully with a lesson, the result is greater levels of dialogue, spontaneous contributions and visible thinking, all of which create opportunities for me to get instant feedback on their learning.

Lastly, the act of puzzling out with peers how a reference system works involves exploration learning, which has a particularly benefit in HE classrooms. New university students can be anxious about their relative intelligence and often worry about not knowing 'right answers'. By providing opportunities for low stakes, collaborative problem solving I can help them overcome the fear of getting things wrong in public. It may even help to break down a fixed learner mindset, which Dweck characterises as 'an urgency to prove yourself over and over' so as not to appear 'dumb' (2012).

However, to achieve the benefits stated above, and effectively teach academic referencing to HE business students, I have to acknowledge that the secondary school classroom is a highly salient aspect of their recent learning experience. It is reasonable for students to expect lessons that involve familiar routines of information transfer and for them to be wary of classrooms where the 'right answers' exist, but are withheld as they are left to puzzle them out for themselves. If I wish to persist with a playful, exploration-based approach, I must scaffold students' return to learning playfully in classrooms. I need, therefore, a way to bridge the gap between what I believe to be good for students' learning and the lessons they are more familiar with. Something that will motivate business students. In other words, I need Steve Jobs.

Innovation: The Link Between Business, Study and Play

Traditionally the adult world into which HE students are transitioning has treated business as the opposite of play: where the former is a nonessential, frivolous use of time and resources, the latter requires a serious, focused effort at creating value. However, the example of Apple guru Steve Jobs cuts through these dominant, at times unexamined ideas, with an alternative business narrative.

Jobs is an aspirational hero figure for many business students. As an innovator he is renowned for his combination of focus and creativity. Stories abound of how his commitment to puzzling out problems has led time and again to extraordinary insights and innovative products. While students tend to see him as a model for business success, I can faithfully promote him as a model for creativity and associative thinking. And, when I promote this side of Steve Jobs, I create a framework for play as 'an effective mechanism ... for encouraging creativity and hence facilitating innovation' (Bateson and Martin 2013).

While Jobs is an exceptional individual, he also exemplifies the now accepted wisdom that businesses need innovators to succeed (for example, see Dyer et al. 2009). In global marketplaces characterised by rapid change, the ability to think ahead and around the competition is key to business survival and success. Stories of Jobs and other innovators that stress their willingness to play with ideas and objects help to make the purpose of play in HE business classrooms clear and encourage students to use learning approaches that support them to become innovative problem solvers like their heroes.

Beyond teaching students how to reference (a technical skill they really do need to succeed in their HE studies) I consider I am teaching students how to learn in ways that are brave, creative and focused on solving puzzling problems—all vital lessons within the business discipline and the professions. The information age has made learning and retention of higher knowledge into an old-fashioned technology—not redundant, but certainly less valuable than it once was. Students add value to their HE qualifications when they become proficient in behaviours that support them to become innovative problem solvers. Already this is acknowledged in the government's plans for the TEF Teaching Excellence Framework (as laid out in the 2016 White Paper *Success as a knowledge economy*) where innovation is linked to both teaching quality and research outputs (Department for Business, Innovation and Skills 2016). More specifically, our QAA Benchmark statement includes 'innovation, creativity and enterprise' on the list of 'Skills of particular relevance to business and management' students in HE (2015: 8).

Steve Jobs and his fellow innovators are my allies as I challenge business students' expectations of how they will learn in HE classrooms and work to convince all students to resist narrowly strategic approaches to learning and solving problems. Innovators (in contrast to inventors) may start from what exists and what is known, but they never stop there. They play with ideas and technologies in order to extend the boundaries of what is currently possible. And, as the CEO of 3M George Buckley knows from experience, innovation needs time and space dedicated to that play: an immediate focus on capturing commercial value will suppress innovation (cited in Berger et al. 2009: 61–62). Insights into the mechanisms of innovation can help students see how classroom tasks that require them to think laterally, act playfully, and take risks, have long-term business benefits. And in this endeavour I am joined by other allies: my Lego and spaghetti wielding colleagues in the business school.

Although the rigid rules of referencing may be forever beyond the reach of student innovators, referencing games and puzzles provide them with practice with the antecedents of innovative thinking. The open, explorative activity of 'puzzling' creates the space for 'what if?' questions and opportunities for students to playfully test possibilities in the search for answers. Through game-based activities, I can even switch the mysterious nature of the referencing code from a turn off, into a motiving force.

For these reasons, despite the challenges, I continue to grow in the belief that the long-term benefits of a playful classroom outweigh any difficulties. Ultimately it will not be just business students who benefit from playful learning opportunities designed to foster problem-solving mindsets. In 2016/2017 in the UK 333,425 students were enrolled in business and administrative studies: it was the largest single subject area (HESA 2018). The future of so many business students will inevitably affect many more people. Surely anything that serious must be worth playing with?

References

Bateson, P., & Martin, P. (2013). *Play, Playfulness, Creativity and Innovation.* Cambridge: Cambridge University Press (E-Book).

Berger, R., Dutta, S., Raffel, T., & Samuels, G. (2009). *Innovating at the Top: How Global CEOs Drive Innovation for Growth and Profit.* Hampshire and New York: Palgrave Macmillan.

Department for Business, Innovation and Skills. (2016). *Higher Education: Success as a Knowledge Economy.* Cm 9258. Available at https://www.gov.uk/government/publications/higher-education-success-as-a-knowledge-economy-white-paper. Accessed July 3, 2017.

Dweck, C. (2012). *Mindset: Changing the Way You Think to Fulfil Your Potential.* London: Little, Brown Book Group.

Dyer, J. H., Gregersen, H., & Christensen, C. M. (2009). The Innovator's DNA. *Harvard Business Review.* Available at https://hbr.org/2009/12/the-innovators-dna. Accessed May 30, 2018.

Entwistle, N. (2001). Styles of Learning and Approaches to Studying in Higher Education. *Kybernetes, 30*(5/6), 593–603.

Gray, P. (2013). *Definitions of Play.* Available at http://www.scholarpedia.org/article/Definitions_of_Play. Accessed July 3, 2017.

HESA. (2018). *Courses: All Students by Subject Area and Sex.* Available at https://www.hesa.ac.uk/data-and-analysis/students/courses. Accessed January 14, 2018.

Jeffery, E. (2012). *A Review of the Literature Examining the Pedagogical Differences Between A Level and University: Executive Summary.* Cambridge: ARD Research Division Cambridge Assessment.

Quality Assurance Agency. (2015). *Subject Benchmark Statement: Business and Management.* QAA1089. Gloucester: The Quality Assurance Agency for Higher Education.

Ratner, C. (1998). *Historical and Contemporary Significance of Vygotsky's Sociohistorical Psychology*. Available at http://www.sonic.net/~cr2/sociohis.htm. Accessed July 3, 2017.

Robinson, K. (2011). *Out of Our Minds: Learning to Be Creative*. Oxford: Capstone Publishing.

Tsibulya, A. (2017). *University Students in 1 Minute*. 7 March. Available at https://www.instagram.com/p/BRVHdY6jj6d/?hl=en. Accessed July 3, 2017.

The Playground Model Revisited: A Proposition for Playfulness to Boost Creativity in Academic Development

Chrissi Nerantzi

Overview

In this exploration, I share my current thinking and reflections about academic development through the playground (Nerantzi 2015). This is a conceptual model I developed based on my practice, experience and related scholarly activities linked to the postgraduate module Creativity for Learning (#creativeHE) as part of the Masters in Higher Education offered at the Centre for Excellence in Learning and Teaching at Manchester Metropolitan University in the United Kingdom, a related open course and open community operating since January 2015 (Nerantzi and Jackson 2018) as well as the institution-wide Greenhouse community for creative practitioners since 2014 (Nerantzi 2016). Offering these professional development opportunities, enabled and supported by social media technologies, has meant that this offer has been opened up to all higher

---

C. Nerantzi (✉)
Centre for Excellence in Learning and Teaching,
Manchester Metropolitan University, Manchester, UK
e-mail: c.nerantzi@mmu.ac.uk

education staff, students and the wider public. These interlinked academic development initiatives that all have a focus on developing creative capacity and capabilities within an academic development context in higher education, enabled me to question my creative and playful practice deeply, deconstruct and re-construct it critically and creatively and develop a framework that first of all helped me frame specific aspects of my practice. Furthermore, it enabled me to propose the Playground model as a design tool and scaffold to be considered by practitioners who are keen to inject and integrate creative play into their teaching practice and create some of the conditions to stimulate creative learning and teaching experiences that feed the imagination and curiosity, therefore bringing learning alive and potentially lead to innovations in teaching.

While I descend into the 'swamp' of my own reflections as Schön (1987: 3) would probably frame it, I plan to use the reflective model by Rolfe et al. (2001) based on three key questions: What? So what? Now what? This model, I feel, gives me the freedom and a loose scaffold at the same time to present my thoughts within a reflective cycle since the original conception of the Playground model, reflect on its use and explore some of the opportunities it now presents to me and others.

In the following section, I will reflect on the development of the Playground model as a continuum to enable and stimulate playful learning as a creativity booster and articulate its relationship to wider theoretical positions around learning and teaching and creativity in the context of higher education.

Zooming In: What Is This All About?

Playful learning seems to have surfaced in the last few years in higher education. The playful experimenters full of curiosity who are not afraid to break the rules, invent new ones and explore new territories, are stepping into the limelight. More of their seeds are germinating and increasingly this happens more visibly. Could it be that the shift towards active, participatory and experiential approaches to learning and teaching as well as game-based learning also contributed to creating a more receptive environment to playful learning? Are we indeed now re-learning the value of play?

There is now a platform to express and share playful learning and teaching approaches more widely through a range of dissemination activities including dedicated (academic) play conferences and publication opportunities such as journals and magazines. Playful practices shared openly via social media and further digital technologies, are helping not only to amplify playful learning and teaching in higher education, strengthen the playful practitioner voices, spread the bug and create a positive climate for its wider use, but also increase playful and creative making. Theoretical and empirical frameworks and models can further support the development of effective pedagogical practices supported by technologies (Reeves and Reeves 1997; Mayes and de Freitas 2013). The Playground model aims to contribute to this.

In the original article, I synthesised and shared my ideas towards a Playground model (Nerantzi 2015) for academic development to support playful interactions in learning and teaching, as I feel that these play a key role in creating the conditions that foster creativity and the multidirectional flowing of ideas, novel problem solving, activities and practices vital to feed our curiosity, question, improvise, develop our criticality and make novel connections and discoveries. Academic development has a focus on the enhancement and transformation of practitioners and practices. We often work with new academics and other professionals who teach or support learning, and inspiring them to become more effective and creative in their teaching is important to us. But is this possible? Watts and Blessinger (2017) note that somebody becomes creative only when they have mastered the discipline and this can take years. Does this mean new practitioners are less creative? Or dare to be playful and creative? Does this apply to teaching a subject too? My approach as defined through the Playground model may challenge this as we often do work with new academics. Bateson and Martin (2013: 43) claim 'play may have opened up new possibilities… that it [is] a source of creativity' or how I might say, it has the power to make the impossible possible. We play on our own, with others collaboratively and we play competitively too (Nussbaum 2013). Playing on own, in collaboration with others but also competing against each other can be valuable depending on the purpose of the approach used in a particular situation. A model dedicated to nurturing playful learning, could, I felt, assist myself and others in designing-in and scaffolding playful learning that would lead progressively to creative empowerment and innovative teaching. But we do need to remember and acknowledge that there are other approaches to boost creativity beyond play and playful learning and that it is advisable to see play as one of the tools in the toolkit and not as the answer to everything.

The Playground model was developed on and informed by related theory and practice. It emerged through the postgraduate Creativity for Learning module and the associated institution-wide Greenhouse community and open and cross-institutional development activities that had collaborative open learning features offered as open educational practices supported by social media which was studied carefully. Findings of a phenomenographic study in which the collaborative open learning experience was explored (Nerantzi 2017) shows, that #creativeHE, which was part of the collective case study and the Playground model was developed within this case, suggest that it enabled cross-disciplinary and cross-institutional development for academics and other professionals who support learning in higher education. The open nature of the module also created opportunities for cross-boundary learning experienced as *anyone* (not just for academics but also with students and the wider public, formally and informally), *anywhere* (not just online and mobile but also offline and locally), with *anyhelp* (supported by course facilitators, peers and public) and *anyhow* (thanks to the elasticity of the pedagogical design and choice) especially within the facilitated collaborative learning groups. The cross-boundary and diverse characteristics of the groups had a positive impact on individual and collective engagement, motivation and sharing of ideas. Furthermore, the pedagogical design appears to have impacted on engagement. One of the categories of description that emerged had a focus on open learning as designed for collaborative learning. The qualitatively different variations within this category of description were constraining, enabling and empowering. The findings suggest that the notion of freedom played a key role in learner empowerment and creative engagement (Nerantzi 2017). This was particularly evident linked to the data collected from #creativeHE where the pedagogical approach was elastic and based on the playground model. The following example from study participant C1 provides some related insights:

> The group we formed, I think was really interesting and engaging at the same time. We tried to, we maintained the main idea of the course, creativity of course. But through discussing and exchanging ideas, and our thoughts, in the hangouts meetings we found it that there are specific dimensions of creativity that we wanted to explore. For example, we agreed all to engage in the project which investigated the role of emotions throughout the community. Participant C1

In the original article about the Playground model, linked it to further frameworks and theoretical positions (see, for example, Ramsden [2008]; Jackson [2015] summarised in Table A.1).

For me, these frameworks offer a representation of teaching and learning as a continuum, as multiple dynamic movements. These movements enable change and transformations through varying the degree and intensity of teacher and learner input and control. A mix of approaches will work better to create stimulating learning experiences (Brookfield 2017). A skillful and effective teacher and learner move dynamically along this

Table A.1 The three main theories of teaching (Ramsden 2008); Creativity and learning ecologies (Jackson 2015); Playground framework (Nerantzi 2015)

Three main theories of teaching (Ramsden 2008)	Creativity and learning ecologies (Jackson 2015)	Playground model (Nerantzi 2015)
Theory 1: Teaching as telling, transmission or delivery—passive	Education 1.0/Creativity 1.0/Learning Ecology 1.0—instructivist	Playground 1.0 supervised>feeling safe, developing trust
Theory 2: Teaching as organising or facilitating student activity—active	Education 2.0/Creativity 2.0/Learning Ecology 2.0—constructivist	Playground 2.0 participatory>gaining playful confidence through guided playful learning
Theory 3: Teaching as making learning possible—self-directed	Education 3.0/Creativity 3.0/Learning Ecology 3.0—connectivist	Playground 3.0 self-determined>autonomy, developing and sustaining play-active practice

continuum depending on the specific situation they are in. Therefore, the whole continuum is equally valuable and needs to be used critically and responsibly. In an attempt to understand the two ends of the continuum using an analogy from chicken farming, one could say that one end of the continuum resembles a more battery-type (reactive or dependent) way of learning and teaching (or passive, according to Ramsden [2008]) or instructivist according to Jackson (2015) while the other end of the continuum has characteristics of a free-range (proactive or independent) way of learning and teaching (or self-directed, according to Ramsden [2008] and connectivist according to Jackson [2015]). Looking closer at this continuum that stretches from dependence to independence, I am wondering where interdependence would be located on this continuum. Taking a closer look at Jackson's (2015) Education 3/0/Creativity 3.0 and its explicit links to connectivism, one might see the relevance of interdependence there, framed as a valuable characteristic for learning. Palmer (2007: 11) wrote 'Good teachers possess a capacity for connectedness. They are able to weave a complex web of connections among themselves, their subjects, and their students so that students can learn to weave a world for themselves'. With these words, Palmer highlights the important role of the teacher and their relationship with the learner and how this is shaping learner attitude and practices. His words made me think about interdependence in a different way and I am wondering if it actually stretches across the whole continuum and perhaps even underpins it as a whole? What varies could be the nature and intensity of interdependence depending on the relationships between teacher, the learner and other learners at different points within the continuum as beautifully written by Palmer (see extract above).

The Playground model depicts the dynamic relationship between theories of teaching more generally and creativity, where playful learning is positioned within these. It provides a scaffold for how playful learning can be integrated into academic development practice but also more widely in learning and teaching based on an informed pedagogical rationale (Nerantzi 2015). So far, this model has been used since its conception in 2015, as far as I am aware, within #creativeHE.

While James and Brookfield (2014: 55) define the vital ingredients of creative reflection as a cocktail of playfulness, creativity, imagination and criticality, I can see that the concept of this cocktail could be extended further and include practice and therefore advocate for a more integrated approach to reflective practice and emphasising empowerment to act, change and transform practice as a result of reflection.

In the next section, I will attempt to analyse and synthesise key pedagogical features of the Playground model and articulate what these could mean for practice.

Zooming Out: So What?

The development of the Playground model (Nerantzi 2015), my relationship with the Creativity for Learning module and associated open and cross-boundary professional development activities through the #creativeHE community, enabled me to use and re-use the model many times in practice as well as reflect on and refine it. This exploration offers an opportunity to share my emerging thoughts about the Playground model and present a more critical and refined version of it while also constructing the theoretical framework around it. Constructing the theoretical framework has helped me organise my thoughts with greater clarity and share these with others so that they can consider it in their practice as a design tool to foster playful learning to boost creativity and innovation in learning and teaching.

Revisiting the pedagogical features of the Playground model, I can see clearly that *connections* and *spaces* feature strongly in these (Nerantzi 2015). Connections to people, ideas and artefacts. *Connections* enabled in *spaces*. These foster learning experiences across the three domains of learning (Bloom 1984), the cognitive (knowing, head), psychomotor (doing, hand) and affective (feeling, heart) domain in *spaces* and *communities* build on trust. Project Zero (2016: 4) makes that link beautifully by stating that 'playful learning offers a pathway for intellectual, social, emotional, and physical development'.

Creating special spaces for play should not be underestimated. Nussbaum (2013: 126 and 142) calls these 'magic circles' where individuals come together, as he says, to 'connect the dots, prototype, make mistakes, and learn from them' but also to share, as he says their 'unfiltered opinions, listening to and building on another's ideas in order to reach insights none of you may have ever discovered on your own'. Brown (2009: 197) also acknowledges the social dimension of play, and claims that 'play sets the stage for cooperative socialization. It nourishes the roots of trust, empathy, caring, and sharing'. Nussbaum (2013) also recognises the importance of trust to make novel discoveries. But trust is not a given. James and Brookfield (2014: 64) talk about 'optimistic trust' as a prerequisite for playful learning and teaching which they define as a state of being where we suspend judgement and let go of fixed preconceptions to open our minds to alternative views in the learning and teaching process which may surprise us.

Sharing as widely as possible, according to Weller (2014: 136), should be 'at the heart of educational practice'. A factor that further promoted wider sharing were the open, collaborative and cross-boundary nature of the communities in which the Playground model was developed supported through social media (Nerantzi 2017). Furthermore, Engeström et al. (1995) recognised that cross-boundary communities foster horizontal working practices that break the monopoly of expertise constructed by the expert and therefore enable diverse views to be shared between expert, novice and the public. Furthermore, Bateson and Martin (2013) acknowledge in the context of cross-disciplinary working that creativity is stimulated especially where there is variety, diversity of individuals, views and ideas. James and Brookfield (2014) add that such interactions can spark original and creative ideas. Cross-boundary learning increases diversity even further and the benefits of novel ideas and perspectives to come together and be formed are amplified significantly. Algers (2016) found that such cross-boundary communities also increase trust, something I have observed myself and it is a fundamental built-in feature of the Playground model. These communities of trust that stretch across online and offline *spaces*, foster and nurture novel and diverse ideas of individuals who are prepared to open up, curious about the world around them, take risks, playfully experiment, have fun but also struggle at times, make mistakes and learn from them but also share their eureka moments with honesty and openness. The practices I observed within #creativeHE, online and offline, through the application of the model, evidence this. Treviranus

(2016: 7) notes 'It is our variability that gives us collective strength' while Nussbaum (2013) translates this collective strength based on diversity and where there is trust into a vehicle that fuels the generation of novel ideas. It is indeed this variability expressed through diversity, respect, togetherness, trust and sharing that seems to create a powerful and motivational playful learning cocktail. Within #creativeHE this was experienced within the wider learning community as well as the smaller collaborative groups.

I can still recognise how the model was synthesised through practice, careful observations and study of relevant literature. The chemistry playful learning created for individual and collective engagement and creative development within and beyond the small collaborative learning groups online and in the open and offline in my private spaces, as well as the choices and opportunities it provided for learning and development was magical. Palmer (2007) emphasises the importance of human connections among teachers and learners and the impact this has on learner to learner interactions. Furthermore, human connections are equally important when fostering creativity and innovations. Playful learning in groups can have a positive impact on creativity and innovation and have a ripple effect across an institution (Bateson and Martin 2013). When these are cross-boundary groups, the ripple effect will stretch beyond institutional walls and magnify the opportunities for collaboration and collective discovery and progress.

Jackson (2015) sees the connections as a key characteristic of Creativity 3.0 that boosts creative learning through creative teaching applying connectivist approaches. The theory behind it, as articulated by Siemens (2006: 15–16), is a recognition that 'learning is primarily a network-forming process' that illuminates the importance these connections play for learning.

The above reflective analysis on the Playground model and its key pedagogical characteristics shows the relationship and interconnectedness of the model with the Three Domains of Learning (Bloom 1984), connectivism (Siemens 2006) and the concept of cross-boundary communities (Engeström et al. 1995; Algers 2016; Nerantzi 2017).

The development of the Playground model within an optional module dedicated to promote Creativity for learning and teaching in higher education and further associated open professional development activities, might be seen by some as a natural home for it. Attracting academics who are already open to the idea of creativity does help secure buy-in and spread the bug for playful learning. However, I should acknowledge that sticking exclusively with those academics might be limiting the opportunities for more rigorous academic dialogue and debate and consider more radical and novel approaches to learning and teaching. Identifying ways to bring in other-minded individuals, more sceptical ones, and immerse them into experiencing the model in practice, would, I think, have the potential to strengthen it more widely and help it develop and evolve into new directions and territories. Adriansen (2010: 84) argues that '… I would advocate using creative teaching methods rather than designing separate courses in creativity. Hence, teaching creativity should be done through creative teaching'. Reflecting critically on this idea, and remembering how the module Creativity for Learning in HE came to life in the first place, due to resistance experienced while using creative and playful learning and teaching approaches more integrated, but also based on my more recent reflections and scholarly activities on co-facilitation the module, I would agree with Adriansen. It is true that developing the model in a safe greenhouse and perhaps less hostile space, has given me the time and space to experiment and play with the ideas, refine and mature them and construct the model, in a way in my own playground. However, as Brookfield (2017) notes, some resistance will always be there when we try something new. It shouldn't stop us though. The space within #creativeHE has helped academics who have engaged with it voluntarily to experience the transformative power of play themselves and establish creative and playful habits and practices. These appear to have boosted their love and passion for teaching and now fuel their curiosity, imagination and practice to create stimulating learning experiences for their students. I couldn't have asked for more.

In the next section, I will explore some of the opportunities the Playground model presents for future practice and research.

Moving On: Now What?

Revisiting the Playground model about two years after its original development and use in relation to the Creativity for Learning module and associated #creativeHE activities online and offline, helped me revisit the original ideas relating to this and articulate with greater accuracy the key features of the model and also position it in related academic literature while also identifying specific ways to take it forward. This is what I will do in this final section.

The Playground model, its continuum and how it relates to existing theoretical perspectives and pedagogical ideas and concepts is helping me now to redesign the model visually (see Fig. A. 1) in relation to relevant theories explored within this chapter so that the model can become a curriculum design tool and be used to model playful learning in academic development to foster and develop creative learning and teaching. Through its application in these settings it may also provide food-for-thought to academics and other professionals who teach in higher education, immerse them into experiencing it as learners, before adopting such approaches in their own practice.

As a result of my reflections on the Playground model and its current application (see previous section), I feel that it is now time to release the Playground model for it to be used in other settings, modules and programmes. It is about time to break free from the safe and welcoming space that was created through #creativeHE and the individuals who engaged and engage with it thanks to their open minds for creative and playful learning and teaching approaches. And while choice plays a key role in learning, experiencing the uncomfortable and alien is equally important in the learning process. Engaging the perhaps more resistant, critical, sceptical practitioners into a discussion, debate and playful interactions to explore the opportunities playful learning present to boost creativity in their practice is equally important, if not more important, as these individuals often don't see themselves as creative (Bateson and Martin 2013) than to continue using it exclusively with like-minded individuals who are already open to more novel approaches to learning and teaching. The time is ripe for me to consider adapting

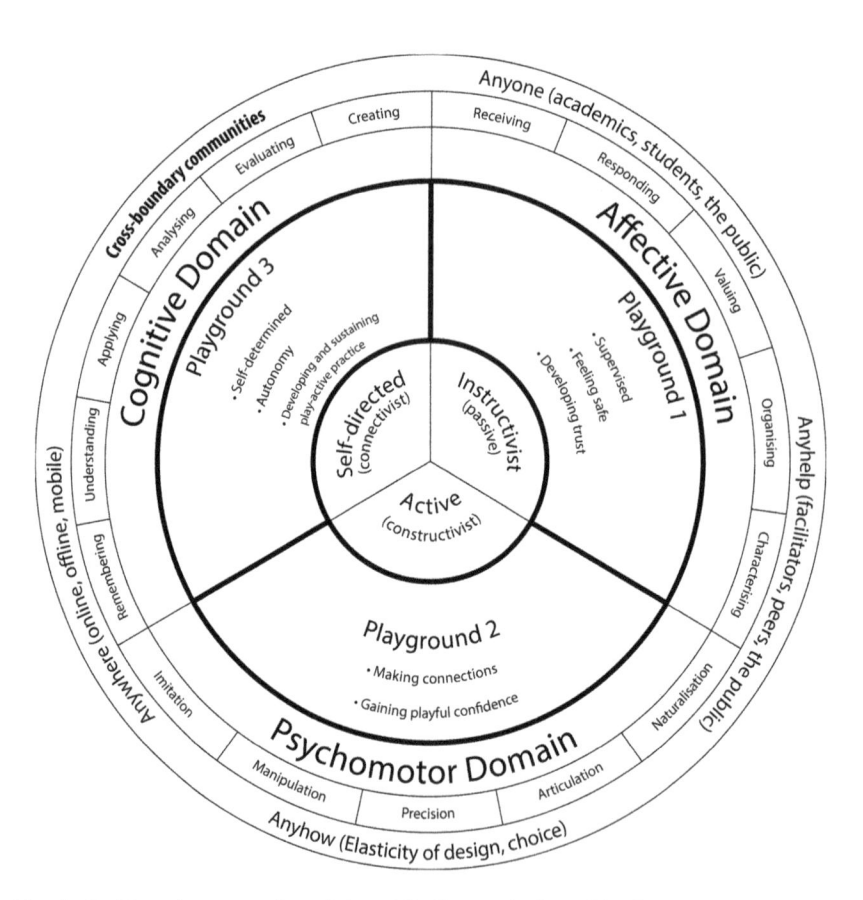

Fig. A. 1 The playground model and its theoretical positioning

the Playground model within the core modules of the Postgraduate Certificate in Learning and Teaching in Higher Education to progressively develop critical and creative playful practices in a more integrated and perhaps surprising way where it is expected the least. My latest readings brought me to a series of articles about the pedagogy of play in childhood (a recent example by Project Zero 2016). Through my wanderings, I discovered significantly less about the role of play after childhood. Farnè (2005) and Resnick (2017), for example, remark that play is a lifelong human activity. More research in this area would help. Perhaps also the articulation of a pedagogy for play or play as learning. Play that is defined as integral and fully embedded into all stages of education, including higher education.

The wider use of the Playground model in formal academic development based on an open and collaborative ethos and using open and social media to extend reach and increase boundary crossing opportunities, may help academics to consider it for their own teaching practice in a range of disciplines and professional areas. Parallel to its use, it will be equally important to build in evaluative research. This will provide valuable insights into its use and help the further development and evolution of it as a response to practice and research.

Final Remarks

Being in the swamp again and critically reflecting and exploring my own Playground creation was a complex and messy task but also an insightful one. I feel, that I have now more clearly articulated for myself and others what this model is about and made connections stronger and more explicit to existing theories and concepts that influence and shape playful learning as I see it, to boost creativity and innovations in learning and teaching. A playground can help diverse individuals and groups create a safe space to develop trust in each other but also in self, open up, be brave, take risks and explore (im)possibilities that we wouldn't otherwise even think of and boost individual and collective creativity. Stefani (2017) notes that the key function of academic development should be more about transformation and less about compliance. However, academics themselves need to be convinced first! Therefore, playgrounds may be especially valuable for modelling practices that academics could consider for their practice to increase creative and innovative teaching and foster stimulating learning experiences for our students. Open-up your playgrounds to enable cross-boundary playful learning! Consider open practices and the use of open and social media to make it happen. I am looking forward to finding out how other practitioners may use the Playground model within academic development and more widely for learning and teaching and evaluating its use in my own wider practices.

Acknowledgements I would like to thank Margy Macmillan who kindly read the first drafts of this chapter and made valuable suggestions to further improve it as well as Liz Walshaw for digitising my hand-drawn image for Fig. A. 1.

References

Algers, A. (2016). *OEP as Boundary Practices—How Academy and Society Can Inform Each Other.* ExplOER Project Webinar. Available at https://connect.sunet.se/p4gxj96aglg/?launcher=false&fcsContent=true&pbMode=normal. Accessed December 28, 2017.

Andriasen, H. K. (2010). How Criticality Affects Students' Creativity. In C. Nygaard, N. Courtney, & C. Holtham (Eds.), *Teaching Creativity—Creativity in Teaching, The Learning in Higher Education Series* (pp. 65–84). Faringdon: Libri Publishing.

Bateson, P., & Martin, P. (2013). *Play, Playfulness, Creativity and Innovation.* Cambridge: Cambridge University Press.

Bloom, B. S. (1984). *Taxonomy of Educational Objectives Book 1: Cognitive Domain* (2nd ed.). New York: Longman.

Brookfield, S. (2017). Creative Approaches to Stimulate Classroom Discussions. In L. S. Watts & P. Blessinger (Eds.), *Creative Learning in Higher Education: International Perspectives and Approaches* (pp. 159–176). Oxon: Routledge.

Brown, S. (2009). Play. In *How It Shapes the Brain, Opens the Imagination, and Invigorates the Soul.* New York: Penguin books.

Engeström, Y., Engeström, R., & Kärkkäinen, M. (1995). Polycontextuality and Boundary Crossing in Expert Cognition: Learning and Problem Solving in Complex Work Activities. *Learning and Instruction, 5*(4), 319–336.

Farnè, R. (2005, September). Pedagogy of Play. *Topoi, 24*(2), 169–181. Available at https://link.springer.com/article/10.1007/s11245-005-5053-5. Accessed May 30, 2018.

Jackson, N. J. (2015). Towards Creativity 3.0: A Narrative for Creativity & Learning Ecologies in Higher Education. *Finding Our Element, Creative Academic Magazine, 1,* 32–37. Available at http://www.creativeacademic.uk/magazine.html. Accessed May 30, 2018.

James, A., & Brookfield, S. (2014). *Engaging Imagination: Helping Students Become Creative and Reflective Thinkers*. San Francisco, CA: Jossey-Bass.

Mayes, T., & de Freitas, S. (2013). Technology-Enhanced Learning. The Role of Theory. In H. Beetham & R. Sharpe (Eds.), *Rethinking Pedagogy for a Digital Age: Designing for 21st Century Learning* (2nd ed., pp. 17–30). Oxon: Routledge.

Nerantzi, C. (2015). The Playground Model for Creative Professional Development. In C. Nerantzi & A. James (Eds.), *Exploring Play in Higher Education, Creative Academic Magazine* (Issue 2A, pp. 40–50). Available at http://www.creativeacademic.uk/. Accessed May 30, 2018.

Nerantzi, C. (2016). Using Ecological Metaphors to Represent Professional Growth: Our Extraordinary 'Greenhouse', Its Creative Academic Gardeners and the Growing of Pedagogical Ideas. *Exploring Creative Ecologies, Creative Academic Magazine, 5*, 64–70. Available at http://www.creativeacademic.uk/magazine.html. Accessed May 30, 2018.

Nerantzi, C. (2017). *Towards a Framework for Cross-Boundary Collaborative Open Learning Framework for Cross-Institutional Academic Development* (Upublished Ph.D. thesis). Edinburgh Napier University, Edinburgh.

Nerantzi, C., & Jackson, J. N. (2018). #CreativeHE: An Animated Google+Platform for Challenging Practitioners to Think Differently. In K. Reedy & J. Parker (Eds.), *Digital Literacy Unpacked* (pp. 123–137). London: Facet Publishing.

Nussbaum, B. (2013). *Creative Intelligence: Harnessing the Power to Create, Connect, and Inspire*. New York: HarperCollins Publisher.

Palmer, P. J. (2007). *The Courage to Teach: Exploring the Inner Landscape of a Teacher's Life*. San Francisco: Jossey-Bass.

Project Zero. (2016). *Towards a Pedagogy of Play*. Harvard Graduate School of Education. Available at http://pz.harvard.edu/resources/towards-a-pedagogy-of-play. Accessed May 30, 2018.

Ramsden, P. (2008). *The Future of Higher Education: Teaching and the Student Experience*. London: Department for Innovation, Universities and Skills.

Reeves, T., & Reeves, P. (1997). Effective Dimensions of Interactive Learning on the World Wide Web. In B. Khan (Ed.), *Web-Based Instruction* (pp. 59–66). Englewood Cliffs: Educational Technology Publications.

Resnick, M. (2017). *Lifelong Kindergarten: Cultivating Creativity Through Projects, Passion, Peers and Play*. Cambridge: The MIT Press.

Rolfe, G., Freshwater, D., & Jasper, M. (2001). *Critical Reflection for Nursing and the Helping Professions: A User's Guide*. Basingstoke: Palgrave Macmillan.

Schön, D. (1987). *Educating the Reflective Practitioner*. San Francisco: Jossey-Bass.

Siemens, G. (2006). *Knowing Knowledge*. Available at www.knowingknowledge.com. Accessed February 20, 2013.

Stefani, L. (2017). Realizing the Potential for Creativity in Teaching and Learning. In L. S. Watts & P. Blessinger (Eds.), *Creative Learning in Higher Education: International Perspectives and Approaches* (pp. 196–209). Oxon: Routledge.

Treviranus, J. (2016). Life-Long Learning on the Inclusive Web. In *Proceedings of the 13th Web for All Conference*, Article 1. Montreal, Canada, April 11–13. Available at https://dl.acm.org/citation.cfm?id=2899476. Accessed May 30, 2018.

Watts, L. S., & Blessinger, P. (2017). History and Nature of Creative Learning. In L. S. Watts & P. Blessinger (Eds.), *Creative Learning in Higher Education: International Perspectives and Approaches* (pp. 3–13). Oxon: Routledge.

Weller, M. (2014). *The Battle for Open: How Openness Won and Why It Doesn't Feel Like Victory*. London: Ubiquity Press.

Coda

In the closing pages of the traditional novel you typically have a grand reveal or a denouement and general tidying of loose ends. This, of course, is not a novel, although it might be considered a collection of short (ish) academic stories. Each has had its own kind of reveal, however subtle, and with so many voices in the text there was never going to be a tidy finish. At this point, you may be reflecting on your own responses to what you have read and where these might take you. As we leave you, we would like to share certain things that have crystallised for us in uniting a plethora of voices.

We have seen that rich and diverse play practices are happening across borders in a wide range of HE disciplines and settings. They confirm that play is a full body experience and that the heart, hand and head are vital ingredients to make it work. Play can transcend contexts or be embedded within disciplinary structures, habits and practices. Our expectations of, and beliefs about, play can be subjective and deeply personal. It finds its shape in us, and we find the right fit of play to suit our preferences. Emotional connections are made through playful learning that really stretches our imagination and curiosity to explore and discover at any age or level. Play definitions are varied and intricate; play types defy enumeration. Objects, models and games are a few threads in a play fabric which has a far richer weave than we might first have thought. The digital is seen to be used as normalised practice alongside learning outdoors; both help our minds wonder and wander. In some stories students became the playmakers, bringing to life the idea of staff–student partnership which can sometimes feel a little worn or too lightly used. The argument for learning through making games or designing play activities has been reinforced in so many ways as a strong motivator for engagement and learning.

What we have seen, too, is that play is not just about having fun, being jolly or escaping hard graft. Inventing play activities can be inspiring but it can take time, and effort and meticulous preparation. Far easier (but less rewarding?) to fish out well-travelled lecture notes that we know will cover the ground. Playing to learn can be uncomfortable; when through play we challenge ourselves to engage in ways we are unsure about, or in using play to tackle matters which are not lighthearted. Through play, we can find ourselves scrutinising aspects of living and learning in our world that make us uneasy. They cause us to question, make us feel wobbly on our feet or in our minds, and destabilise our views of accepted norms.

Above all, these stories show that the potential for play in higher education is wide open, with ground still to be broken. Our examples include playful learning within undergraduate and postgraduate provision but few mention doctoral studies. Anecdotally we know that play is being used as part of doctoral supervision and within creative research methods and practices, and yet those examples are mostly lying under the surface of publication at the moment. Play in HE is an exciting area which is under-researched and which is wide open for further investigation. Many of the contributions focus on using play for classroom activities and informal learning, integrated into the everyday learning and teaching process. We talk less of its use relating to assessment, although again we are aware of experimentation in this area. What are the opportunities that this offers? Is there a place for playful assessment? And what about the differences that can be explored, such as those between play and games, or other play types? And who will tackle the tensions inherent within our views of free play as part of a university curriculum?

If we are just getting the hang of purposeful play, then how much more of a road we have to travel in allowing ourselves permission for purposeless and open-ended playing.

It is very bad form in essay writing to post rhetorical questions and then leave them unanswered. We are not writing an essay, thankfully. Such questions are among the many that we are pondering, and which we invite our fellows at university—educators, researchers, administrators, managers, students and those in our wider community—to answer. We now hand this book (and its online companion) over to you, whatever your relationship to higher education. How might you extend your own ways of reflecting, creating, and playing in life, work and learning?

Index

abstract, building 227–36
academic development 199–201, 240, 317–19, 322, 327, 329
academics 9, 11, 319–20, 326–7, 329
  ESCAPE 33, 35
  GBL resources 285–6
  LEGO® 241
  Ludic model 29
  module co-designing 300
  referencing 296
accomplishment 61, 132, 168
accountability 12, 218
achievement 13, 28, 62, 153, 217–18
Ackerman, Diane 7
acquaintances 95
actions (action plans) 58, 68, 80, 240, 267, 274
  places 95–6, 98

activities 69, 95, 265, 266
adaptation 48, 68, 267, 286
Adriansen, H. K. 326
adults 216
adventure 11, 34–5, 46, 94, 187
agency 34, 39, 94, 278
Algers, A. 324
algorithms 268
ambiguity 94, 106, 115
Ambiguity of Play, The 177
analysis 134, 182, 270, 305
anatomy 233, 236
anecdotes
  birthday candles 136
  chalk breaking 137
  mobile phone tossing 135
  pomegranates 131–2
  wooden blocks 133–4
Anglia Ruskin University 295
answers 124, 247

anticipation 104, 108
anxiety 69, 71, 124, 179, 217, 224
applications 169, 324, 327
   building the abstract 235
   GBL resources 286
   LEGO® 240
   maths 160
   players' perspective 264
   PM 142
   public engagement 150
   referencing 296
   theory representations 248
   Wardopoly 276
   worms and waste 164
Apprentice, The 286
appropriateness 13, 51
arches, building 133–4
art 161, 255
art and design 68–9
artefacts 17, 103, 323
   building the abstract 228
   classrooms 104–5
   curiosity and play 105–6
   HE 106–7
   Ludic model 25
   play and creativity model 68–9
   professional love 244
   referencing 309
   student experience 107–9
   urban learning spaces 176. *See also* cabinets of curiosities
artists 105, 164, 190
arts, digital 59
aspirations 62, 216, 217, 243
assessment 60–2, 71, 103, 137–8, 257–8, 284
assignments
   building the abstract 235

cityscapes 190
communications factory 205
dancer and writer 255, 257
dopamine 129
engineering 138
play and creativity model 70
PM 141
writing PAD 209. *See also* briefs
Association of Business Schools 179
attainment 6, 204
Attfield, Jane 59, 64
attitudes 7, 12, 167, 322
   building the abstract 232
   engineering 135
   play and creativity 70
   public engagement 155
audiences 151, 154, 155, 185, 190, 266
authenticity 45, 51
authority 12
autonomy 124, 266, 278
avatars 265
awareness
   ESCAPE 37
   HE 81
   Ludic model 25
   Park Life 293
   places 98
   professional love 244
   public engagement 164
   Wardopoly 277
awe and wonder 160

B

badges 13, 284
Bailly, J. C. 194
balloon waterfalls 48–50

Banerjee, T. 267
Bangkok traffic jam 50
Barnett, L. A. 277
barriers 72, 209
Baryshnikov, Mikhail 254
Bassok, D. 52
Bateson, P. 68, 69, 309, 319, 324
Bech, Tine 178
becoming 23–5
  essentials 26–7
  projects 27–8
  student feedback 28–9
  team's evaluation 29–30
  thirdspace and freedom 25–6
bed spaces 274–5
behaviours (behavioural traits) 9, 38, 58, 268, 311
  sports coaching 45, 50
being, state of 68, 70, 72
belonging, sense of 186, 192, 193, 204, 286
benefits 169
  building the abstract 231, 234
  clinical simulations 220
  ESCAPE 37
  GBL resources 286–7, 289
  referencing 311, 313
Bereiter, C. 137
Blessinger, P. 319
blogging 24, 187, 190, 192. *See also* writing
bodies, physical 95, 260
bonding (bonds) 5, 12, 48, 81, 172, 243
books, stud 292–293
Borsdorf, Henk 62
boundaries 46, 97, 193, 218, 244, 313. *See also* cross-boundaries

Bowles, T. A. 104
boxes, shoe 117–19
bricks, building 173–4
bridges, building of 167–9
briefs 72–3, 288
Bright Sparks Theatre Arts Company 223
Bristol ChemLabS Centre for Excellence in Teaching and Learning 146, 147, 152, 155
Bristol University 146
Brookfield, S. D. 93, 193, 228, 322, 324, 326
Brooks, D. 51
Brown, Stuart 9, 10, 12, 45
Buckley, George 313
Budd, Chris 9
building. *See* modelling
Bushnell, Nolan 260
business education 172, 174, 176, 179
Butcher, C. 51

cabinets of curiosities 103–9
camaraderie 4, 277
cameras 114, 128–9
campaigns, political 181
camps, residential 148
campuses 94, 114, 164, 179, 186–7, 255
Captain Kangaroo 254
Cardiff Metropolitan University 67, 113, 114
Cardiff School of Art & Design 67
care 133, 164, 263, 275. *See also* healthcare

careers 45, 155
caring 324
Carlson, N. R. 233
Cass Business School 171
ceremonies 95
certainty 94
chairs, musical 46–7
challenges 169
   building the abstract 234–5
   dancer and writer 258
   ESCAPE 34, 37
   module co-designing 299
   players' perspective 266
   PM 141
   urban learning spaces 178
   Wardopoly 277, 279
change 142, 177, 279, 312, 323
characteristics 320, 322
   games 303
characters 45, 256, 265
Chatterjee, H. 107
Chazan, S. 58
childhood 46, 68, 115, 309, 328
children 50–1, 57–9, 94, 114, 167, 216
chocolate 129, 149
choices 124, 278, 327
circles, magic 106, 109, 323
citations. *See* referencing, academic
cityscapes 185–94
classrooms
   cabinets of curiosities 104–6
   cityscapes 185, 188–90
   dancer and writer 255–6
   dopamine 124, 128
   engineering 133
   history 181–2
   Ludic model 29–30

   players' perspective 264
   referencing 311
   Wardopoly 279
clients 164, 223–4, 248. *See also* audiences
clinical simulations 213–20
clues 33, 36–8, 308
coaching, sports 43–52, 240. *See also* teamwork
cognition 107, 264
cohesiveness (cohesion) 11, 80, 265
collaboration 171–2, 319–20, 324–5
   building the abstract 236
   conclusion 179–80
   context 172–4
   dancer and writer 259
   dopamine 126, 129
   ESCAPE 34
   GBL resources 284–7, 289
   innovation 59–60
   LEGO® 240
   place 98
   play and creativity 69
   players' perspective 267
   referencing 311
   reflection and follow up 178–9
   Spaces 2050 175–8
   sports coaching 45
   Wardopoly 277
colleagues 16
collegiality. *See* camaraderie
communication 15, 169, 203–5, 223–5
   dancer and writer 259
   ESCAPE 34
   players' perspective 267
   PM 142
   public engagement 153, 155

Index

word play 200
worms and waste 163–4
communities 15, 95, 98, 114, 265, 323–4
communities of practice 113, 286, 289
compartmentalisation 104
competence (competencies) 94, 142, 264
competitions 128–9, 136, 149, 153, 178
   dancer and writer 254, 256–7
competitiveness (competition) 255, 287, 289, 308, 312, 319
complexity 24, 96, 141, 235, 241, 267, 275
computer science 266–267, 269
concepts 227, 230, 232, 233, 248, 293
conferences 149, 179, 240, 319
confidence 138, 286
   innovation 57, 62
   play and creativity 69, 71
   public engagement 149, 154
conflicts 132, 182, 216, 217
confusion 38, 279
connectedness 322
connectedness (interconnectedness) 16, 106, 193, 325
connections 4, 15, 319, 323, 325
   cabinets of curiosities 106–7
   cityscapes 187
   dancer and writer 259
   sports coaching 48
   theory representations 247–8
   word play 200
connectivism 322, 325
connessione 106
consequences 68

conservation 163, 291–3
Constructionism 228–9, 233
constructions 240
constructivism 167
contentment 124
contents 24–5, 38, 44, 104, 105, 142
contexts
   engineering 136
   GBL resources 284, 286
   HE 240
   innovation 60
   play and creativity 68–9
   PM 142
   sports coaching 51
   urban learning spaces 172–4
   Wardopoly 274
   word play 200
contribution 265, 277, 300, 311
control 12, 321
   dopamine 124
   ESCAPE 34–5, 39
   GBL resources 284
   innovation 59, 62
   PM 141
   Wardopoly 278–9
conversations 16, 243
costs 142, 259, 279
Counterplay 8
creative block 69, 71, 72
Creative Entrepreneur in Residence 171–2, 175, 178
creative thinking 50, 204, 305
Creativeworks 171–2, 179
creativity 7, 9, 319–20, 322–7
   building the abstract 228, 232
   cabinets of curiosities 106, 108
   communications factory 208

dancer and writer 257, 259
ESCAPE 34
innovation 60, 64
maths 160
OLC 113
play and creativity 67, 70, 72–3
referencing 310–12
sports coaching 45, 48, 50–1
theory representations 247
Wardopoly 279
credibility 12, 14
crises 174, 179–80, 214
critical consciousness 105
criticality 322
critical reflection 109
critical thinking 34, 103, 106, 236, 277
cross-boundaries 320, 324, 325
cross-disciplinary 320
cross-institutions 320
cultural communication 117
culture 97, 126, 204, 232, 305, 309
   cityscapes 185–6, 188
   shoe boxes 117–19
curiosità 105–6
curiosities. *See* cabinets of curiosities
curiosity 318–19, 326
   dopamine 128–9
   ESCAPE 34
   GBL resources 284
   referencing 310
   Wardopoly 279. *See also* cabinets of curiosities
curricula 327
   cityscapes 194
   GBL resources 285, 289
   innovation 59, 61–2
   Ludic model 25–6
   module co-designing 300

   OLC 114
   places 94, 96
   referencing 307
   sports coaching 44
Curveball 288

D

dance 253–61
Dark Would, The (TDW) 77–91
data 114, 216, 231, 232, 320
da Vinci, Leonardo 105–6
Dean, Roger T. 62–3
debates 29, 181
debriefs 37, 38, 231, 276, 277
debts, student 259
Deci, E. L. 134–5
decisions 58, 274, 279, 284
Deininger, Gina 68
deliveries. *See* presentations (deliveries)
demonstrations 135, 136, 150
De Montfort University 59, 207–8
dental students (professionals) 117–18
dépaysement 194
depression 10
deprivation 9
design 105, 181, 323, 327. *See also* named tools
Deterding, S. 263
Develop@City 179
developers 228, 277–8
development, academic 199–201, 240, 317–19, 322, 327, 329
Dewey, J. 95
dialogues 95, 105, 277, 311, 326
Diamond, Marian 9
diaries 70–1

DiCarlo, S. E. 138
disciplines 69, 96, 311. *See also* cross-disciplinary
Disclosure Barring Service (DBS) 152
discoveries 124, 159, 160, 319, 324
discovery 38, 108, 160, 279, 325
 cityscapes 190, 194
discussions 70
 building the abstract 227, 229, 232–4
 clinical simulations 217
 communications factory 204
 culture shoe box 119
 imagination 304
 LEGO® 240
 novelty 181–2
 places 98
 professional love 244
 sports coaching 48
 Wardopoly 278
 worms and waste 164
dishes 204, 208
dissemination 240, 319
diversity 235, 324, 325
dolls, dress-up 208
dopamine 123–30
dropout (rates) 234, 267
durability 292
Dweck, C. 311
Dyrssen, Catharina 59
dyslexia 232, 234

E
Early Childhood Educators (ECEs) 307, 308–9
Early Years 52, 57–8, 113

East Midlands Writing PAD Centre (EMWPC) 207
eco-tourism 292
Edinburgh, University of 300
education
 building the abstract 228
 dancer and writer 258
 Ludic model 29
 places 95–6, 98
 public engagement 149
 sports coaching 44
 theory representations 247
 urban learning spaces 174
educators 37, 95, 118, 219
effectiveness 152, 267, 296
effort 37–8, 137, 259, 289, 310–12, 324
Egan, Kieran 134
egg-dropping 141
Einsteins 4–6
Electrical Engineering 236
Eliot, T. S. 188
emotions 69, 95, 216, 264, 321
 sports coaching 44, 51
empathy 51, 108, 164, 244, 324
empowerment 259, 320, 323
encounters 35, 82, 95–6, 98
encouragement 235
engagement 169, 320, 325
 building the abstract 231
 cabinets of curiosities 104, 108–9
 cityscapes 190
 culture shoe box 118
 engineering 138
 GBL resources 284, 286, 289
 novelty 181–2
 places 95, 97–8
 referencing 310

urban learning spaces 176
Wardopoly 274, 277
writing PAD 209. *See also* public engagement
engineering education 131–8
enhancement 51, 319
enjoyment 48, 264, 269, 278
enquiry 95–6, 310
enthusiasm 16, 26–7, 244, 254
envelopes (scenario) 12–13
environments 318
  building the abstract 232
  cityscapes 185–6, 194
  communication 224
  dancer and writer 259
  dopamine 128
  engineering 131, 137
  ESCAPE 33–9
  GBL resources 284, 286–7
  innovation 59–62
  learning 109
  Ludic model 30
  outdoor 113–15
  places 95
  play and creativity 70
  players' perspective 265
  referencing 309
  sports coaching 46, 51
equality 15, 108, 224, 260
escape rooms 33–9
e-science 59, 60
ESCP Europe 174
ethics 117, 285
Euler, Leonhard 160
European Conference on Games Based Learning (ECGBL) 287
evaluation 64, 234, 240, 293
  building the abstract 231–2
events, special 152

evidence 58, 126, 127, 232, 240
exaggeration 217
exams 30, 124, 137–8
exchanges 4, 16, 96, 194–5, 219
excitement 96, 118, 136, 217, 264
exhibitions 24, 73, 105
expectancy theory 278
expectations 37, 132, 254, 277, 313
experience, double 107
Experience Points (XPs) 257
experiences 326–7
  cityscapes 187
  dancer and writer 256
  LEGO® 240
  play and creativity 69
  poetry writing 196
  sports coaching 46
experiences, personal 45
experimentation 30, 60–2, 107, 260, 279
  play and creativity 68–9, 72
expertise (experts) 35, 37, 51, 300, 324
exploration 200, 220, 240
  Bangkok traffic jam 50
  children doing research 58–9
  musical chairs 46–7
  play and creativity 68
  in practice 59–65
  training game 51–2
  water balloons 48–50
exposure 14, 244

F
facilitators 277, 278
failure
  clinical simulations 217, 219
  dancer and writer 258

dopamine 123
engineering 133–4, 137
imagination 305
innovation 60
professional love 244
sports coaching 51
urban learning spaces 174
fantasy 34, 216, 224
Farnè, R. 328
fascination 94, 107
fears 14, 124, 234
feedback 16
  communications factory 204
  dopamine 123
  ESCAPE 37–8
  GBL resources 284
  LEGO® 233–4
  Ludic model 28–9
  Park Life 291
  players' perspective 266–7
  public engagement 151, 154
  referencing 296–7, 311
  sports coaching 50
  urban learning spaces 177
feelings 10, 216, 217
females 215, 268
fencing 244, 292
festivals 15–16
findings, building the abstract 232–4
flâneurs 186, 192
flexibility 119, 164, 309
  dancer and writer 256, 259
  innovation 60, 62, 64
flow 36–7, 70
focus groups 28–9
Forencich, F. 45
Forest of Plinths 114
Forest Schools 4–6
formulae 160–1

fossil tracks 125–6
frameworks 319, 321, 323
Francis, P. 207
freedom 11, 46, 62, 248, 279, 320
  building the abstract 232, 235
  play and creativity 68–9, 72
free play 12–13, 38, 80, 114, 334
Free to Learn 61
Frissen, V. 107
Frogger 295–7
frustration 37, 169, 219, 255
fun 34, 138, 142, 161
funding 178, 219, 286, 297
futures 174, 177

G

Gaba, D. M. 218
game developers 277–8
gamers 35
games 7
  balloon waterfalls 48–50
  Bangkok traffic jam 50
  dancer and writer 253, 255–6
  maths 160
  military 174
  module co-designing 300
  musical chairs 46–7
  referencing 310
  urban learning spaces 179. *See also* simulation-games
games-based learning (GBL) 283–9, 318
games design 265–6, 285
games masters 36–7
game studies 106
gamification 7, 264, 265, 266–9, 283–9
gases 127, 150

Gauntlett, David 232, 240, 248
Gelb, M. 105–6
geography 95
geometry 160
gestures 196
goals 68, 169, 240, 279, 284
    dancer and writer 256, 258–9
    ESCAPE 34, 37
gold 199–200
Gordon, Gwen 68, 69
Graham, S. 107
graphics 295, 296
Gray, Peter 7, 60, 61, 62, 228, 308
Greenhouse community 317, 320
Gregoire, C. 45
Gregory, J. 160–1
grief 197
grocery bags 131–2
Gröppel-Wegener, A. 207
growth, cognitive 34

H

Hand, B. 284
handling (object-handling) 106, 107
handprints, action 209
hands 229
Harvard Referencing 295
Harvard University Press 177
#creativeHE 320, 323, 324, 326
healthcare 224, 274
healthcare professionals (workers) 214, 224, 233
health, mental 10
health sciences 227–8
    activity 230–1
    author's practices 235
    challenges 234–5
    evaluation 231–2

    findings and discussion 232–4
    related work 235–6
    theory 228–9
    workshops 228–9
Heubner, D. 98
Higher Education (HE) 106–7
Higher Education Academy (HEA) 25, 286, 289
Higher Education Statistics Agency (HESA) 314
history teaching 181–2
Hollander, J. B. 267
Holtham, Clive 178
homelessness 195–6
Hudson, Seth 254–5
Huizinga, Johann 8, 106
humour 94, 244
Hutt, C. 58

I

Ideal Gas Law 127
ideas 16, 320, 323–4
    cabinets of curiosities 107, 109
    dancer and writer 257
    dopamine 123
    LEGO® 240
    module co-designing 300
    play and creativity 68–70
    referencing 313
    theory representations 247
identity 8, 12, 14, 200, 248, 260
    cityscapes 185, 188, 192
    ESCAPE 35
    places 94
    professional 244
illustrations 71, 168, 188
imagery 94, 104

imagination 10, 167, 303–5, 318, 322, 326
  cabinets of curiosities 106
  cityscapes 186, 190, 194
  clinical simulations 218
  communication 228
  engineering 134
  innovation 64
  maths 159
  module co-designing 303–5
  places 95, 97
  play and creativity 69
  poetry writing 196–7
  sports coaching 45–6
  urban learning spaces 172, 175
Imaginative Approach to Teaching, An 134
immersion 193, 279
Immersive Game (IG) 265
imperfection 132–4
improvisation 38, 70, 71, 224, 259, 319
incentives 310
inclusion 108, 232, 278
independence 97, 277, 322
indisciplinary 175
individuals 9, 33–4, 177, 232, 305
  model revisited 324, 326–7, 329
inference 125, 126, 127
Inkwell Arts 223
innovation 57–65, 318, 323, 325
  building the abstract 235
  cabinets of curiosities 108
  referencing 312–14
  urban learning spaces 175
Innovative Learning Week 300
innovators 312–13
inquiry 69, 134, 248
inquisitiveness 105, 193

insights 103, 240, 276, 312–13, 324, 329
inspiration 61, 182
installations 175–8, 179
Institute of Creative Technologies (IOCT) 59
instructions 168, 195–7, 248, 253, 259, 274
integration 52
interactions 319, 324–5, 327
  cityscapes 192
  communication 223
  dancer and writer 253, 258
  GBL resources 284
  places 98
  players' perspective 264, 266
  public engagement 145
  sports coaching 48
  Wardopoly 278. *See also* social interactions
interconnectedness 106, 325
interdependence 322
International Preparation for Fashion (IPF) 203
Internet 159, 186
interpretation 126, 177
interventions 46. *See also* games
interviews 267, 269
involvement 264, 283
Issenberg, S. B. 214
items. *See* artefacts
iterations 36, 83, 257–8

Jackson, N. J. 322, 325
James, Alison 322, 324
  building the abstract 228, 233
  cityscapes 193

Ludic model 30
  places 93
Jarvis, J. 107
Jobs, Steve 311–12, 313
journeys 95–6, 97, 188, 255
joy 68, 96, 209
judgement 72, 284, 324
Judkins, Rod 45
Jung, Carl 229
justification 51, 137, 149

K

Kane, Pat 8
Kangas, M. 279
Kasworm, C. E. 104
Kaufman, S. B. 45
Keats, John 199
Kinetic Molecular Theory 126–7
knowing 95, 97
knowledge 169
  building the abstract 228–9, 235
  cityscapes 192–3
  clinical simulations 217
  dopamine 123, 125–6
  GBL resources 285–6
  innovation 58, 60–1, 63–4
  OLC 115
  places 95
  play and creativity 69
  players' perspective 269
  poetry writing 196
  public engagement 146
  sports coaching 45
  urban learning spaces 174–5, 177, 180
  Wardopoly 274, 279
  word play 200
Knowles, M. S. 52

Kolb, D. A. 141
Kuh, G. 203

L

Lagadothon 297
landscapes 96, 97
language 107, 118, 185–94, 232
laughter 43, 46, 48, 126, 204, 255
laws 126–7
leadership 267, 275, 277, 279, 286
  health-care 274
learners 167, 321–2
  culture shoe box 119
  ESCAPE 34–5
  imagination 303
  innovation 59, 61–2
  places 94, 97
  players' perspective 264
learning 6, 13, 318–19, 321, 323–4, 327
  building the abstract 228–9, 232, 234–5
  cabinets of curiosities 103, 107
  cityscapes 190, 193–4
  clinical simulations 218
  communication 224
  culture shoe box 115
  dancer and writer 259
  dopamine 123, 128
  engineering 133, 138
  ESCAPE 36, 38
  GBL resources 285
  innovation 59
  LEGO® 240
  Ludic model 24, 30
  motivation 169
  places 94
  players' perspective 264, 267, 269

professional love 244
referencing 309, 311, 313
urban learning spaces 172, 179
Wardopoly 274, 276
word play 200
learning, active 45, 135, 169
learning communities 98, 203–4, 325
learning, experiential 44, 52, 141. *See also* Wardopoly
learning objectives 34, 129, 278
learning opportunities 51, 95, 313
learning outcomes 60, 62, 263, 277, 284, 289, 310
learning, playful 11, 318–20, 322–7
   building the abstract 235
   GBL resources 284
   HE 83
   Ludic model 30
   places 94
   referencing 310–11, 313
   sports coaching 45
   urban learning spaces 174, 179
   Wardopoly 277
   writing PAD 209
lecturettes 149
Lefebvre, H. 26
legislation 57, 115
LEGO® 14–16, 167, *168*, *169*, 243–4, 247–8
LEGO® SERIOUS PLAY® (LSP) 233, 235–6, 239–41
Lejeune, Chad 72
Leonardo da Vinci 105–6
Leverhulme Trust 164
levity, semantic 199–201
Lewis, Marianne 175
lighting 104, 175, 255
linearity 38, 96

Listen, Connect, Do (LCD) 68
literacies 25, 34, 50
literature 325, 327
   building the abstract 227–8
   clinical simulations 214, 216, 218
   dopamine 129
   engineering 132
   GBL resources 283, 288
   imagination 304
   innovation 64
   places 95
   players' perspective 264
   poetry 195
   urban learning spaces 172
locals (localness) 185, 186, 188, 190, 193
Loi, D. 105
London College of Fashion 203
love, professional 243–5
Ludic model 23–30
ludic spaces 300
Lynch, B. 107

M

Mabey, R. 95
MacLure, M. 107
magic 161
Malbert, R. 105
Malone, Gareth 30
Malone, T. W. 267
management (management education) 146, 174, 275, 277
   clinical simulations 217, 219, 220
Manchester Metropolitan University 179
manifestos 8, 105, 208
mannequins (manikins) 213, 215
marketing 181

marketplaces, global 312–13
Martin, P. 68, 69, 309, 319, 324
Marton, F. 235
maths 159–61, 167–9
Maton, K. 200
Meaning 36
   building the abstract 230
   cityscapes 190
   communications factory 204
   ESCAPE 34
   LEGO® 240
   OLC 115
   places 96
   Wardopoly 276
   word play 200
meaningfulness 218, 278
meaning-making 98
measurements 126, 228
Meccano® 167–9
media, digital 129
medical education 213
memory 107, 115, 197, 231, 233
mentors 153, 154
Meyer, Dan 132
Mezirow, J. 234
Mid-Staffordshire NHS Foundation Trust 273
misconceptions 123, 126, 127
mistakes 70, 284, 323, 324. *See also* failure
mobile phones 135, 160
mobility 279
modelling 227–8
   activity 230–1
   author's practices 235
   challenges 234–5
   evaluation 231–2
   findings and discussion 232–4
   related work 235–6

   theory 228–9
   workshops 228–9
   models 174, 230–1, 232, 233, 240, 319
Modular Game (MG) 265
module, design 299–300
Morrison, K. 228
motivation 167–9, 320
   cabinets of curiosities 108
   dancer and writer 259
   GBL resources 284, 287, 289
   innovation 63
   LEGO® 240
   play and creativity 69–70, 72–3
   players' perspective 263, 265
   PM 142
   referencing 309
   sports coaching 51
motivation, intrinsic 134–5
movement 45, 68, 259–60
Mozilla Foundation 13
Multiplayer Classroom: Designing Coursework as a Game, The 257
Murray, Jane 58
music (musicians) 104, 105, 161
Myers, D. 267
mystery 9, 94, 96, 126–7, 160

N

Nachmanovitch, S. 12
narratives
   cityscapes 188
   clinical simulations 214, 216
   dancer and writer 254
   ESCAPE 34, 38–9
   places 94
   sports coaching 45
   Wardopoly 274, 278

National Government Bodies of Sport (NGBs) 44
National Student Survey (NSS) 25
nature 96, 255
Neagu, Paul 105
negotiation 224, 267, 275, 309
Nerantzi, Chrissi 30
neuroscience 9, 124, 229, 234, 244
Nicholson, S. 34
Norgard, R. 106
notions, preconceived 126
novelty 181–2, 324–6
  building the abstract 234
  culture shoe box 119
  dancer and writer 259
  dopamine 124
  play and creativity 68
nurse leadership education 273–80
nurses 220, 227. *See also* Wardopoly
Nussbaum, B. 323, 324, 325

O

objectives 300
observations 124–5, 127, 132, 188, 197, 325
observers 62, 231
obstacles 179–80, 305
Open Laboratories Programme (OLP) 147–8
openness 10, 14
  building the abstract 235
  cityscapes 193
  module co-designing 300
  places 95
  play and creativity 73
  word play 200
opportunities 97, 152, 169, 224, 311, 329

Wardopoly 277, 279
organisations 11, 12, 152, 174, 177–8
otherness 107
outcomes
  cabinets of curiosities 108
  clinical simulations 220
  communication 224
  dancer and writer 257
  dopamine 124
  Ludic model 30
  referencing 311
  sports coaching 46
outcomes, learning 78, 268, 277, 310
  GBL resources 284, 289
  innovation 60, 62
Outdoor Learning Centres (OLC) 113–15
outreach 146–7, 152, 153–5, 240
ownership 115, 286
Oxbridge 25

P

Pac-Man 295
Palmer, P. J. 322, 325
Palpable Art Manifesto! 105
Papert, S. 228
Park Life 291–3
Parr, R. 9
participants
  building the abstract 230, 233
  communication 224
  LEGO® 240
  module co-designing 300
  places 96
  professional love 244
  public engagement 146
  sports coaching 44, 48

urban learning spaces 175–6, 179
participation 167, 318
  cabinets of curiosities 106
  cityscapes 188
  communication 224
  LEGO® 240
  referencing 309
partnerships 240, 299–300
patients 214, 273, 274, 275, 279
patterns 36, 94, 160
pauses 37. *See also* reflection
Peabody, M. A. 234
pedagogy, playful 11. *See also* learning, playful
peers 71, 153, 154, 195, 269, 277, 289
Pellis, Sergio 9
perceptions 3, 37, 195, 232, 234, 264, 266–9
performance (acting out) 6, 28, 35, 173, 182
persistence (persevere) 35, 48, 135
personalities 244
personality 26, 109
perspectives 15, 324
  building the abstract 229
  communication 204
  innovation 63
  places 94
  theory representations 247
photographs 137, 178, 231, 240, 255
Piaget, J. 284
place 93–9
places 163–4, 185
plagiarism 307, 308
planning 141, 177, 182, 186, 236, 266–7
play 17–18, 104, 108, 124
  challenges 13–14
  characteristics 60, 132

Creativity Festival 15–17
dangers of deprivation 9–10
definition 6–7
fear of free play 12–13
how and why 7–9
science of 9
thirdspace and freedom 25–6
types 10–11
play and creativity 67–73
Play and Creativity Festival 15–17
play culture 106
Play-Doh® 227–36
players 263–70
  building the abstract 228
  cabinets of curiosities 107
  cityscapes 190
  dancer and writer 253
  ESCAPE 36
  referencing 310
  Wardopoly 276, 278, 279
Play Ethic, The 8
Playful Learning Conference 179
playfulness 322
  dancer and writer 254
  places 96
  play and creativity 69, 71
  referencing 308
  urban learning spaces 173
  word play 200
playground model 317–18, 329–30
  moving on 327–9
  zooming in 318–23
  zooming out 323–6
playgrounds 44, 106. *See also* Outdoor Learning Centres (OLC); urban learning spaces
playscapes 113–15
Play Tents 16–17
pleasure 34, 124, 169, 195

poetry 195–7, 199
possibilities 61, 68, 95, 96, 106
Potternewton Fulfilling Lives and Aspire Centres 223
power 224, 284, 300, 326
Powers, J. D. 152–3
practices 123, 180, 227, 319, 323
   classroom 108
   pedagogical 16
   personal 277
   Stead 235
   teaching 318, 326. *See also* communities of practice
practitioners 318, 327
preconceptions 13, 126, 247, 324
presentations (deliveries) 129, 149, 150, 151, 305. *See also* writing, science
pretending, cooperative 215
Pritchard, A. 45
proactivity 181
Problem Based Gaming (PBG) 284
Problem Based Learning (PBL) 284, 287
problems (activities) 37, 60, 135
problem solving 319
   building the abstract 228
   dancer and writer 259
   dopamine 124
   engineering 132
   ESCAPE 34
   GBL resources 284
   play and creativity 69–70
   players' perspective 269
   referencing 310–11, 313
   Wardopoly 274, 277
production 291
professional development 179, 235, 259, 317, 326

ESCAPE 33, 35
professional practices 52, 176, 218
proficiency 141, 269, 312
progress 37, 169, 278, 325
project management (PM) 141–2, 204
projects 27–8, 129, 136, 267
Project Zero 323
promenadology 95
prompts 33, 83, 94, 190
props 14, 38, 39, 70, 71
Prown, J. 108
Pryor, Karen 55–6
Psychology Today 7
publications 151, 178–9, 319
public engagement 145–56
public spaces. *See* urban learning spaces
purpose (purposeful) 6, 11, 13–14, 319
   cabinets of curiosities 106
   cityscapes 193
   clinical simulations 217
   engineering 131
   ESCAPE 34
   HE 80–81, 83
   innovation 57
   Ludic model 25
   play and creativity 68
   professional love 244
   referencing 297, 312
   sports coaching 46
puzzles 36, 38, 70, 128, 160, 310

Quality Assurance Agency (QAA) 25, 313
quatrains 195–6

questioning 108, 124, 193, 240, 319
questionnaires 59, 231, 267, 269, 293
questions 69, 279

R

randomness 56, 204, 267–8, 292
reactivity 51, 148, 200, 322
readers 188
reading 115, 181
realia 118
realism 51
realities 216, 217
reality 8, 125, 141, 218, 219, 220
receptive 10
receptiveness 95, 124
recollections 45–6
record-keeping 218
recycling 164
referencing, academic 295–7, 307–14
reflection 34, 37–8, 52, 108, 322, 327
reflections, student 60
   assessment 62
   building the abstract 227–30
   cityscapes 192–3
   communication 224
   computing 63–4
   dancer and writer 254, 258
   GBL resources 284
   knowledge 63
   learning environments 61–2
   LEGO® 240
   module co-designing 300
   perspectives 63
   play and creativity 70
   PM 142
   research 61
   responsibility 62
   skills 64–5
   urban learning spaces 178
   Wardopoly 274, 277
   worms and waste 164
   writing PAD 208–9
relationships 8, 322
   building the abstract 229
   cabinets of curiosities 108
   communication 224
   dopamine 126–7
   GBL resources 285
   places 94
   professional love 243
   sports coaching 46
   Wardopoly 277, 279
   worms and waste 164
research
   building the abstract 232
   dopamine 129
   evaluative 329
   GBL resources 285–6
   innovation 58–9, 61–2
   LEGO® 240
   methods 114, 287
   public engagement 146, 152–5
   urban learning spaces 172
   writing PAD 207. *See also* gamification
researchers 59, 149
research plait 208
research, reframing 208
resistance 13–14, 96, 247, 288, 326
Resnick, M. 328
resources 103, 219, 292
   culture shoe box 117–19

management 279
teaching materials 286, 308. *See also* gamification
responses 2–4, 231–3, 240, 269, 309
  clinical simulations 216, 219
  places 95, 97–8
responsibility 62, 164, 267, 279, 285
retention 182, 312
revision, academic. *See* Park Life
rewards 138, 153, 265, 284
  ESCAPE 34, 36, 38
risk-taking (trial and error) 324
  building the abstract 235
  innovation 60
  OLC 115
  referencing 313
  sports coaching 51
  urban learning spaces 179
Robinson, Sir Kenneth 17, 44, 69, 247, 310
Roe, Andrea 164
role-playing 174, 279
roles 6, 190
Rolfe, G. 318
RollWithIt 288–9
Romanek, D. 107
Rubio y Degrassi, Lleonard 178
rules 318
  building the abstract 228, 234
  dancer and writer 257–258
  engineering 136
  GBL resources 284
  module co-designing 300
  players' perspective 265
  urban learning spaces 172
  Wardopoly 278
Runco, M. 44
Russel Group 25

safety 68, 244, 274, 275
Saljo, R. 235
satisfaction 168, 279
scavenger hunts 128–9
scenarios 216, 217, 219, 224, 277
  Yelnats 35–9
Schön, D. 318
schools 94, 146–8, 150, 154, 240, 310
sciences 95. *See also* neuroscience; students, chemistry
Science, technology, Engineering and Mathematics (STEM) 152
scientists 59, 132. *See also* neuroscience
searching 128, 268
Secret Life of Campus, The 15
Selborne 95
self 26, 29, 71–2, 243, 258, 277
self-expression 232, 260
semantic levity 199–201
seniority 12
sensazione 106
serendipity 186
sfumato 106
Shakespeare, William 197
sharing 240, 320, 323, 324, 325
Sheldon, Lee 257
Shields, R. 26
Siemens, G. 325
Significance of Enrichment, The 9
simplicity 48, 161
simulation-games 141, 274. *See also* name simulations
simulations 174, 213–20
situations 217, 322
skills

acquisition 4
building the abstract 228
cityscapes 192
clinical simulations 218
communication 224
communications factory 204–5
ESCAPE 37
GBL resources 284, 286
innovation 61, 64–5
play and creativity 69, 71
players' perspective 269
public engagement 146, 152–3
word play 200
Smith, Hazel 62–3
Social Animal: A Study of How Success Happens, The 51
social interactions 266, 309
socialization 9, 324
social media 317, 319–20, 324, 329
   LEGO® 240
   public engagement 151
   urban learning spaces 176
social sciences 285–6, 287
society 45, 172, 260
software 134, 255–6
soils 163
Soja, E. W. 26
sonnets 197
Sotto, E. 229
sounds (noise) 255, 279
soundtracks 188
Southampton University 13
Sovic, S. 204
spaces 323–7
   cabinets of curiosities 105–6
   cityscapes 188–90
   dancer and writer 258
   ESCAPE 34–5, 38
   module co-designing 299

places 96
   transitional 26
   Wardopoly 277, 279
SPACES 2050: Seeing and Seers 175–8
spaces, urban learning 171–80
spectroscopy tours 150–1
spontaneity 6, 277
Spontaneous 254–5
sports. *See* coaching, sports
stakeholders 114, 115, 267
status 35, 50, 224
Statutory Framework for Early Years Foundation Stage 57
Stead, Rachel 235
Stefani, L. 329
stereochemistry 148
stereotyping 105
stimulation 172
stimuli 4, 9, 229
strength, collective 325
stress 69, 70, 234, 247
Structured Active In-Class Learning (SAIL) 131
stuckness 240
stud books 292–293
students
   business 310–11
   cabinets of curiosities 104, 107–9
   cityscapes 186–8, 190, 194
   communication 223–5
   communications factory 204
   culture shoe box 119
   dancer and writer 253, 259
   dopamine 124, 128–9
   engineering 133
   ESCAPE 37
   game producers 285
   innovation 59–60

Ludic model 26–7
novelty 182
places 94–5
play and creativity 69
players' perspective 266–9
professional love 244, 247–8
public engagement 154
urban learning spaces 179
worms and waste 164
writing PAD 207
students, chemistry 145–6, 156
   competitions 149
   effectiveness 152–3
   lecturettes 149
   less positive aspects 155
   looking forward 155
   OLP 147–8
   primary workshops 148
   residential camps 148
   scene setting 146–7
   schools lectures 150
   science writing 151
   special events 152
   spectroscopy tours 150–1
   students' gain 153–5
   types of play 147
success 135, 137, 138, 169
supervisors 146, 155
support 164, 190, 243
surprise 62, 81–2, 160, 248
Surrey, University of 235
surveys 129, 274. *See also* named surveys
survival 79, 153, 177, 268, 312
suspense 87, 108
sustainability 15, 70, 163–4
Sutton-Smith, Brian 7, 10, 177, 216–18, 220
Swick, D. C. 152–3
swollage 208
symptoms 217
synthesis 129

tactile play 105, 107
tasks 310, 311, 313
teacher education 94, 103
   classrooms 104–105
   curiosity and play 105–6
   HE 106–7
   student experience 107–9
teachers 119, 147, 167, 321, 322
teacher training. *See* teacher education
teaching 169, 318–20, 323–4, 327
   cabinets of curiosities 103, 107
   cityscapes 193
   dancer and writer 259
   GBL resources 284–5
   LEGO® 240
   Ludic model 29
   public engagement 153–5
   sports coaching 44–5
   urban learning spaces 180
   word play 200
teaching assistants (TAs) 125–8
Teaching Excellence and Student Outcomes Framework (TEF) 17
Teaching Excellence Framework (TEF) 313
teaching methods 97, 124, 326
teaching practices 285, 329
teams 279
teamwork 142, 169, 204
   players' perspective 267, 269
   Wardopoly 274, 277–8

technology 60, 117, 264, 283, 312–13, 319
testing 142, 152
texts 186, 190, 192, 199
The Dark Would (TDW) 77–91
themes 28, 94, 224, 232–3, 248, 304
Theorems 160
theories 69, 126, 142, 227, 228–9, 327
theory, LEGO® representations 247–8
thinking 9
  building the abstract 233
  cabinets of curiosities 108
  communication 208
  dancer and writer 255
  imagination 305
  places 96–7
  play and creativity 68–9
  players' perspective 270
  referencing 311, 313
  theory representations 247–8
  urban learning spaces 173, 175
  Wardopoly 277
Thomas, D. 267
Three Domains of Learning 325
threshold concept 299
Tine Bech Studio 175
Toffler, Alvin 17–18
toolkits 79, 244, 320
touching, active 107
tourists 185, 190
tower building 133–4
trainees 217
Training Game, The 55–6
traits 216, 268
transformation 319, 329
  HE 85–6
transition 26, 97, 196, 287, 312

travelling 98
Treviranus, J. 324–5
trial and error. *See* risk-taking (trial and error)
trickery 6
tricks, card 161
trust 108, 124, 323, 324, 325
Tsibulya, Alan 307
turn-taking 274, 277
Tutchell, S. 109

U

UK Professional Standards Framework (UKPSF) 25
UK Teaching Excellence Framework 36
uncertainty 8, 10, 96
understanding
  building the abstract 236
  cityscapes 193
  communication 224
  engineering 132
  professional love 243
  public engagement 153
  theory representations 248
  Wardopoly 274
unfreezing 177–8
University of Leeds 295
University of London 171
University of Warwick 36
University of Winchester 15
unpredictability 187
urban learning spaces 171–80

V

validity 61, 63
value 312–3
valued 225, 257

value-discovery 128
values 70, 72, 117, 128
variability 177, 325
versatility 118, 279
Veterinary Medicine 236
veterinary professionals 163–4
videos 135, 136
virtual reality 195
visas 305
visitors 190, 192
vorticity 135–6
Vygotsky, L. S. 284

W

walls 190–2
Wardopoly 273–80
Warwick Medical School 296
waste 163–4
Watts, L. S. 319
well-being 70, 164, 195, 234, 244
Weller, M. 324
Whitebread, D. B. 277
Whitton, N. 284
whoosh bottles 150
wildlife conservation 291–3
Willingham, D. 138
Willis, Boris 254–5
Wilson, F. 229, 233
wind turbines 136
Winnicott, D. W. 8, 26, 107
winning 278, 287, 292
women (females) 268
wonder 9
    cabinets of curiosities 105–6
    cityscapes 186
    dopamine 129

engineering 135
ESCAPE 34
maths 160
places 94, 96, 98
poetry 194
Wood, Elizabeth 59, 64
Wordplay (Word Play) 195, 199–201
words 187–8
working conditions 219
working, modes of 59
workplaces 61, 64
workshops 204, 207–8, 230, 267, 286–9, 300
workshops, primary 148
worms 163–4
writers 253–61. *See also* writing
writer's block 233, 248
writing 185–94, 253–61
    building the abstract 233
    Ludic model 24–5
    OLC 115
    science 151
    theory representations 248. *See also* poetry
Writing PAD 207–9

Y

Yelnats, Stanley 35–9
Yue, X. D. 277
Yu, P. 277

Z

Zhao, C. 203
Zhao, Yong 71, 73

Lightning Source UK Ltd.
Milton Keynes UK
UKHW011026060219
336828UK00008B/349/P